this Constitution

this Constitution
Our Enduring Legacy

American Political Science Association
American Historical Association

Congressional Quarterly Inc.

Printed in the United States of America

Library of Congress Cataloging-in-Publication Data

This Constitution.

Collection of essays chosen from This Constitution magazine, published by Project '87.
Bibliography: p.
Includes index.
Summary: A collection of essays discussing the theoretical origins and revolutionary context of the Constitution, its application to issues such as civil liberties and national versus state powers, and the evolution of the three branches of government.
1. United States—Constitutional history. [1. United States—Constitutional history. 2. United States—Politics and government]
I. American Political Science Association. II. American Historical Association. III. Project '87. IV. This Constitution.

KF4541.T45	1986	342.73	86-16764

ISBN 0-87187-396-6

Illustration Acknowledgments appear on p. 317.

Contents

Preface

How will we celebrate the most significant birthday of our time—the 200th anniversary of the drafting of the Constitution? With balloons? Tall ships in the harbor? Fireworks? Spread-eagle speeches? Surely all of these.

There are those who believe, however, that the Constitution merits also a more serious commemoration. This great charter deserves first of all to be fully understood by the people who are governed by it. It is not a simple grant of authority to a national government but a complex separating, blending, and balancing of powers. Hence as a nation we need to "go back to school" in the Constitution.

Even more, some of us believe if we wish truly to honor this document we should celebrate the men who framed it. Theirs was the most formidable feat of institutional creativity in the history of this nation, perhaps even of the West. We may acclaim their creative vision in recognizing the rising needs of Americans, their bold institutional innovations that mock those who say that humans can advance only by tiny, incremental steps through "practical," piecemeal changes.

And even more still, we should commemorate the incomparable political leadership of the framers. It all seems so obvious today—the Articles of Confederation could not do the job, and naturally the system of the 1780s had to be replaced. But it was not so obvious at the time. Many Americans were perfectly content with their Confederation. Many feared this new federal "Leviathan" that was about to be put on their backs. Many deplored the absence of a Bill of Rights—which the framers were astute enough to promise to add to the new charter.

Can we emulate today the supreme achievement of the framers: their capacity to stand back from the existing system, to evaluate its performance, to grasp the intensifying demands on government, and then to propose drastic changes in our political system? We do not need blindly to worship our constitutional system in order to celebrate it. We can say now that the framers planned in terms of centuries; they built a structure of government that still stands essentially intact today. Can a Constitution drafted in the days of the stage coach and the schooner survive for another two centuries, in the face of the dire problems—poverty, terrorism, legalized injustice, illiteracy, communal violence, drugs, massive malnutrition and ill health—that girdle the globe?

Can the Constitution survive for the long-run future—indeed can it survive *today*? One reason for its longevity—let us confess—is that we have partially evaded the fragmentation of government caused by the constitutional checks and balances among the executive, legislative, and judicial branches of the federal government, and by the division of powers between the national and state levels of government. We have overcome the fragmentation through the political parties' role in occasionally uniting the diverse parts of the government, through giving to the president emergency powers that we now recognize as dangerous, through putting heavy policy responsibilities on the courts (as in the Supreme Court antisegregation cases), and through various makeshifts and gimmicks that enable the system to work temporarily. An example of the latter is the Gramm-Rudman-Hollings Act Congress enacted in 1985. Challenged in the courts, this forced-budget measure put automatic brakes on federal spending, on the theory that the president and Congress could not act decisively and unitedly enough.

The following pages seek to illuminate some of these problems. The distinguished historian Richard B. Morris and I list thirteen crucial questions that were hammered out by the historians and political scientists who compose the committee in charge of Project '87. This whole volume, indeed, is a reflection of the mission of Project '87, a joint enterprise of the American Historical Association and the American Political Science Association, to promote scholarly research and to solicit both celebratory and critical writings on the constitutional system. The reader will find these thirteen issues discussed in the article that begins this book.

The editors of Congressional Quarterly and the directors of Project '87 have selected from among the essays commissioned those that in their judgment contribute most to this book's overall mission. While there is always room for argument about any individual selection in such a process, I believe that the overall result of the selection is balanced and judicious. It would not have been practical or economical to have included all the commissioned essays in this volume, despite their uniformly high quality.

"Eighteenth-Century American Constitutionalism" by Gordon S. Wood is one of the first essays in *this Constitution*. It sets the stage by describing the view of our founding fathers that contrary to the thinking in England there was a distinction between "legal" and "constitutional." All of British constitutional tradition (from which American ideas mainly evolved) focused on establishing fundamental principles that would protect the people from the despotic power of the crown. Thomas

Jefferson and his colleagues saw a threat in elected legislators that British constitutionalism did not take into account. Jefferson wrote: "173 despots would surely be as oppressive as one." This thinking led to the concept of constitutional conventions and a process of ratification that made the people the actual constituent power. The written Constitution and its underlying philosophy led in less than two decades to the introduction of judicial review, America's special contribution to the governance of nations.

Essays later in the book treat the conspicuously close relationship between the Constitution and the federal courts charged with interpreting it. The essay by Philip B. Kurland deals with the origin of the national judiciary and another by Frank J. Sorauf presents a perspective on the courts and constitutional change.

There have been occasions—and they may persist in some quarters today—when the Fourteenth Amendment has been viewed as a disruptive instrument designed to expand "equal justice under law" beyond the intent of the framers or reason. Howard N. Meyer articulates another view: the Fourteenth Amendment was an effort "to give constitutional force to the human rights principles of the Declaration of Independence."

The reader will find the same unifying theme in the remaining essays in *this Constitution:* enduring relevance. This is our ultimate appreciation, our final tribute to the draftsmen.

James MacGregor Burns

The Constitution:
Thirteen Crucial Questions

James MacGregor Burns and Richard B. Morris

1. Too Much—or Too Little—National Power? Are the limits placed on the federal government's powers by the Constitution realistic and enforceable?

The framers wanted a national government strong enough to exercise certain general powers but not so powerful as to threaten peoples' liberties. In their reading of history and their own experience they had seen all too many republics turn into despotisms. "In framing a government which is to be administered by men over men," wrote James Madison, "the great difficulty lies in this: you must first enable the government to control the governed; and in the next place oblige it to control itself." Thus the framers carefully enumerated the powers delegated to the national government while, in the Bill of Rights, reserving the rest to the states and the people. Congressional legislation, executive acts, and decisions by the federal judiciary have broadened national power enormously in the face of internal and external threats to our national security and economic well-being. Has this trend gone too far? Or is the national power in fact inadequate in the face of social unrest, economic instability, and international turbulence? Will it be even less adequate in our third century—the age of continuing technological change, nuclear danger, and intense pressure on national and global resources?

2. Does Federalism Work? Is the Constitution maintaining an efficient and realistic balance between national and state power?

The United States did not invent federalism, but under our Constitution it has a distinctly indigenous form—equality of the states in the Senate, and a Bill of Rights which, through the Tenth Amendment, reserves to the states or the people powers not delegated to the United States by the Constitution. Nevertheless, the American union exercises its power directly

1

on the individual, and under the Constitution's supremacy clause congressional statutes and treaties constitute the supreme law of the land. Drastic changes in the direction of centralization have taken place since the Civil War, especially during and after the New Deal, including the nationalization of most of the Bill of Rights. The Income Tax Amendment of 1913, which has led to the federal government's collecting an overwhelming portion of the tax revenue, has further weakened state power. To sustain state solvency, Congress promulgated a Revenue Sharing Act in 1972, but it is doubtful whether the ensuing limited fiscal relief to the states has restored the balance of power of the federal structure. Can federalism work without continued federal handouts? Must federal control of revenue mean federal domination of state action?

3. Is the Judicial Branch Too Powerful? Are the courts exercising their powers appropriately as interpreters of the Constitution and shapers of public policy?

A whole cluster of cases—from Dred Scott through the New Deal decisions, the recent civil libertarian cases and culminating in *Brown v. Board of Education* (1954—desegregation), *Baker v. Carr* (1962—reapportionment), and *Roe v. Wade* (1973—abortion)—show that where Congress fails to act, the Supreme Court has ventured into the field of policy making, in areas ranging from human freedom to definitions of

Signing of the Constitution

privacy. It has been asserted that "the Constitution is what the judges say it is." Is this role for the courts a proper and necessary one in a democracy? Does it bespeak a vacuum of power in Congress and a tendency of the representative body to evade making decisions in cases where public opinion is sharply divided? Could the current move to limit the jurisdiction of the federal courts endanger the Bill of Rights, among other safeguards to individual freedom? Can a federal union survive without lodging somewhere a power to declare laws unconstitutional, to ensure separation of powers, to apply to laws a strict scrutiny in instances of impaired fundamental rights, and to make explicit the avowed intent of the Preamble, "to establish justice"?

4. Balancing Liberty and Security: How can republican government provide for national security without endangering civil liberties? For the framers, liberty—the protection of individual rights against governmental or religious interference—lay at the heart of a constitutional republic. The Bill of Rights is the enduring and eloquent testament to their commitment to liberty. But Americans have differed over the meaning of liberty—does it mean the right to speak, to assemble, to print, to pray, to bear arms without limit of any kind? Is the essential role of republican government simply to leave people alone in their exercise of these rights, or to take a positive role in expanding these liberties, or even to broaden some rights—such as free speech—and to narrow others—such as the right to bear arms? And are civil and political and religious liberties enough—what about economic and social rights? During World War II Franklin D. Roosevelt promulgated the Four Freedoms—freedom of speech and of worship, but also freedom from want and from fear. Does government have the right and duty under the Constitution to guarantee all these "freedoms" and at the expense of whose liberty? Finally, what is the proper role of government in resolving conflicts between individual rights and national needs—for example, the right of free speech and assembly during war? Can republican government provide for national security without endangering civil liberties?

5. Suspects' Rights: How can republican government protect its citizenry and yet uphold the rights of the criminally accused?

The rise of crime in the United States has raised tensions between certain guarantees in the Bill of Rights, the capacity of the legal system, and measures intended to curb lawlessness.

Article II protects the right to bear arms, but gun control measures seek to restrain gun ownership. Article IV protects citizens from governmental searches without warrants, but conflicts arise over collection of evidence in potentially criminal situations. Articles VI, VII, and VIII stipulate the rights of the criminally accused to counsel, trial by jury, and protection from excessive bail and cruel punishment, but the complexity of procedures required to administer the criminal justice system, including constitutionally mandated rights, results in practices like plea-bargaining which are often troublesome to observers. These issues are of immense concern to the public, which demands personal security and at the same time supports the basic principles of criminal justice in a democratic society. Can these conflicting interests be reconciled?

6. "All Men Are Created Equal": What kinds of equality are and should be protected by the Constitution and by what means?

A major contemporary issue is the distinction between equality before the law and equality in distribution of resources and benefits. The former deals with a limited set of governmental procedures, like voting. The latter embraces all interests and would require social policy to achieve equality. Questions are constantly arising about equality: Can a state deny welfare to a person only briefly resident? Can a state, by using property taxation as a basis for school finance, allocate less money to poor districts? Can universities use quotas to promote affirmative action? Does the Constitution guarantee equality of opportunity or equality of result, and which do we want? Finally, we must address the question of how much the government should intervene in sensitive areas like health, education, and housing, in order to equalize economic and even "social" opportunity.

7. Women's Rights: Does the Constitution adequately protect the rights of women?

Women are not mentioned in the original Constitution. Nonetheless, the description of the qualifications of a representative as a "person" permitted a woman to be elected to Congress in 1916 even before they were guaranteed the right to vote by a federal constitutional amendment. The Fourteenth Amendment too speaks of "all persons" being entitled to citizenship, bars any state from enforcing any law which shall "abridge the privileges or immunities of Citizens of the United States," prohibits any state from depriving "any person of life, liberty, or property without due process of law" and from

IS *THIS* A REPUBLICAN FORM OF GOVERNMENT? IS *THIS* PROTECTING LIFE, LIBERTY, OR PROPERTY? IS *THIS* THE EQUAL PROTECTION OF THE LAW?

MR. LAMAR (*Democrat, Mississippi*). "In the words of the inspired Poet, 'Thy Gentleness has made thee Great.'" [Did Mr. LAMAR mean the Colored Race?]

Harper's Weekly, September 2, 1876

denying "to any person within its jurisdiction the equal protection of the laws." While none of these provisions discriminates on the basis of sex, the Supreme Court to date has not interpreted them to bar sex distinctions in law outright. The Constitution, through the Nineteenth Amendment, specifically prohibits only one form of sex-based discrimination; no state may now deny women the franchise. In a variety of other crucial areas, however, the Constitution contains no explicit guarantees of women's rights. The defeat of ERA raises anew the question of whether the present protections of the Constitution can be interpreted as providing affirmative guarantees of sexual equality, and if not, what alternatives should be pursued?

8. Safeguarding Minorities: Does the Constitution adequately protect the rights of blacks, native Americans, ethnic groups, and recent immigrants?

The Constitution historically has protected various economic and regional groups against national interference—nineteenth-century industrial capitalists, slave holders, religious minorities, political dissenters. On the other hand, it has failed to protect American blacks, both before and after Emancipation, other racial groups, including native Americans and Japanese-Americans, and leaders and members of alleged "radical" groups suspected of "subversion." The trend in this century, as a result of congressional legislation, presidential action, judicial decisions, the efforts of organized minorities and civil liberties and civil rights groups, has been toward much stronger constitutional guarantees of minority rights. Will this trend continue? Is it imprudent to depend so heavily on federal judicial sensitivity to minority concerns? Can we strengthen majority rule *and* protect minority rights?

9. The Constitution Faces Outward: Does the president possess adequate power—or too much power—over war-making and foreign policy?

Except in his capacity as commander in chief, the president receives the bulk of his powers under delegation and authority of Congress. The experience of the Civil War, World War II, and the Vietnam War reveals that the president can exercise extraordinary powers in wartime both to subvert civil liberties and to dispatch troops into war zones without explicit direction of Congress. Are such measures necessary for the national defense? The recent War Powers Act was designed to make the commander in chief more responsive to the people's representatives in Congress. Whether it will do so has yet to be tested, especially in view of the recent Supreme Court decision invalidating the legislative veto.

In foreign affairs, the president under the Constitution is the principal actor, although treaties require the assent of the Senate to be valid. While in most instances the consent of the Senate has become a formality, there have been and continue to be occasions when the necessity for Senate ratification does produce a struggle between the president and the Senate. Such contests took place over the adherence to the Covenant of the League of Nations, the Panama Canal Treaty, and the Canadian Fisheries compact. Should the two-thirds requirement for a treaty be lowered to a simple majority or a three-fifths majority in order to minimize such conflicts, or should the Senate be a more active partner than it has been?

10. Too Many Checks and Balances? Does the constitutional separation of powers between the president, the Congress and the judiciary create a deadlock in governance?

Determined to make government their servant and not their master, the framers contrived a most ingenious system of pitting the legislative branch against the executive, Senate against the House, and, in effect, the judiciary against either or both the other branches. The "accumulation of all powers, legislative, executive, and judiciary, in the same hands," Madison said, was the "very definition of tyranny." The framers not only gave different branches different powers but required their members to be chosen by—and hence responsive to—diverse and conflicting "constituencies." "Ambition," Madison summed it up, "must be made to counteract ambition." Their handiwork can still be seen on the front page of virtually any newspaper today. Is the checks-and-balance system out of date, a relic of the "horse-and-buggy" era? Does it unduly hobble the federal government as it seeks to cope with an overwhelming tide of problems? Or is governmental quarreling, inefficiency, delay, and even impotence a price we must pay—are willing to pay—to keep "government off our backs"?

11. "Government by the People": Does the evolving constitutional system, including political parties and interest groups, strengthen fair and effective representation of the people or undermine it?

We are used to majority rule in House and Senate, town meetings, city councils, student governments. Counting heads, and deciding in favor of the side having the votes of a majority seems an easy, practical, and fair way to settle differences. The Constitution, however, was not established solely on the basis of majority rule, but on the protection of regional and local minorities as well. By controlling one body, such as the Senate, a regional, economic, or political minority could veto actions by the majority. This arrangement differs sharply from the parliamentary system, where simple majorities can and do make crucial decisions. Over the years the extension of the right to vote, the rise of a national party system that united like-minded presidents, senators, and congressmen, and such changes as the direct election of United States senators, tended to make national government somewhat more majoritarian. Recent decades, however, have often seen the executive and legislative branches politically divided, inhibiting simple majoritarian decisions. Moreover, even leaders and parties winning nation-wide majorities have trouble putting through their programs in the face of the strength of economic and social interest groups. Do these groups advance or threaten the goal of "government by the people"? Have we ever in our history attained this goal?

12. The Constitution and the Economy: Can the Constitution be utilized more effectively to provide economic security and promote the well-being of all Americans?

The Constitution was created not in a vacuum, but largely in response to the severe depression which the Articles of Confederation were powerless to arrest. Hence, the charter granted to Congress powers over commerce and taxation and included various fiscal prohibitions on the states in the full-faith-and-credit clause, the export-import clause, and the clause against impairing the obligation of contracts. Hamilton's enunciation of implied powers, his interpretation of the taxing power, and his insistence on honoring the public credit contributed to the upward economic thrust in the first decade of our history. Thus, from the start the government was a friend of private enterprise. The degree to which the Constitution has been employed to promote business enterprise and yet discipline its abuses has varied with national administrations and the personnel of the federal courts. But the power to promote the public welfare resides in the Constitution, and its use depends finally upon the public conception of its necessary and proper function, especially in the times of economic crisis. Are we satisfied with its performance today?

13. Constitutional Flexibility: Should we make changing our fundamental charter of government simpler and more democratic?

The Constitution provides two formal ways for amending it: 1) by a two-thirds vote of Congress and a three-quarters vote of the state legislatures or state conventions; 2) by a convention to be called by the legislatures of two-thirds of the states, whose amendments shall be ratified by the legislatures of three-quarters of the states. This procedure was a modification of the Articles of Confederation, which required a unanimous vote of *every* state to amend the Articles. The states have made no use of their power to initiate amendments. From the start all amendments to the Constitution have been proposed by Congress and not by the state legislatures, and only one of them, the Twenty-first Amendment repealing prohibition, was

Resolution of the Constitutional Convention to submit the newly adopted Constitution to the Congress of the Confederation

effected through ratification by convention rather than state legislatures. The defeat of recent amendments and the prospect of a cluster of other proposals have given rise to serious questions: Do we need further amendments to the Constitution? Is the present amendment procedure too restrictive or have judicial interpretation, legislative and executive actions proven adequate to meet most needs for constitutional flexibility? If a constitutional convention is called by the states, can its proposals be restricted to the terms of its summons? Does the convening of a new constitutional convention threaten the very foundation of the original document?

Richard B. Morris is Gouverneur Morris professor of history emeritus at Columbia University and editor of the Papers of John Jay. He is now working on a book about the forging of the federal union to be published by Harper & Row.

James MacGregor Burns is Woodrow Wilson professor of government at Williams College. He is now writing a three-volume political and intellectual history of the United States since the founding period; it is being published by Alfred A. Knopf, Inc.

I. Roots of the Constitution

Eighteenth-Century American Constitutionalism

Gordon S. Wood

The era of the American Revolution was the greatest and most creative age of constitutionalism in American history. During the last part of the eighteenth century Americans established the modern idea of a written constitution. There had been written constitutions before in Western history, but Americans did something new and different. They made written constitutions a practical and everyday part of governmental life. They showed the world not only how written constitutions could be made truly fundamental, distinguishable from ordinary legislation, but also how such constitutions could be interpreted on a regular basis and altered when necessary. Further, they offered the world concrete and usable governmental institutions for the carrying out of these constitutional tasks. All in all it was an extraordinary achievement, scarcely duplicated by any modern country in such a brief period of time.

Lord Bolingbroke

Before the era of the American Revolution a constitution was rarely ever distinguished from the government and its operations. Traditionally in English culture a constitution referred not only to fundamental rights but also to the way the government was put together or constituted. A constitution was the disposition of the government; it even had medical or physiological connotations, like the constitution of the human body. "By constitution," wrote Lord Bolingbroke in 1733, "we mean, whenever we speak with propriety and exactness, that assemblage of laws, institutions and customs, derived from certain fixed principles of reason, directed to certain fixed objects of public good, that compose the general system, according to which the community hath agreed to be governed." The English constitution, in other words, included both fundamental principles and rights and the existing arrangement of governmental laws, customs, and institutions.

13

By the end of the Revolutionary era, however, the Americans' idea of a constitution had become very different from that of the English. A constitution was now seen to be no part of the government at all. A constitution was a written document distinct from and superior to all the operations of government. It was, as Thomas Paine said in 1791, "a thing *antecedent* to a government; and a government is only the creature of a constitution." And, said Paine, it was "not a thing in name only; but in fact." For Americans a constitution was like a bible, possessed by every family and every member of government. "It is the body of elements, to which you can refer, and quote article by article; and which contains . . . everything that relates to the complete organization of a civil government, and the principles on which it shall act, and by which it shall be bound." A constitution thus could never be an act of a legislature or of a government; it had to be the act of the people themselves, declared James Wilson in 1790, one of the principal framers of the federal Constitution of 1787; and "in their hands it is clay in the hands of a potter; they have the right to mould, to preserve, to improve, to refine, and to furnish it as they please." If the English thought this American idea of a constitution was, as Arthur Young caustically suggested in 1792, like "a pudding made by a recipe," the Americans had become convinced the English no longer had a constitution at all.

It was a momentous transformation of meaning. It involved not just a change in the Americans' political vocabulary but an upheaval in their whole political culture. In the short span of less than three decades Americans created a whole new way of looking at government.

The colonists began the imperial crisis in the early 1760s thinking about constitutional issues in much the same way as their fellow Britons. Like the English at home they believed that the principal threat to the people's ancient rights and liberties had always been the prerogative powers of the king, those vague and discretionary but equally ancient rights of authority that the king possessed in order to carry out his responsibility for governing the realm. Indeed, eighteenth-century English citizens saw their history as essentially a struggle between these conflicting rights, between a centralizing monarchy on one hand and localist-minded nobles and people on the other. Eighteenth-century colonists had no reason to think about government much differently. Time and again in the colonial period the colonists had been forced to defend themselves against the intrusions of royal prerogative power. They relied for defense on their colonial assemblies, their rights as Englishmen, and what they called their ancient charters. In the seventeenth century many of the colonies had been established by crown charters, corporate or proprietary grants made by the king to groups like the Massachusetts Puritans or to individuals like William Penn and Lord Baltimore to found colonies in the New World. In subsequent years these written charters gradually lost their original purpose in the eyes of the colonists and took on a new importance, both as prescriptions for government and as devices guaranteeing the rights of the people against their royal governors. In fact, the whole of the colonists' past was littered with such charters and other written documents of various sorts to which the colonial assemblies had repeatedly appealed in their squabbles with royal power.

In appealing to written documents as confirmations of their liberties the colonists acted no differently from other Englishmen. From almost the beginning of their history, Britons had continually invoked written documents and charters in defense of their rights against the crown's power. "Anxious to preserve and transmit" their liberties "unimpaired to posterity," the English people, observed one colonist on the eve of the Revolution, had repeatedly "caused them to be reduced to writing, and in the most solemn manner to be recognized, ratified and confirmed," first by King John with Magna Carta, then by Henry III and Edward I, and "afterwards by a multitude of corroborating acts, reckoned in all, by Lord Cook, to be thirty-two from Edw. 1st to Hen. 4th and since, in a great variety of instances, by the bills of rights and acts of settlement." All of these documents, from Magna Carta to the Bill of Rights of the Glorious Revolution of 1689, were merely written evidence of those "fixed principles of reason" from which Bolingbroke had said the English constitution was derived.

Although eighteenth-century Englishmen talked about the fixed principles and the fundamental law of the English constitution, few of them doubted that Parliament, as the representative of the nobles and people and as the sovereign law-making body of the nation, was the supreme guarantor and interpreter of these fixed principles and fundamental law. Parliament was in fact the bulwark of the people's liberties against the crown's encroachments; it alone defended and confirmed the people's rights. The Petition of Right, the act of Habeas Corpus, the Bill of Rights were all acts of Parliament, statutes not different in form from other laws passed by Parliament.

For Englishmen therefore, as William Blackstone, the great eighteenth-century jurist pointed out, there could be no distinction between the "constitution or frame of government" and "the system of laws." All were of a piece: every act of Parliament was part of the English constitution and all law, customary and statute, was thus constitutional. "Therefore," concluded the English theorist William Paley, "the terms *constitutional* and *unconstitutional,* mean *legal* and *illegal.*"

Nothing could be more strikingly different from what Americans came to believe. Indeed, it was precisely on this distinction between "legal" and "constitutional" that the American and the British constitutional traditions diverged at the Revolution. During the 1760s and seventies the colonists came to realize that although acts of Parliament, like the Stamp Act of 1765, might be legal, that is, in accord with the acceptable way of making law, such acts could not thereby be automatically considered constitutional, that is, in accord with the basic principles of rights and justice that made the English constitution what it was. It was true that the English Bill of Rights and the act of settlement in 1689 were only statutes of Parliament, but surely, the colonists insisted, they were of "a nature more sacred than those which established a turnpike road." Under this pressure of events the Americans came to believe that the fundamental principles of the English constitution had to be lifted out of the law-making and other institutions of government and set above them. "In all free States," said Samuel Adams in 1768, "the Constitution is fixed; and as the supreme Legislature derives its Powers and Authority from the Constitution, it cannot overleap the Bounds of it without destroying its own foundation." Thus in 1776, when Americans came to make their own constitutions for their newly independent states, it was inevitable that they would seek to make them fundamental and explicitly write them out in documents.

It was one thing, however, to define the constitution as fundamental law, different from ordinary legislation and circumscribing the institutions of government; it was quite another to make such a distinction effective. In the years following the Declaration of Independence, many Americans paid lip service to the fundamental character of their state constitutions, but like eighteenth-century Britons they continued to believe that their legislatures were the best instruments for interpreting and changing these constitutions. The state

James Madison

legislatures were the representatives of the people, and the people, it seemed, could scarcely tyrannize themselves. Thus in the late 1770s and early eighties, several state legislatures, acting on behalf of the people, set aside parts of their constitutions by statute and interpreted and altered them, as one American observed, "upon any occasion to serve a purpose." Time and again the legislatures interfered with the governors' legitimate powers, rejected judicial decisions, disregarded individual liberties and property rights, and in general, as one victim complained, violated "those fundamental principles which first induced men to come into civil compact."

By the mid-1780s many American leaders had come to believe that the state legislatures, not the governors as they had thought in 1776, were the political authority to be most feared. Legislators were supposedly the representatives of the people who annually elected them; but "173 despots would surely be as oppressive as one," wrote Thomas Jefferson. "An *elective despotism* was not the government we fought for." It increasingly seemed to many that the idea of a constitution as fundamental law had no real meaning after all. "If it were possible it would be well to define the extent of the Legislative power, but," concluded a discouraged James Madison in 1785, "the nature of it seems in many respects to be indefinite."

No one wrestled more persistently with this problem of distinguishing between statutory and fundamental law than did Jefferson. In 1779 Jefferson knew from experience that no legislature "elected by the people for the ordinary purposes of legislation only" could restrain the acts of succeeding legislatures. Thus he realized that to declare his great act for Establishing Religious Freedom in Virginia to be "irrevocable would be of no effect in law; yet we are free," he wrote into the bill in frustration, "to declare, and do declare, that ... if any act shall be hereafter passed to repeal the present or to narrow its operation, such act will be an infringement of natural right." But such a paper declaration was obviously not enough; he realized that something more was needed. By the 1780s both he and Madison were eager "to form a real constitution" for Virginia; the existing one was merely an "ordinance" with "no higher authority than the other ordinances of the same session." They wanted a constitution that would be "perpetual" and "unalterable by other legislatures." But how? That was the rub. Somehow or other, if the constitution were to be truly fundamental and immune from legislative tampering, it would have to be created, as Jefferson put it, "by a power superior to that of the legislature."

By the time Jefferson came to write his *Notes on the State of Virginia* in the early 1780s the answer had become clear. "To render a form of government unalterable by ordinary acts of assembly," said Jefferson, "the people must delegate persons with special powers. They have accordingly chosen special conventions to form and fix their governments." In 1775-76 conventions or congresses had been legally deficient legislatures made necessary by the refusal of the royal governors to call together the regular and legal representatives of the people. Now, however, these conventions were seen to be special alternative representations of the people with the exclusive authority to frame or amend constitutions. When Massachusetts and New Hampshire wrote new constitutions in the early 1780s, the proper pattern of constitution-making and constitution-altering was set: constitutions were formed by specially elected conventions and then placed before the people for ratification. Thus in 1787 those who wished to change the federal government knew precisely what to do: they called a convention in Philadelphia and sent the resultant document to the states for approval. Even the French in their own revolution several years later followed the American pattern. Conventions and the process of ratification made the people the actual constituent power. Such institutions, historian R. R. Palmer has said, were the most distinctive contributions the American Revolution made to Western politics.

Thomas Jefferson

But these were not the only contributions. With the idea of a constitution as fundamental law immune from legislative encroachment more firmly in hand, some state judges during the 1780s began cautiously moving in isolated cases to impose restraints on what the assemblies were enacting as law. In effect they said to the legislatures, as George Wythe, judge of the Virginia supreme court did in 1782, "Here is the limit of your authority; and hither shall you go, but no further." These were the hesitant beginnings of what would come to be called judicial review—that remarkable American practice by which judges in the ordinary courts of law have the authority to determine the constitutionality of acts of the state and federal legislatures. There is nothing quite like it anywhere else in the world.

The development of judicial review came slowly. It was not easy for people in the eighteenth century, even those who were convinced that many of the acts of the state legislatures in the 1780s were unjust and unconstitutional, to believe that unelected judges could set aside acts of the popularly elected legislatures; this prerogative seemed to be an undemocratic judicial usurpation of power. But as early as 1787 James Iredell of North Carolina, soon to be appointed a justice of the newly created Supreme Court of the United States, saw that the new meaning Americans had given to a constitution had clarified the responsibility of judges to determine the law. A constitution in America, said Iredell, was not only "a fundamental law" but also a special popularly created "law in writing ... limiting the powers of the Legislature, and with which every exercise of those powers must necessarily be compared." Judges were not arbiters of the constitution or usurpers of legislative power. They were, said Iredell, merely judicial officials fulfilling their duty of applying the proper law. When faced with a decision between "the *fundamental unrepealable* law" made specially by the people and an ordinary statute enacted by a legislature contrary to the constitution, they must simply determine which law was superior. Judges could not avoid exercising this authority, concluded Iredell, for in America a constitution was not "a mere imaginary thing, about which ten thousand different opinions may be formed, but a written document to which all may have recourse, and to which, therefore, the judges cannot witfully blind themselves." Although Iredell may have been wrong about the number of different opinions that could be formed over a constitution, he was certainly right about the direction judicial authority in America would take. Through the subsequent development of the doctrine of judicial review judges in America came to exercise a power over governmental life unparalleled by any other judiciary in the world.

These then were the great contributions to constitutionalism that Americans in the Revolutionary era made to the world—the modern idea of a constitution as a written document, the device of a convention for creating and amending constitutions, the process of popular ratification, and the practice of judicial review. The sources of these constitutional contributions went back deep in Western history. For centuries people had talked about fundamental law and the placing of limits on the operations of government. But not until the American Revolution had anyone ever developed such regular and everyday institutions not only for controlling government and protecting the rights of individuals but also for changing the very framework by which the government operated. Americans in 1787 and in numerous state constitutional conventions thereafter demonstrated to the world how a people could fundamentally and yet peaceably alter their forms of government. In effect they had institutionalized and legitimized revolution. After these American achievements, discussions of constitutionalism could never again be quite the same.

Edward S. Corwin, *The "Higher Law" Background of American Constitutional Law* (1959).

J. W. Gough, *Fundamental Law in English Constitutional History* (1961).

Andrew C. McLaughlin, *The Foundations of American Constitutionalism* (1932).

Gordon S. Wood, *The Creation of the American Republic, 1776-1787* (1969).

SUGGESTED ADDITIONAL READING

Gordon S. Wood is professor of history at Brown University, and the author of *The Creation of the American Republic, 1776-1787* (University of North Carolina Press, 1969).

From Confederation to Constitution: The Revolutionary Context of the Great Convention

Lance Banning

Most Americans recall our Revolution in decidedly selective ways. As a people, we are not as eager as we used to be to recollect how truly revolutionary are our roots. Our Bicentennial celebration, for example, focused overwhelmingly on independence and the war with Britain, not on the genuinely revolutionary facets of the struggle. Too often, we commemorated even independence with hoary myths about tyrannical King George and clever minutemen who used the woods and fences to defeat the British regulars. Perhaps, then, it is not so inexcusable as it would first appear for some Americans to think that Thomas Jefferson wrote the Constitution as well as the Declaration of Independence in 1776. If we think of the American Revolution as no more than a sudden, brave attempt to shake off English rule, perverse consistency leads easily to a mistake that lumps together all the documents and incidents connected with the Founding. For a better understanding, as another Bicentennial approaches, we would do well to fit the Constitution back into the revolutionary process from which it emerged.

As John Adams said, the American Revolution was not the war against Great Britain; it should not be confused with independence. The Revolution started in the people's minds at least ten years before the famous shots at Lexington and Concord. It was well advanced before the colonies declared their independence. It continued for perhaps a quarter of a century after the fighting came to an end. It dominated the entire life experience of America's greatest generation of public men. And it was fully revolutionary in many of the strictest definitions of that term. The men who made it wanted not just independence, but a change that would transform their own

23

societies and set a new example for mankind. They wanted to create, as they put it on the Great Seal of the United States, "a new order of the ages" which would become a foundation for the happiness of all of their descendants and a model for the other peoples of the world. To their minds, the federal Constitution was a revolutionary act, an episode in their experimental quest for such an order.

A Republican Experiment

From a twentieth-century perspective, the American Revolution may appear conservative and relatively tame. There were no mass executions. Social relationships and political arrangements were not turned upside down in an upheaval of shattering violence, as they would be later on in France or Russia or any of a dozen other countries we might name. To people living through it, nonetheless—or watching it from overseas—the American Revolution seemed very radical indeed. It was not self-evident in 1776 that all men are created equal, that governments derive their just authority from popular consent, or that good governments exist in order to protect God-given rights. These concepts are not undeniable in any age. From the point of view of eighteenth-century Europeans, they contradicted common sense. The notions that a sound society could operate without the natural subordination customary where men were either commoners or nobles or that a stable government could be based entirely on elections seemed both frightening and ridiculously at odds with the obvious lessons of the past. A republican experiment had been attempted once before on something like this scale—in England during the 1640s and 1650s—and the ultimate result had been a Cromwellian dictatorship and a quick return to the ancient constitution of King, Lords, and Commons.

Nevertheless, the Americans dreamed revolutionary visions of perfection, comparable in many ways to revolutionary visions of later times. They sought a new beginning, a rebirth, in which hereditary privilege would disappear and all political authority would derive exclusively from talent, public service, and the people's choice. And their commitment to the principles of liberty and equal rights did touch and change most aspects of their common life.

No essay of this length can possibly describe all of the ways in which the Revolution altered American society. To understand the Constitution, though, we have to realize, at minimum, that as they fought the War for Independence, Americans were equally involved in a fundamental transforma-

tion of political beliefs and thus of political institutions. The decision to separate from England was also a decision that Americans were a people different from the English, a separate nation with a special mission in the world. This people had no way to understand their new identity except in terms of their historical mission, no way to define or perfect their national character except by building their new order. To be an American, by 1776, was to be a republican, and to become consistently republican required a thorough reconstruction of existing institutions.

A republican experiment, in fact, required rebuilding governments afresh. For in the months between the clash at Lexington and the Declaration of Independence, formal governments dissolved in one American colony after another. The people, who had ordinarily elected only one branch of their local governments, simply transferred their allegiance from their legal governmental institutions to extra-legal revolutionary committees, state conventions, and the Continental Congress. Through the first months of the fight, the conventions

25

A Declaration by the Representatives of the UNITED STATES OF AMERICA. in General Congress assembled.

When in the course of human events it becomes necessary for ~~a~~ one people to ~~dissolve the political bands which have connected them with another, and to~~ as-sume among the powers of the earth the ~~separate and equal~~ station to which the laws of nature & of nature's god entitle them, a decent respect to the opinions of mankind requires that they should declare the causes which impel them to ~~the~~ ~~the~~ separation.

We hold these truths to be ~~sacred & undeniable~~ self-evident; that all men are created equal ~~& independent~~; that ~~from that equal creation they derive~~ they are endowed by their creator with ~~equal~~ ~~rights some of which are~~ inherent & inalienable, rights; that among these are life, ~~&~~ liberty, & the pursuit of happiness; that to secure these ~~ends~~ rights, go-vernments are instituted among men, deriving their just powers from the consent of the governed; that whenever any form of government ~~shall~~ becomes destructive of these ends, it is the right of the people to alter or to abolish it, & to institute new government, laying it's foundation on such principles & organising it's powers in such form, as to them shall seem most likely to effect their safety & happiness. prudence indeed will dictate that governments long established should not be ch~~anged~~ for light & transient causes: and accordingly all experience hath shewn that mankind are more disposed to suffer while evils are sufferable than to right themselves by abolishing the forms to which they are accustomed. but when a long train of abuses & usurpations [begun at a distinguished period &] pursuing invariably the same object, evinces a design to ~~subject~~ reduce them under absolute Despotism, ~~to arbitrary power~~, it is their right, it is their duty, to throw off such ~~government~~ & to provide new guards for their future security. such has been the patient sufferance of these colonies; & such is now the necessity which constrains them to expunge their former systems of government. the history of the present king of Great Britain is a history of unremitting injuries and

and committees managed very well. Power rested with the people in a wholly literal sense, the people followed the directives of these revolutionary bodies, and those bodies turned the popular determination into armies and materials of war.

Some revolutionaries might have been content to see their states continue indefinitely under governmental bodies of this sort. Many patriots were intensely localistic, and they had learned a fierce distrust of any power much beyond the people's easy reach. Other patriots, however, many more of those who exercised great influence, never saw the revolutionary agencies as anything but temporary. A structure that depended so immediately on the people was good enough for an emergency, but hardly suitable for the longer term. For permanence, most patriots admired a governmental structure that balanced and divided power between different and independent parts, not one that concentrated it in single bodies which performed both legislative and executive functions.

The revolutionaries had been reared as Englishmen, in a tradition that instructed them that liberty was incompatible with the unchecked rule of the majority or with a government composed of only a single branch. Proper constitutions, they believed, depended on consent, but governments existed in order to protect the liberties of all. The revolutionaries had decided that good governments should have no place for aristocrats or kings, but they continued to believe that immediate and undiluted rule by the majority could not provide the wisdom and stability that governments require, nor could it offer proper safeguards for the rights of all. Thus, as they moved toward independence, the revolutionaries started a long search for a governmental structure in which liberty and representative democracy could be combined. This was what they meant by a "republic."

Most of the revolutionary states established written constitutions before the end of 1776. Although they differed greatly in details, these constitutions tended to be similar in broader lines. The colonial experience, together with the quarrel with Great Britain, had taught a powerful fear of the executive and of the executive's ability to undermine the independence of the other parts of government by use of patronage or "influence." Accordingly, most states created governors too weak to do such harm. Most stripped the governors of the majority of their traditional powers of appointment and deprived them of the traditional right to veto legislation. Most provided for election of the governors by the legislative branch. Most confined the chief executives, in short, to the job of enforcing the legislatures' wills.

According to these constitutions, the legislative power would remain within the people's hardy grip. The concept of a balance required two legislative houses, but hostility to privilege was far too sharp to let the second house become a bastion for any special group, in imitation of the English House of Lords. Moreover, in societies without hereditary ranks, it was difficult to reach agreement on a genuinely republican method for selecting the few men of talent and leisure whose superior wisdom, lodged in an upper house, was traditionally supposed to check the passions of the multitude. The revolutionary senates differed relatively little in their makeup from the lower houses of assembly. Democratic Pennsylvania did without an upper house at all and placed executive authority in the hands of a council, rather than a single man, though this was such a radical departure from general ideas that it quickly created an anti-constitutional party in that state.

Nearly all the revolutionaries would have failed a modern test of loyalty to democratic standards. Even the most dedicated patriots were eighteenth-century men, and eighteenth-century thinking normally excluded many portions of the people from participation in the politics of a republic: adherents to unpopular religions, women, blacks, and even very poor white males.

Accordingly, not even Pennsylvania departed so far from tradition as to give the vote to every male adult. And yet most states moved noticeably in that direction. Most lowered the amount of property one had to own in order to possess the franchise. Several gave the vote to every man who paid a tax. All the states provided for annual elections of the lower house of legislature and, often, for annual elections of the senate and governor as well. Every part of these new governments would be chosen by the people or by those the people had elected. And the legislatures in particular were filled with men whose modest means and ordinary social rank would have excluded them from higher office in colonial times. In a variety of ways, these governments were far more responsive to the people than the old colonial governments had been. They were also far more closely watched. The revolutionary air was full of popular awareness of the people's rights.

The revolutionary movement disestablished churches, altered attitudes toward slavery, and partly redefined the role of women in American society. Eventually, of course, revolutionary concepts paved the way for an extension of the rights of citizens to all the groups that eighteenth-century patriots excluded. But whatever else the Revolution was or would become, its essence lay originally in these thirteen problematic experiments in constructing republican regimes. It would succeed or fail, in revolutionary minds, according to the success of these regimes in raising the new order and fulfilling expectations that republicanism would defend and perfect this special people and the democratic social structure that they hoped would become the envy of the world.

Americans did not intend, at the beginning, to extend the revolutionary experiment in republican government from the states to the nation as a whole. Republics were expected to be small. The Revolution had begun as an attempt to protect the old colonial governments from external interference by a distant Parliament and king. Traditional loyalties and revolutionary ideas were both keyed to the states.

A Permanent Confederation

Still, the argument with Britain taught Americans to think that they were a single people, and the War for Independence built a growing sense of nationhood. There was a Continental Congress before there were any independent states. *Congress* declared American independence and recommended that new state governments be formed. *Congress* assumed the direction of the war.

The Continental Congress was an extra-legal body. It had simply emerged in the course of the imperial quarrel and continued to exert authority with the approval of the people and the states, all of which sent an unspecified number of delegates to help take care of common concerns. As early as June 12, 1776, these delegates initiated consideration of a plan to place their authority on formal grounds. But the experiences that had led to independence made Americans powerfully suspicious of any central government, and there were many disagreements in the Congress. Meanwhile, there was also the necessity of managing a war.

Not until November 17, 1777, did Congress finally present a formal proposal to the states. This plan, the Articles of Confederation, called upon the sovereign states to join in a permanent confederation presided over by a Congress whose authority would be confined to matters of interest to all: war and peace; foreign relations; trade with the Indians; disputes between states; and other common concerns. Each state would continue to have a single vote in Congress. In matters of extreme importance, such as war and peace, Congress would act only when nine of the thirteen states agreed. Since Congress would not directly represent the people, troops or money could be raised only by requisitioning the states.

The Articles of Confederation did not issue from a systematic, theoretical consideration of the problems of confederation government. For the most part, they only codified the structure and procedures that had emerged in practice in the years since 1774. Most of the country scarcely noticed when they finally went into effect, which was not until February 1781—three years after they were first proposed. Maryland, which had a definite western border, refused its consent until Virginia and the other giant states, whose colonial charters gave them boundaries which might stretch from coast to coast, agreed to cede their lands beyond the mountains to the Confederation as a whole. Then, for most of the rest of the 1780s, Americans lived in a confederation of this sort.

Historians have long since given up the old idea that the Confederation years were a period of governmental folly and unmixed disaster. The Articles established a genuine federal government, not merely a league of states. The union was to be permanent, and Congress was granted many of the usual attributes of sovereign authority. Great things were accomplished. The states secured their independence and won a generous treaty of peace, which placed their western border at the Mississippi River. The country weathered a severe post-war depression. Congress organized the area northwest of the Ohio for settlement and eventual statehood. In fact, the Northwest Ordinance of 1787 established the pattern for all the rest of the continental expansion of the United States, providing that new territories would eventually enter the union on terms of full equality with its original members and thus assuring that America would manage to escape most of the problems usually confronted by an expanding empire. It was not an unimpressive record.

Thirteen Squabbling States

Nevertheless, the Articles of Confederation came under increasing criticism from an influential minority even before they formally went into practice. This minority was centered in the Congress itself and around the powerful executive officials created by the Congress, especially Robert Morris, a Philadelphia merchant who was appointed Superintendent of Finance in 1781. Morris and his allies were necessarily concerned with the Confederation as a whole, and they found it almost impossible to meet their responsibilities under this kind of government. By the time the war was over, the Confederation's paper money was entirely worthless—"not worth a Continental," as the phrase still goes. The Confederation owed huge debts to army veterans, to citizens who had lent supplies or money during the war, and to foreign governments and foreign subjects who had purchased American bonds. Dependent on the states for revenues, Congress could not even pay the interest on these obligations. All the states had war debts of their own, and in the midst of a depression, their citizens were seldom willing or even able to pay taxes high enough to make it possible for the republics to handle their own needs and meet their congressional requisitions as well. By 1783, Morris, Alexander Hamilton, James Madison, and many other continental-minded men were insisting on reform. They demanded, at the very least, that Congress be granted the authority to levy a tax on foreign imports, which might provide it with a steady, independent source of revenue.

The need for revenue, however, was only the most urgent of several concerns. Lacking a direct connection with the people, Congress had to work through and depend on the states for nearly everything. Unable to compel cooperation, its members watched in futile anger as the sovereign republics went their separate ways. Some states quarreled over boundaries. Troubled by the depression, others passed competitive duties on foreign imports. The states ignored Confederation treaties, fought separate wars with Indians, and generally neglected congressional pleas for money.

As this happened, American ambassadors in foreign lands—John Adams in England and Thomas Jefferson in France—discovered that the European nations treated the American Confederation with contempt. The European powers refused to make commercial treaties that would lower their barriers to freer trade and ease America's commercial problems. England refused to remove her soldiers from forts in the American northwest, insisting that she would abide by the treaty of peace only when the states began to meet their own obligations to cease persecuting returning loyalists and to open their courts to British creditors who wanted to collect their debts.

Nevertheless, the nationalists in Congress were frustrated in their desire for reform. The Articles of Confederation could be amended only by unanimous consent, but when Congress recommended an amendment that would give it the authority to levy a five percent duty on imports, little Rhode Island refused to agree. When Congress asked for power to retaliate against Great Britain's navigation laws, the states again could not concur.

Repeatedly defeated in their efforts at reform, increasingly alarmed by mutual antagonisms between the states, which had grown serious enough by 1786 to threaten an immediate fragmentation of the union into several smaller confederacies, the men of continental vision turned their thoughts to fundamentals. A much more sweeping change, they now suspected, might be necessary to resolve the pressing problems of the current central government. And if the change went far enough, a few of them began to think, it might accomplish something more. It might restore the Revolution to its proper course.

The Revolution, after all, involved a dream of national greatness; and the dream was going wrong. A people who had hoped to be a model for the world was fragmented into thirteen petty, squabbling states. The states would not—or could not—subordinate their separate interests to the good of the Confederation as a whole. Even worse, too many of the states fell short of fulfilling revolutionary expectations within their individual bounds. The early revolutionary constitutions had delivered overwhelming power to the people's immediate representatives in the lower houses of assembly. As these lower houses struggled to protect the people from hard times, they frequently neglected private rights and seldom seemed to give a due consideration to the long-term good. As clashing groups in different states competed to control their house of representatives, nobody could feel certain what the law might be next year, when one majority replaced another. The lower houses of assembly were essentially unchecked by the other parts of government, and to many revolutionaries it appeared that the assemblies proceeded on their ways with slight regard for justice and little thought about tomorrow. The rule of law appeared to be collapsing into a kind of anarchy in which the liberty and property of everyone might depend on the good will of whichever temporary majority happened to control his state. No one could feel secure in the enjoyment of his rights.

Liberty in Peril   During the 1780s, in other words, the feeling grew that liberty was once again in peril. Alarm was most intense among the men whose duties, education, or experience encouraged them to pin their patriotic feelings on the continent as a whole: certain members of Congress; most of the best-known revolutionary thinkers; most of the former officers of the continental army; many merchants, public creditors, and other men of wealth. Men of social standing were distressed with the way in which the revolutionary principles of liberty and equality seemed to shade into a popular contempt for talent or distinction. Too often, to their minds, the best men lost elections in the states to self-serving, scrambling demagogues, and the revolutionary constitutions made it far too easy for these demagogues to set an ill-considered course or even to oppress the propertied minority in order to secure the people's favor. Continued confiscations of the property of people who had sympathized with Britain and continued use of paper money, which threatened men's investments and their right to hold their property secure, were grievances of particular importance to those who had investments and positions to defend.

And yet the sense of fading hopes and failing visions was not exclusively confined to men of wealth. Anyone whose life had been immersed in revolutionary expectations might share in the concern. Every state seemed full of quarrels. Every individual seemed to be on the scrape for himself. No one seemed to have a real regard for common interests, a willingness to recognize that selfish interests must be limited by some consideration for the good of all. Public virtue, to use the phrase the revolutionaries used, seemed to be in danger of completely disappearing as every man and every social group sought private goods at the expense of harmony and other people's rights. But virtue, revolutionaries thought, was the indispensable foundation for republics, without which they could not survive. If public virtue was collapsing, then the Revolution was about to fail. It would degenerate into a kind of chaos, from which a tyrant might emerge, or else the people, in disgust, might eventually prefer to return to hereditary rule.

So, at least, did many fear. Guided by the same ideas that had impelled them into independence, they saw a second crisis, as dangerous to liberty as the crisis that had led them into Revolution. As they had done in 1776, they blamed their discontents on governments that lacked the character to mold a virtuous people and fit them for their special role. Once more, they turned to constitutional reform. They saw in the problems of the Confederation government not merely difficulties that would have to be corrected, but an opportunity that might be seized for even greater ends, an opportunity to rescue revolutionary hopes from their decay.

The constitutional reformers of the 1780s had several different motives and several different goals. Some had an economic interest in a constitutional reform that would enable the central government to pay its debts and act to spur the economic revival. All wanted to make the government adequate to its tasks and able to command more respect from the rest of the world. Some wanted more: to reconstruct the central government in such a way that its virtues might override the mistakes that had been made in some of the states. They wanted to redeem the reputation of democracy and save the republican experiment from a process of degeneration which threatened to destroy all that they had struggled for.

Shays' Rebellion handed them their chance. Out in western Massachusetts, hard times, large debts, and the high taxes prompted by the state's attempt to handle its revolutionary debt drove many farmers to distress. They first petitioned for relief, but when the legislature refused to issue paper money or to pass the laws required to protect their property from seizure, petitions gave way to rebellion. Farmers forced the courts to close in several counties, and Daniel Shays, a revolutionary captain, organized an armed resistance. The rebels were defeated with surprising ease. The state called out

Massachusetts militiamen firing into the ranks of Shays' rebels

the militia during the winter of 1786, and Shays' forces disintegrated after a minor fight. The incident was nonetheless, for many, the final straw atop a growing load of fears. Armed resistance to a republican government seemed the ultimate warning of a coming collapse.

Earlier in 1786, delegates from five states had met at Annapolis, Maryland, to consider better means of regulating interstate and international trade. Nationalist sentiment was strong among the delegates. Hamilton and Madison were there. The participants quickly agreed that little could be done about commercial problems without a revision of the Articles of Confederation. They said as much in a report to Congress and their states, and Congress endorsed their recommendation for the meeting of a national convention to consider ways to make the central government "adequate to the exigencies of the union." Badly frightened by events in Massachusetts, whose constitution was widely thought to be among the best, every state except Rhode Island answered the call. From this context and in hope that it might save both liberty and union, the Constitutional Convention emerged.

Gordon S. Wood, *The Creation of the American Republic, 1776-1787* (1969).

H. James Henderson, *Party Politics in the Continental Congress* (1974).

Jack N. Rakove, *The Beginnings of National Politics: An Interpretive History of the Continental Congress* (1979).

Willi Paul Adams, *The First American Constitutions: Republican Ideology and the Making of the State Constitutions in the Revolutionary Era,* translated by Rita and Robert Kimber (1980).

Jackson Turner Main, *The Sovereign States, 1775-1783* (1973).

SUGGESTED ADDITIONAL READING

Lance Banning is associate professor of history at the University of Kentucky. A former N.E.H. and John Simon Guggenheim Fellow, he is the author of *The Jeffersonian Persuasion: Evolution of a Party Ideology* (Cornell University Press, 1978). He is currently engaged in a study of the life and thought of James Madison.

The Imperial Roots of American Federalism

Jack P. Greene

"This government is so new, it wants a name." Thus complained Patrick Henry, one of the most articulate, prominent, and formidable opponents of the new Constitution in June 1788 during the Virginia ratifying convention. Scholars have since argued over whether the government formed under the Constitution was democratic. But virtually all of them—of whatever ideological hues or methodological orientations—have agreed that Henry was correct, that the new federal political system created by the Constitution was an entirely new, even quite a radical, departure in political institutions.

Mislabeled by its opponents as a *consolidated* government, it was, in response to hostile critics like Henry, called by its supporters first a *confederal* and then a *federal* government, a name that has stuck with it ever since. Whether this creation was in fact entirely new and, if so, whence it derived and what precisely was new about it are the principal questions that will be taken up in this article.

Precedents

We can perhaps best begin this discussion with a brief definition of the term *federalism*. Federalism is a political arrangement in which the basic powers of sovereignty are distributed among several governments, each of which has its own distinct share of those powers. A federal state differs from a *unitary*, or *consolidated* or *centralized*, state such as those that have existed throughout most of western Europe since the Renaissance. A unitary state concentrates sovereign authority in a single government.

A federal system can be further distinguished from a *confederation*, like the Holy Roman Empire or the United States between 1776 and 1788. Merely an association or league of sovereign governments organized for some designated purposes of mutual interest, a confederation places ultimate

authority in the several member states, which delegate a few carefully limited powers to the general government. Whether a government is unitary, confederal, or federal depends primarily on the location of the basic powers of sovereignty.

Opponents of the Constitution in 1787-88 charged, and its supporters freely admitted, that there were no other examples in the contemporary world of a federal state. As James Madison pointed out in *The Federalist,* Nos. 19 and 20, those few European states that were not unitary in structure—Poland, the Swiss Cantons, and the Netherlands—were all loose confederations.

The ancient world also included several non-unitary polities that were familiar to the men who framed the United States Constitution. The "most considerable" of these, Madison wrote in *The Federalist* No. 18, was "that of the Grecian

38

republics, associated under the Amphictyonic council." According to "the best accounts transmitted of this celebrated institution," it bore "a very instructive analogy" to the Articles of Confederation, the government the Philadelphia Convention was proposing to replace. But it in no sense corresponded to the new federal scheme of government devised by the convention.

By contrast, two other unions of Grecian republics, the Archaen League and the Lycian Confederacy, seem to have resembled the American federal government somewhat more closely. In each, Madison noted in *The Federalist,* "it is probable that the federal head had a degree and species of power, which gave it a considerable likeness to the government framed" at Philadelphia. As Madison admitted, however, "such imperfect monuments" remained of those "curious political fabric[s]" that they threw much less "light . . . on the science of federal government" than the founding fathers would have liked.

As the great American constitutional historian Andrew C. McLaughlin pointed out over fifty years ago, however, another precedent existed much closer to home and was much more familiar to the framers of the American constitution. That precedent was to be found in the structure of the British Empire as it had functioned in fact, if not in theory, over much of the period from its founding in 1607 until its partial dissolution as a result of the American Revolution.

"Anyone even slightly familiar with the American constitutional system," wrote McLaughlin, "will see at once the similarity between the general scheme of the old empire and the American political system of federalism." In theory, the central, or metropolitan, government in Britain had unqualified authority. In practice, however, power was distributed between the metropolitan government and the several colonial governments. Each colonist, McLaughlin noted, obviously lived "under two governments." One was imperial in scope and exercised full authority over foreign affairs, war, peace, and intercolonial and foreign trade. The other was a colonial government that exercised *de facto* and virtually exclusive jurisdiction over almost all matters of local concern. Far from being "a thoroughly consolidated and centralized" political entity, the early British Empire thus actually embodied the most basic principles of federalism.

**Theory and Practice
in the Early Modern
British Empire**

But if such a *de facto* division of power characterized the early modern British Empire, it certainly had no firm *de jure* status. Indeed, the question of how authority was distributed between the metropolitan government at the center and the several colonial governments in the periphery of the empire in America was the principal source of political contention within the old empire. As the debate over this question gradually took shape during the last four decades of the seventeenth century, the central underlying issue was to what extent—and in what cases—the authority of the metropolitan government in London limited the scope of the powers of the colonial legislatures.

Colonial assemblies could neither pass laws nor, in most colonies, even meet without the consent of the governor. Like the British monarch, governors continued to play an influential role in the legislative process. Nevertheless, the assemblies early claimed full legislative authority over their respective jurisdictions. They based these claims upon two foundations. First, they stood upon the inherited right of their constituents not to be subject to any laws passed without the consent of their representatives, a right that for most colonies seemed to have been confirmed by their early charters from the crown. Second, they relied upon precedent. By the middle of the eighteenth century, they had actually exercised such authority for many decades and in some cases for well over a century.

Even though they had been so long in possession of such extensive authority over local affairs, the colonial assemblies never managed to persuade the metropolitan government to admit in theory what they had achieved in fact. As a result, their authority in relation to that of the crown and Parliament in London remained in an extremely uncertain state. To have eliminated that uncertainty would have required, as the English economic writer Charles Davenant recognized as early as the 1690s, a clear delineation of the "bounds between the chief power [in Britain] and the people" in the colonies in a way acceptable to both. No matter how much power they actually exerted within their respective spheres, in the absence of such an arrangement, the colonial legislatures could never be entirely secure from the overwhelming might of the metropolitan government. They could never be sure that their constituents would enjoy the same degree of protection of their liberties and properties as did their fellow Englishmen in Britain.

Before the 1760s, the recurrent debates over this subject focused on whether crown orders to colonial governors—they were called royal instructions—actually had the force of law within the colonies. In 1757, Lord Granville, president of the King's Privy Council, elaborated the official metropolitan view during an interview with Benjamin Franklin. Because the royal instructions were drawn up by the Privy Council and because the "King in Council is THE LEGISLATOR of the Colonies," Granville insisted, such instructions constituted "the LAW OF THE LAND" in the colonies "and as such *ought to be* OBEYED."

In reply, Franklin admitted that the colonial legislatures could not "make permanent laws" without the king's consent: all legislation in most colonies required the royal approval. But, he argued, instructions were not laws because, by both charters and longstanding custom, colonial "laws were to be made by [the colonial] . . . Assemblies," and the king could not "make a law for [the colonists] without" their consent.

Although the subject was never fully explored and certainly never resolved, the fundamental issue in this debate was the location of the basic powers of sovereignty within the

Benjamin Franklin

Parade of the Stamp Act in New York

British Empire. According to the logic of Granville's position, those powers were concentrated solely in the King-in-Council which had total authority over the colonies. By contrast, Franklin's reply assumed that at the time of initial settlement the king had delegated some of that authority to the colonial governments and could not subsequently act in the areas so delegated without the consent of the colonial legislatures.

This running dispute elicited almost no discussion of the role of Parliament in relation to the colonies, the issue that would eventually stir so much controversy during the 1760s and 1770s. Prior to the 1760s, Parliament exerted its legislative authority over the colonies only in very limited spheres, primarily involving defense, trade, and other matters of strategic and economic concern to the empire as a whole. Nevertheless, to the extent that they considered Parliament's relationship to the colonies at all, people on both sides of the Atlantic seem to have regarded its authority as being unlimited.

The many contemporary references to Parliament as the ultimate protector of colonial, as well as metropolitan, rights and privileges strongly suggest that the colonists did not yet think of Parliament as a threat to the authority of their own legislatures. "There was no Doubt," Franklin wrote in 1756, "but the Parliament understand the Rights of Government" and, he implied, could be trusted to protect them, in the colonies quite as much as in Britain itself.

Everybody knew of instances in which crown officials, acting in their executive capacity, had, through either ignorance or malice, taken oppressive measures against the colonists. But no one could trace a single such action to Parliament. Indeed, when the crown's ministers in 1744 and 1749 had proposed that Parliament pass a statute "to make the King's instructions laws in the colonies," Parliament voted it down, an action, Franklin later recalled, "for which we adored them as our friends and [as] friends of liberty."

Because they regarded Parliament as a potential ally in the efforts of their legislatures to hold on to their authority over local affairs, colonial political thinkers made no systematic attempt prior to the 1760s to argue that Parliament's colonial authority had any limits. Nevertheless, in response to proposals in the early 1750s that Parliament might tax the colonies for defense, some colonists did suggest that, because "the Colonists have no Representatives in Parliament" and because it was "suppos'd an undoubted Right of Englishmen not to be taxed but by their Consent given thro' their [own] Representatives," Parliament had no authority to tax the colonies.

Again, this suggestion implied that, far from being concentrated entirely in the metropolitan government, the essential powers of sovereignty were distributed between it and the several colonial governments and that each colonial government had exclusive power to tax the inhabitants in the area for which it had responsibility. Meanwhile, notwithstanding the absence of theoretical agreement about the distribution of power within the empire, the empire continued to function in practice with a rather clear demarcation of authority; the colonial governments handled virtually all internal matters and the metropolitan government in London oversaw most external affairs.

Searching for a Principle

Parliament's explicit effort to impose taxes on the colonies in the mid-1760s, in particular through the Stamp Act of 1765, prompted a fuller exploration of the distribution of power within the British Empire. In response to that measure, the colonists took the position that they could not be taxed except by their own legislatures and that Parliament had no authority to tax them for revenue. This position implied that Parliament could legislate for the colonies and levy duties for purposes of regulating trade as opposed to raising a revenue.

But in a significant number of instances, colonists denied not only Parliament's authority to tax but also its right to pass laws relating to the "internal polity" of the colonies. Thus did the Virginia Assembly in a petition to the king in December 1764 protesting against the proposed Stamp Act claim for Virginians the "ancient and inestimable Right of being governed by such Laws respecting their internal Polity and Taxation as are derived from their own Consent." The Virginia House of Burgesses reiterated this claim in resolutions in May 1765, and the legislatures of Rhode Island, Maryland, and Connecticut repeated it in one form or another later that year.

To discover precisely what Virginians and others were claiming in 1764-66 when they denied Parliament's right to pass laws respecting the internal polity of the colonies, we can turn to the writings of the Virginia lawyer and antiquarian Richard Bland. In two pamphlets, *The Colonel Dismounted,* published in 1764 just a few weeks before the Virginia legislature prepared the petition to the king referred to above, and *An Inquiry Into the Rights of the British Colonies,* published early in 1766 after Parliament had enacted the Stamp Act, Bland claimed for the colonists the "right . . . of directing their *internal* government by laws made with their own consent." In addition, he argued that each colony was "a distinct State, independent, as to their *internal* Government, of the original Kingdom, but united with her, as to their *external* Polity, in the closest and most intimate LEAGUE AND AMITY, under the same Allegiance, and enjoying the Benefits of a reciprocal intercourse."

Bland did not make clear exactly what specific matters were subsumed under the term *internal* and what under *external.* But he clearly implied that Parliament's authority over the colonies stopped somewhere short of the Atlantic coast and did not extend over any affairs relating exclusively to their internal life. Although he acknowledged that the colonies were subordinate to Parliament, he denied that they were "absolutely so." He contended that Parliament could not constitutionally pass tax measures or any other laws that violated the colonists' essential rights as Englishmen, especially their right to be governed in their internal affairs by laws made with their own consent as expressed through their elected representatives.

Most of the colonial protests against the Stamp Act, especially the official protests of the Stamp Act Congress in the fall of 1765, did not go so far as the Virginians in excluding Parliament from all jurisdiction over the internal affairs of the colonies. Rather, they mostly tended to exclude Parliament only from any authority to tax the colonies for revenue. Probably, as Edmund S. Morgan has remarked, because "the issue of the day was taxation" and "Parliament at this time was not attempting to interfere" with other aspects of the internal affairs of the colonies, few saw the need to consider explicitly the larger question of the general limits of Parliament's colonial authority. But the Virginia protests suggest the existence of a strong impulse in the colonies to deny Parliament's jurisdiction over all internal colonial matters.

Whether they drew the lines between taxation and legislation or between internal and external spheres of government, *all* colonial protests displayed a common concern to specify the jurisdictional boundaries between Parliament and the colonial assemblies. This concern clearly implied a conception of empire in which the essential powers of sovereignty were not, as most metropolitan political writers and officials maintained, concentrated in Parliament but were distributed among several distinct polities within the empire, much in the manner of the American federal system contrived in 1787. This concern also underlined the fact that in practice the essential powers of sovereignty were already distributed among those polities and pointed to the need for some explicit definition of exactly how and by what underlying principles those powers were distributed.

The metropolitan response to colonial protests against the Stamp Act revealed that no one in Britain shared the colonial conception of empire, except for a few Americans like Benjamin Franklin. Although a few British political leaders accepted the colonial claim of no taxation without representation and denied Parliament's right to tax the colonies for revenue, Sir William Blackstone, the eminent professor of English law at Oxford, sounded the predominant opinion.

In his influential *Commentaries on the Laws of England,* the first volume of which was published in 1765 during the Stamp Act crisis, Blackstone argued that the King-in-Parliament had absolute and indivisible authority over all matters relating to all Britons everywhere. "What the Parliament doth" with reference to any of the British dominions, he declared, "no authority upon earth can undo." The colonies were perforce subject to its jurisdiction. In the British view, the basic powers of sovereignty were not distributed among the metropolitan and colonial governments but were concentrated in the hands of the King-in-Parliament.

To most Britons in the home islands, in fact, the colonial position appeared incomprehensible because it seemed to suggest the existence of more than one sovereign power in a single political entity. Sovereignty, they believed in common with virtually all contemporary political thinkers in Britain and Europe, could not be divided. *Imperium in imperio,* a sovereign authority within a sovereign authority, seemed to them a contradiction in terms. The colonies were either part of the British Empire and therefore under the sovereign authority of the King-in-Parliament or entirely separate states, each of which was sovereign over its own territory and inhabitants. According to British theory and in total disregard of the experience of a century and a half of imperial governance, no half-way ground between these two positions could exist.

For the next eight years, the controversy over the question of the respective jurisdictions of Parliament and the colonial legislatures, what McLaughlin has referred to as "the problem of imperial organization," lay at the heart of the deepening conflict between Britain and the colonies. While British political and constitutional theorists continued to deny that "powers could be distinguished one from the other" and to assert that Parliament either had "all powers or none," a long line of colonial thinkers persisted in their efforts to try to draw a line between the jurisdiction of Parliament and that of the colonial legislatures.

As writers such as John Dickinson followed out the logic of the line drawn by the Stamp Act Congress, most colonists from 1767 to 1774 seem to have held that Parliament could legislate for the colonies but could not tax them for revenue. But an increasing number of Americans, looking at the problem with a more penetrating eye, began to view it in terms closer to those of Bland and the Virginia legislature. For instance, as early as 1766 Franklin had begun to think of the colonies as "so many separate little States, subject to the same Prince, but each with its own Parliament." "The Sovereignty of the King is therefore easily understood," he wrote the Scottish philosopher Lord Kames from London in early 1767. But, he complained, "nothing is more common here than to talk of the *Sovereignty of Parliament,* and the *Sovereignty of this Nation* over the Colonies," and these kinds of sovereignties he found difficult to reconcile with the *de facto* situation of government as it had existed within the empire for the previous century. Franklin did admit, however, that it seemed "necessary for the common Good of the Empire, that a Power be lodg'd some-where to regulate its general Commerce" and other matters of broad concern.

William Blackstone

Over the next several years, one thinker after another came to similar conclusions. Two lawyers, James Wilson of Pennsylvania and Thomas Jefferson of Virginia, both published pamphlets in 1774 in which they argued that the colonies were distinct and independent governments bound to Britain only through their mutual allegiance to a common monarch, that the British Parliament had no authority to exercise any jurisdiction over them, and as Wilson put it, that "the only dependency, which [the colonists] . . . ought to acknowledge, is a dependency on the Crown."

The First Continental Congress endorsed this position in its Declaration and Resolves in October 1774. In that docu-ment, Congress explicitly denied that Parliament had any authority to legislate for the colonies, albeit it did commit the colonists to abide by such Parliamentary statutes for regulating the external commerce of the colonies as were genuinely designed to secure "the commercial advantages of the whole empire to the mother country, and the commercial benefits of its respective members." But this offer, Congress emphasized, did not constitute an admission of Parliament's right to institute such regulations but was made only because of "the necessity of the case."

Congress thus drew a line very similar both to existing practice within the empire and to the boundary suggested by Bland and the Virginia legislature at the very beginning of the great constitutional debate over the problem of imperial orga-nization. According to Congress, the colonial governments, acting in conjunction with the king, had clear title to all of the essential powers of sovereignty relating to matters concerning the internal affairs of the colonies, just as the King-in-Parliament had similar title for those matters relating to the internal affairs of Britain. That much now seemed obvious, at least to the leaders of American resistance.

But other areas did not obviously belong within the jurisdiction of any one of the several governments within the British Empire. Constitutionally, it was not clear that those areas belonged to the government of any one of the individual states any more than to that of one of the others. But because the metropolitan government had conventionally exercised such authority for the whole empire, the colonies agreed, for the time being, to obey all Parliamentary measures that seemed to them to be for the general welfare of the whole.

The First Continental Congress thus not only asserted the possibility of distinguishing among various categories of the essential powers of sovereignty in a political association of distinct states like, according to their conception, the British Empire. It also specified the crucial line of demarcation between those powers relating to the purely internal and local affairs of each member state and those concerning matters in which all of the states had some common interest.

More important, perhaps, in terms of the history of the development of the idea of federalism, Congress had identified—without clearly recognizing that it had done so—the need within such an association for one central authority with the power to deal with all matters of mutual concern. This need could not be constitutionally met within the existing structure of the empire.

The Principle Defined

In many respects, much of the constitutional history of the next twelve years, from the Declaration and Resolves of the First Continental Congress in 1774 to the Federal Convention in 1787, revolved around the search for some way to meet the need for a central authority without destroying the sovereignty of the individual states. The new United States had, in a sense, merely inherited the problem of imperial organization from the British Empire.

Though it scarcely articulated the problem so succinctly, one of the main questions of the first decade of independence was, in the words of McLaughlin, "whether federalism was possible as a theory of political organization." The early modern British Empire might indeed have been characterized by a *de facto* distribution rather than by a concentration of authority. But could the founders devise any theory or set of constitutional principles by which to divide the essential powers of sovereignty?

The Articles of Confederation, the first national government, obviously did not solve this problem. The Articles clearly distinguished those powers that should belong to the national government from those that should be left to the states. In general, it drew the line precisely where the First Continental Congress had decided it had been drawn in the empire: between matters of purely local concern, which remained entirely in the hands of the states, and matters of common concern to all the states, which came within the jurisdiction of the Confederation Congress.

In effect, however, the Articles of Confederation established no more than a league of sovereign states, each of which had agreed that the general government should have authority over certain concerns of general interest, including war, peace, and disputes among states. But the Articles did not provide the general government with power sufficient to carry its authority into existence. As John Adams remarked, Congress under the Articles was "not a legislative assembly, nor a representative assembly, but only a diplomatic assembly." All of the essential powers of sovereignty remained in the hands of the states. They did not relinquish any of them because they had not yet devised a theory that would permit them to resolve the problem that had brought the empire to grief, the problem of whether the essential powers of sovereignty could be divided. Prior to 1787, no one had yet found a way to disprove Blackstone's maxim that sovereignty, "the Summa imperii," was indivisible.

By 1787, the weakness of the national government under the Articles of Confederation had caused many to fear for the future of the American union. Called together for the explicit purpose of strengthening the national government, the Philadelphia Convention of that year quickly found itself confronted with the old problem, as McLaughlin has phrased it, of imperial order, the problem of how to create a strong "national government without destroying the states as integral, and, in many respects, autonomous parts of" the political system.

The members of the Convention soon, in McLaughlin's words, "found themselves engaged in the task of constructing a new kind of body politic," one that was "neither a centralized system on the one hand nor a league or confederation on the other." They had relatively little difficulty in allocating powers between the national and the state governments. Their experi-

Alexander Hamilton

ence with both the empire and the Articles of Confederation provided clear guidance in that. But they confronted a vastly more difficult task in devising a system through which the basic powers of sovereignty could not only be divided between the national and state governments but divided in such a way as to keep one level of government from encroaching upon the other.

The old and as yet unresolved question of by what principles the essential powers of sovereignty could be distributed still constituted the main difficulty in this enterprise. As McLaughlin has said, the Convention's solution to this question was both its "signal contribution . . . to the political life of the modern world" and the most important American contribution to political theory and practice. So original was the Convention's solution that its members did not fully understand what they had done until after the Constitution had been completed and they had—in the crucible of debate—to explain the principles behind the new government and how it would operate.

As Gordon S. Wood has shown in *The Creation of the American Republic,* a crucial intellectual breakthrough made the contrivance of an acceptable federal system possible: the idea that sovereignty lay not in governments (and hence not in the governments of individual states) but in the people themselves. If, as the new Constitution assumed, sovereignty resided in the people, the "state governments could never lose their sovereignty because they had never possessed it." In addition, the sovereign people could delegate the basic powers of sovereignty to any government or governments they wished, and they could divide up those powers in any way they saw fit, delegating some to one level of government and others to another, while retaining still others in their own hands.

Thus, as Madison wrote in *The Federalist,* both the state governments and the national government were equally creatures of the people: "both [were] possessed of our equal confidence—both [were] chosen in the same manner, and [both were] equally responsible to us." "The federal and state governments," said Madison, "are in fact but different agents and trustees of the people, constituted with different powers, and designed for different purposes." Although the supremacy clause in Article VI of the Constitution ensured that federal laws would take precedence over state laws whenever the two came into conflict, both the national government and the state governments were to have full authority within their respective spheres.

The framers had thus fashioned a government that was neither a consolidated government nor a mere confederation of sovereign states. In the words of Alexander Hamilton in *The Federalist,* the former implied "an entire consolidation of the States into one complete national sovereignty with an entire subordination of the parts" to that national sovereignty, while the latter suggested simply "an association of two or more states" into one polity with all sovereignty remaining in the states. The new federal government was something in between. It aimed, said Alexander Hamilton in *The Federalist* No. 32, "only at a partial . . . consolidation" in which the states clearly retained all those rights of sovereignty that they had traditionally exercised, except for those that through the Constitution had been reallocated by the people to the federal government.

**Something Old and
Something New**

As McLaughlin argued, the American federal state was indeed "the child of the old British empire." In contriving the Constitution, the framers clearly drew, if in many ways only half consciously, upon the experience and precedents of the empire. Like the empire, the American federal system did not concentrate power in a single government but distributed it among different levels of government. It thus "gave legal and institutional reality to the principle of diversification of powers and ... crystallized a system much like that under which the colonists had grown to maturity."

But if the American federal system was not so radical in form, it was fundamentally so in principle. By locating sovereignty in the people rather than in the government or in some branch thereof, the framers of the Constitution had contrived a radical new scheme of governance whereby the basic powers of sovereignty could be divided without dividing sovereignty itself. This intellectual—and political—invention not only finally made possible the solution of the imperial problem of the relationship between local and national authority in its American context. It also provided a structure that was—and, in principle, still is—capable of a variety of permutations and combinations as sovereign groups of people seek to work out forms peculiarly appropriate for governing themselves.

**SUGGESTED
ADDITIONAL READING**

Bernard Bailyn, *The Ideological Origins of the American Revolution* (1967).

Jack P. Greene, *The Quest for Power: The Lower Houses of Assembly, 1689-1776* (1963).

Andrew C. McLaughlin, *The Foundations of American Constitutionalism* (1932).

Edmund S. Morgan and Helen M. Morgan, *The Stamp Act Crisis: Prologue to Revolution* (1953).

Jack N. Rakove, *The Beginnings of National Politics: An Interpretive History of the Continental Congress* (1979).

Gordon S. Wood, *The Creation of the American Republic, 1776-1787* (1969).

Jack P. Greene is Andrew W. Mellon Professor in the Humanities at Johns Hopkins University. He is now finishing a book on British-American constitutional development, 1607 and 1788.

II. Designing the Government

53

Framing a Congress to Channel Ambition

Michael J. Malbin

Debates over the role and structure of Congress took up well over half of the 1787 Constitutional Convention. In fact, the convention probably owed its success to the way profound, divisive issues were presented in the context of specific choices about institutions and about representation. Much of the credit goes to James Madison and other Virginians who helped draft, and then persuaded the respected Governor Edmund Randolph to introduce, a series of fifteen concrete resolutions that were much more far-reaching in their overall effect than they may have seemed on first appearance.

The Convention began its substantive work on May 30. For two weeks, until June 13, the Virginia plan dominated the agenda, as delegates considered and amended its proposals twice through clause by clause. During these weeks, as historian Forrest McDonald has said, "the delegates spoke and voted as if the question before them were *what kind* of a national government would be created. . . . [But] the real issue, throughout, was whether there would be a national government—and therefore a nation—at all."

The basic issue was not joined directly until William Paterson of New Jersey presented a set of counterproposals to the convention on June 15. The New Jersey plan would have "revised, corrected and enlarged" the Articles by creating a new executive and judicial branch of government and by increasing Congress' power. But the Paterson plan sharply disagreed with Virginia's on a key feature of the confederal system. The Virginia plan provided for a two-chamber legislature with each chamber allocating representatives on the basis of population. The New Jersey plan maintained Congress as a unicameral legislature, as it was under the Articles of Confederation, with each state having an equal vote. The dispute between the two plans over representation became the core issue dividing delegates who wanted to preserve the Confederation from those who wanted a more national government.

In his classic 1913 study of the convention, Max Farrand wrote:

> It is altogether possible, if the New Jersey plan had been presented to the convention at the same time as the Virginia plan, that is on May 29, and if without discussion a choice had then been made between the two, that the former would have been selected.... But in the course of the two weeks' discussions, many of the delegates had become accustomed to what might well have appeared to them at the outset as somewhat radical ideas.

On June 19, the convention voted 7 to 3 (with one state divided) to proceed with the Virginia plan. One vote did not settle the matter, however. Over the next month the original supporters of the New Jersey plan tried numerous times to reargue the basic issue, first by trying unsuccessfully to gain equality of state representation in the House, and then finally by winning a compromise that tilted heavily toward the nationalists, but gave the states equality in the Senate.

Because the representational issues dividing the New Jersey and Virginia plans were seen by the delegates as being the most crucial ones before them, the convention's records pose some problems for understanding how the Framers might have intended Congress to perform. The primary question was: "What should the government represent, people or states?" (A few delegates, including Pennsylvania's Gouverneur Morris and South Carolina's General Charles Pinckney wanted to add property to the basic two-part dispute.) The question of "what" is conceptually distinct from and logically prior to the question of "how." *How* representatives ought to behave can only be determined once you know *what* they are supposed to represent and *why*. But these concerns became thoroughly intertwined in the convention and ratifying period, and so they must remain here. To understand how the Framers were hoping Congress would behave, we must start with more basic issues. In so doing, we will be able not only to learn about Congress, but also to understand the role of institutions more generally in the thinking of the Constitution's framers.

Basic Premises   Most of the participants in the 1787 Convention, and most Federalists and Anti-Federalists in the subsequent debate over ratification, had remarkably similar views about both the bedrock nature of human beings and the desired ends of government. They agreed, for example, that people are naturally selfish creatures whose equal and natural rights derive from their self-interested origins. They also agreed that without civil society, people's natural and equal rights to life, liberty, and the pursuit of happiness were constantly imperiled. Finally, to use the language of the Declaration of Independence on the purpose of government, they agreed that "to secure these rights, Governments are instituted among men, deriving their just powers from the consent of the governed." In other words, the American debate of 1787-89 was conducted, as Herbert Storing has shown, among people who agreed both about the unchangeable starting point (human nature) and about the

The Virginia plan, in George Washington's hand

desired end. In both these matters, the disagreeing Americans stood squarely within a common, modern, philosophic framework.

If the two contending sides of 1787-89 agreed about where their discussion should begin and end, they disagreed sharply about how to get from one place to the other. The Federalist and Anti-Federalist agreement on the primacy of self-interest led both to be concerned that people in government might use power to serve their own ends at the expense of ordinary citizens. The first level of protection against this, for both Federalists and Anti-Federalists, lay in the people's ability, directly or indirectly, to choose their own representatives. From this point on, their arguments diverged.

For the Anti-Federalists, keeping the government true to its proper end would require the people to maintain a vigilant watch and zealous control over the actions of their representatives. As presented in the state ratifying conventions, this meant frequent elections, the ability to instruct representatives on specific legislative issues, the ability to recall representatives in mid-term and, most of all, it meant legislative districts that were small enough for people to know and judge their representatives personally.

If districts are to be kept small then so must the nation, or else the legislature would become so large as to be unwieldy. But many—not all, but many—of the Anti-Federalists had another, more basic, reason for preferring small republics to large ones. For them, the preservation of liberty required citizens not only to be vigilant but also to exercise self-restraint, to moderate their self-interest in the name of the general welfare. These Anti-Federalists also believed preserving freedom required the government to educate citizens to care about the public good, and that such education was only possible in a regime that was small enough for citizens to feel they belonged to a common community.

The supporters of the Constitution rejected the Anti-Federalist notion that zealous watchfulness, even if supplemented by citizenship education, could preserve liberty in a small republic. This disagreement was central to the Federalists' ideas about institutions in general, and Congress in particular.

FEDERAL HALL

The Seat of CONGRESS

Printed & Sold by A. Doolittle New-Haven 1790

Senate chamber during John Adams' presidency

Federalists on Faction and Representation

The clearest statement of the Federalists' rejection of the small republic argument is in James Madison's *Federalist* No. 10. Vigilance is not enough to protect freedom in a small republic, Madison argued, because a vigilantly self-interested majority could still use its power to oppress a minority. The problem, Madison argued, is that human beings by nature will have different passions, opinions, and interests, and that groups of people with similar passions, opinions, and interests will tend to band together to form factions that will try to take actions that are adverse either to the rights of other citizens or to the permanent and aggregate interests of the community. The problem of faction, Madison went on, could not be avoided by educating citizens to be virtuous, or to act in the name of the common good. Even if citizens could be made to care about the common good, they could not all be given the same opinions. Inevitably, their opinions will be colored by their self-interest, replacing factions founded on low calculations of self-interest with even more dangerous ones founded upon selfishly informed, uncompromising righteousness.

The constitutional solution, as is well known, was an extended or large, commercial republic in which factions would be encouraged to multiply. The more factions there were, the less likely would it be that any one could become a majority and use its position to oppress the minority. From a multiplicity of factions immediately flows a legislative process in which legislators must think of others' needs to achieve their own objectives. If no single faction comprises an electoral majority by itself, legislative majorities in a large republic ordinarily have to be made up of coalitions of minorities that come together only after a process of accommodation and compromise. Factions that help form today's legislative majority will moderate their demands because they may be part of tomorrow's minority. For the same reason, today's minorities will not feel so frustrated as to think of rebellion, because they might well help form tomorrow's majority.

But large republics do more than produce multiple factions and the Constitution provides for something more than a pluralistic politics of compromise and coalition. Large republics are representative rather than direct democracies, and representatives do not simply reflect the opinions or factions that exist in the general public. Instead, Madison said in No. 10, the effect of representation *necessarily* is to "refine and enlarge the public views"—sometimes by improving them, and sometimes by making them worse. The aim of the Constitution was to create institutions that would improve as they refined.

Self-Interest and the Electoral Connection

One reason legislators "refine and enlarge the public views" is that they, like everyone else, act primarily from self-interested motives. Legislators may share some of their constituents' interests and passions, but they will also have some of their own. The framers saw self-interest as anything but a monolithic passion. The fact is, as they noted, that people define their interests differently: some want wealth, others want small tokens of honor, and a few will be satisfied with nothing less than lasting fame. (See *The Federalist* Nos. 57, 25, and 71.)

The danger of representative government is that greedy legislators may use the policy arena to their private advantage or that, more rarely but more seriously, great-souled people in search of lasting fame may seek to usurp power for themselves. The challenge to a constitution writer is to create institutions within which both great and not-so-great people will be motivated to satisfy their personal ambitions by behaving in ways that in fact serve the public interest. Alexander Hamilton put the issue this way during the New York state ratifying convention in a speech outlining the dangers of mandatory term limits: "Men [i.e., legislators forced to retire] will pursue their interests. It is as easy to change human nature as to oppose the strong current of the selfish passions. A wise legislator [i.e., constitution writer] will gently divert the channel, and direct it, if possible, to the public good." A great deal of the discussion about Congress in the Constitutional Convention and, especially, in the state ratification debates was about how the self-interests of legislators might be channelled in just such a fashion.

The point can be seen in a cursory examination of the topics that were discussed. Given the importance of institutions to the framers, it is remarkable how little time they spent talking about the way Congress should be organized, apart from the crucial suffrage and apportionment issues involved in the basic nation-state dispute. Except for a few details, the United States Constitution is silent about procedure and focuses instead on the powers of Congress and the electoral relationship between constituency and representative.

We will not spend much time in this article on the powers of Congress. They are important for defining the scope of the national government and for providing each branch of Congress with the ability to resist domination by another branch of government. Congressional power also does help channel the ambitions and motivations of legislators: it is hard to attract able people to puny offices. But congressional power was not discussed primarily in this context at the convention.

The relationships between legislators and their constituents, in contrast, had the incentives of members as their central focus. This can be seen in discussions in both the convention and the states over how large congressional districts should be and how long senators and representatives should serve. It can also be seen in state ratifying convention disputes over whether constituents should be able to instruct members of Congress how to vote on specific legislative issues, whether voters should be able to recall members in mid-term and, finally, whether the Constitution should provide for mandatory rotation in office by limiting the number of consecutive terms a member may serve.

Size of Congressional Districts

The Constitutional Convention placed no upper limit on the size of congressional districts, but did stipulate that they should be no smaller, after each census, than an average of

30,000 people per district, with each state having at least one. The Anti-Federalists objected that there was no telling how large districts might become in the future and, in any case, 30,000 was too large a district to permit effective representation. (After the 1980 census, congressional districts averaged about 500,000 inhabitants.)

The Anti-Federalist position rested on three different concerns. First, they argued that a legislature with so few representatives, and such large districts, could not possibly contain members who would have the detailed knowledge of local conditions necessary to assure representation of the country's full multiplicity of interests. "Our federal representatives," said Virginia's George Mason, in his state's ratifying convention, "must be unacquainted with the situation of their constituents. Sixty-five members cannot possibly know the situation and circumstances of all the inhabitants of this immense continent."

George Mason

Even more serious, from the Anti-Federalist perspective, was the fact that the people would not know their own representatives personally. "The number of the House of Representatives [is] too small," said John Smilie in the Pennsylvania ratifying convention. "They will not have the confidence of the people, because the people will not be _known_ by them as to their characters."

Finally, a large number of Anti-Federalists mentioned that large districts would result in an aristocratic legislature. People advancing this argument included Mason, Smilie, Patrick Henry of Virginia, the anonymous Pennsylvania pamphleteer Centinel, "Hampden" (probably William Findley) in the _Pittsburgh Gazette,_ John Lansing of New York and, especially, New York's Melancton Smith, who argued that large districts would exclude "middling yeomen" from Congress and favor what he called the "natural aristocracy," among whom he included the learned and able as well as the well-born and _nouveau riche._

The Anti-Federalists' concerns about "aristocracy" reflected their view of representation. The _Letters from a Federal Farmer_ (authorship disputed, usually attributed to Richard Henry Lee) put the point this way:

> A full and equal representation is that which possesses the same interests, feelings, _opinions,_ and _views_ the people themselves would were they all assembled—a fair representation, therefore, should be so regulated that every order of men in the community, according to the common course of elections, can have a share in it.

Thus, for the Federal Farmer, the reason for having a legislature that mirrored the electorate was to make sure it would reflect the electorate's "opinions and views." Since it would be impossible to have a legislature for the whole nation that would be large enough to satisfy these requirements without becoming absurdly unwieldy, the Federal Farmer concluded that "the idea of one consolidated whole, on free principles, is ill-founded."

The Federalists rejected these arguments in all of their parts. Liberty was not well secured, they maintained, by a legislature that simply reflected the electorate's opinions and views—particularly not if the electorate were the relatively undifferentiated one of a small republic. The framers wanted a legislature that would also be free to exercise reason to overcome transient passions that may overwhelm public opinion.

Reason presumes knowledge, of course. The Federalists generally accepted the criticism that large districts would mean representatives who were less aware of local details. They denied, however, that this would be important for federal legislation. As one anonymous Connecticut pamphleteer put it:

> The federal legislature can take cognizance only of national questions and interests, which in their very nature are general, and for this purpose five or ten honest and wise men chosen from each state, men who have had previous experience in state legislation, will be more competent than an hundred.

Neither did the Federalists believe that a "fair representation" required a legislature that mirrored the social composition of the citizenry. "The idea of an actual representation of all classes of the people by persons of each class is altogether visionary," wrote Hamilton in *The Federalist* No. 35. More importantly, the Federalists flatly rejected the notion that rewarding ability is "aristocratic" (today's code word would be "elitist"). Permitting the voters to choose those who were best able to serve was just the opposite, in their view, from a conventional aristocracy that rewards people without regard to ability. If rewarding merit meant creating a "natural aristocracy" of people who would rise to prominence through careers in public service, so much the better. The whole point of the framers' concern with ambition was to find a way to encourage its healthy forms and attach it to serving the Constitution.

The discussion of aristocracy still fails to reach the heart of the framers' response. The Anti-Federalist concerns about the size of legislative districts began, the framers thought, from the wrong end of the problem. The place to begin was with the purpose of the government's democratic branch, not with its size or structure. The framers saw the legislature as a forum within which elected representatives accountable to different local constituencies could deliberate together—ideally about what would be good for the nation, but at least about what compromises would be needed to forge majority legislative coalitions from a multifactional constituency base.

The legislature was not supposed to be a place in which a multiplicity of interests simply came together and clashed. Peaceful resolution consistent with the protection of liberty presupposed deliberation—informed, direct discussion among the elected members. For this reason, the framers' discussions about legislative structure put the requirements of deliberation first. The House had to be large enough to insure "free consultation and discussion," but not so large as to produce the "confusion and intemperance of a multitude" (*The Federalist* No. 55). How large would be too large in their eyes is something we do not know. *The Federalist* confidently predicted a House with 400 members. But at some point, too large a legislature would produce the form of democratic control without the content. (They would have said the same thing about direct initiatives and referendums.) The actual result would be demagogic leadership by a few. "In all very numerous assemblies," Madison continued in *The Federalist* No. 55, "passion never fails to wrest the sceptre from reason. Had every Athenian citizen been a Socrates, every Athenian assembly would still have been a mob."

Thus, the framers' concern with the legislature's size reflected their desire to promote deliberation, and that desire in turn grew out of a markedly different view of representation than the one put forward by Anti-Federalists. But controlling the size of Congress can only, at best, make deliberation possible. It cannot by itself make self-interested, ambitious legislators, who owe their jobs to their constituents, *want* to resist their own constituents' momentary passions. To address that issue, we must turn to the length of the congressional term, recall, and mandatory rotation.

Length of Terms   The Anti-Federalists, in keeping with their general view that legislators should be checked closely by the people, thought democratic principles should require House members to face reelection every year. Elbridge Gerry expressed what later became a widely shared Anti-Federalist opinion when he upheld "annual Elections as the only defense of the people against tyranny," during the Constitutional Convention. At the time, Gerry was opposing a three-year term. After a compromise of two years was reached, the convention's debate on this point cooled off. Nevertheless, the desire for one-year terms continued to surface in many states during the ratification period.

Three different arguments were advanced against one-year terms. In at least four different state ratifying conventions, Federalist speakers said people would need at least two years to become sufficiently knowledgeable to deliberate intelligently about national legislation. Maryland's Daniel of St. Thomas Jenifer also opposed annual elections in the Constitutional Convention because they "made the best men unwilling to engage in so precarious a service," a view echoed by many others.

But the third and most important argument was that it would take more than a year, according to future House Speaker Thomas Sedgwick of Massachusetts at his state's ratifying convention, for a representative to "divest himself of local concerns." If elections were held too frequently, James Madison said in the Constitutional Convention, "none of those who wished to be reelected would remain at the seat of Government." By staying in the capital instead of constantly returning home, members might be led to think about national issues from at least somewhat of a national vantage point. Two-year terms were *not* meant to divorce members from their constituents' immediate, local concerns, as the Anti-Federalists charged. But they were intended to give members time to live near, talk to, and work with their colleagues and thus broaden the perspectives they brought with them from home.

Everything just said about two-year House terms applies even more forcefully to the Senate's six-year term. The Senate is often portrayed in popular writings as if it were intended to be a collection of quasi-ambassadors from the states—the true heir to the Congress of the Articles of Confederation. This view is superficially plausible. Article I does give states equal representation in the Senate, senators were elected by state legislatures, a few people in the convention did speak of senators as the guardians of states' interests, and many more spoke in these terms decades later, after slavery became the overriding political issue.

But the dominant view of the Senate at the convention focused on national, not state interests. One good clue comes from the important but often overlooked fact that senators vote as individuals: in the Congress of 1774-89 and in the Constitutional Convention, votes were cast by state, with each delegation having one vote. Another clue comes from the debate over paying senators from the national instead of the several state treasuries. But the clearest statements came when the convention considered the length of Senate terms.

The Senate, as everybody knows, was expected to have the will to resist temporary fits of popular passion that sweep over the House. Two-year terms might help House members gain somewhat of a national perspective for their deliberations, but electoral uncertainty was expected to keep them tied closely to the people's immediate desires. Longer terms, to use Governor

Edmund Randolph's words at the convention, would give senators the firmness to resist the House's "democratic licentiousness." They would do so by giving senators a purely self-interested reason for avoiding a simply short-term view: at any given moment, as the provision was finally worked out, one-third of the Senate would be held accountable for its decisions not in one or two years but in five or six, after the decisions had been in effect for a while.

Recall and Rotation   The value of six-year Senate and two-year House terms would be lost, however, if members could be recalled in the middle of their terms or barred from running for reelection. The original Virginia plan for the Constitution followed the Articles of Confederation (Article V) by including rotation and recall provisions for the House (but not for the Senate). These were dropped later in the convention without controversy, but many Anti-Federalists tried to revive the ideas during the state ratifying debates. The argument in the ratifying conventions over recalling members in mid-term went over ground that should be familiar by now: Anti-Federalists wanted to keep legislators closely tied to their constituents; Federalists wanted some degree of legislative independence to permit a nationally focused process of deliberation.

In contrast with the recall debate, rotation raised some new issues that are important for understanding legislative self-interest and ambition. "Rotation is an absurd species of ostracism," said Robert Livingston in the New York state ratifying convention. "It takes away the strongest stimulus to public virtue—the hopes of honors and rewards." If the legislator's self-interest, or love of honor, is the source of his or her public virtue, how would a legislator faced with a term limitation react? Richard Harrison predicted in the New York ratifying convention that most would simply become lazy, unambitious, and "regardless of the public opinion." But Alexander Hamilton warned the same convention that without a constitutional outlet for their ambition, many legislators would greedily use their office to line their pockets, while the most ambitious, feeling thwarted, might well think seriously of usurping power for themselves, or otherwise undermining the Constitution.

The way the Constitution's supporters talked about mandatory term limits helps clear up an important misconception about how they viewed political careers. A number of people today seem to yearn nostalgically for the "good old days," when members of Congress were political amateurs. These people seem to want—and to think the Constitution's framers wanted—members of Congress to be men or women of the people who would see their legislative service as brief interruptions in a basically private career. It is true that most of the framers expected the normal congressional career to be short. They expected that large numbers of sitting members would be defeated for reelection, and that others would find travel and life away from home unattractive. But whatever the framers may have expected, they also wanted to encourage able politicians to satisfy their ambitions through careers in public service. That is why mandatory rotation was such an anathema to them.

Ambition and the National Perspective

The issue of rotation shows that the Constitution's supporters believed a successful government must provide outlets for, and even encourage, political ambition. But what made the framers think legislators would satisfy their ambition in a useful way? Specifically, since the people are the source of all honors and rewards in a democracy, what made them think ambitious legislators ever would be willing to act in the name of the national long-term good, instead of the immediate gratification of their own constituents?

There are three answers to these questions. First, by lengthening House and, especially, Senate terms, the Constitution gives representatives a good reason to worry about the long-range implications of their policy choices.

Second, by getting members of Congress to live in the capital for a substantial portion of every two-year period, the framers tried to put them in a setting where they would be concerned about their reputations in the eyes of their colleagues as well as about the immediate opinions of their constituents. Along these lines, it is worth noting that the members of the First Congress, many of whom attended the Constitutional Convention, apparently expected congressional leadership on individual issues to be based not on formal positions—the early congresses were relatively undifferentiated bodies formally—but on a member's ability to lead debate and persuade his colleagues of his point of view.

Finally, no position in the government set up by the 1787 Constitution was elected directly by the people except that of representative. To become a senator, president, judge, or cabinet officer, a politician had to gain the respect and support of other practicing politicians. And in the case of the presidency—unlike today's situation with its primary-dominated nomination system—there was no way to attain the country's highest office without the support of a national cross-section of political leaders. The legislator who wanted to "move up," in other words, would simply have to broaden his vision beyond the immediate constituency to gain the respect of his colleagues.

The Framers' Argument as a Model for Contemporary Understanding

We can distill the Federalist argument still further. Because people are by nature selfish, it would be foolhardy to rely either on watchfulness or virtue for the protection of liberty. Therefore, institutions must be created that will supply people with self-interested reasons for acting in the public interest. Private vice does not equal public virtue, in the framers' argument. Rather, private interest is a given, and properly shaped institutions can encourage—not guarantee, but encourage—private interest to seek satisfaction through behavior that will benefit the public.

Among the many kinds of institutional features the framers might have considered for mediating the role of self-interest, two were given prominence. One was not discussed in this article: the checks and balances that make the branches of government powerful enough to protect themselves, and important enough to make capable officeholders want to serve in them. The other set related to constituencies, election, reelection and advancing from one office to the next. By focusing on these two kinds of features, while remaining largely silent about others, the framers seemed to be saying these were the most crucial. Internal structures and procedures were less important and therefore perhaps not worthy of being in the Constitution for that reason alone. They also were seen, at least to some extent, as being derivative: internal structures and procedures would, after all, be devised by legislators whose characters and interests would be shaped by the incentives the Constitution did address.

The contemporary Congress is very different from the Congress of 1789. The most important changes of the past two centuries are well known: the growth of the government's and, with it, of Congress' agenda, the increased legislative power of the president, the direct election of senators, the growth in the importance of incumbency in House elections, the revolution in communications technology, and the highly differentiated organization of the House and Senate along both party and committee lines. But despite all of this change, the arguments of 1787-89 contain an underlying logical structure that still seems useful for organizing one's thought about Congress.

Many of Congress' internal institutional changes over the past two centuries were brought about directly or indirectly because of prior changes in the two kinds of features the framers had identified as crucial. The committee system, for example, originally grew out of Congress' desire to assert its independence of the executive branch. The roles that members have been willing to let committee and party leaders play

Unfinished dome of U.S. Capitol, 1868

within Congress at different times have related directly to the members' changing views about their own reelection and career objectives.

Over the years, the Congress has departed from many of the framers' specific intentions. Direct election, for example, has produced a very different Senate from the one originally envisioned. The reelection rate for House incumbents is much higher than originally expected and reflects a changed relationship between constituent and representative. The growth of the government and of the legislative agenda has substantially reduced the opportunity for deliberation by the full membership of either the House or Senate, as committees and their staffs perform tasks members once did themselves in the Committee of the Whole. So, even though the framers' model for understanding incentives and results seems to remain useful, the contemporary Congress does not, in many ways, live up to their original expectations.

Before we become completely negative, however, we should recognize that at least some of the framers' more important objectives have been met. The framers wanted to be sure that members of Congress—in the face of inevitable pressures from their constituencies—would have some incentive for taking unpleasant, but needed actions. That the specific incentives have changed should be obvious. That members have not always taken unpleasant actions is clear, and no surprise. What is more remarkable in a democracy is how often the members have done so. That is no small matter. Congress remains by far the world's most important national legislature; the regime and its fundamentally free character have endured. These two facts, though not cause and effect, seem incontrovertibly related.

Michael J. Malbin, a resident fellow at the American Enterprise Institute for Public Policy Research in Washington, D.C., is currently working on a new book, *Congress in Perspective.* This article is based on research he did under a grant from Project '87.

The Origins of the American Presidency

Thomas E. Cronin

The invention of the American presidency in 1787 is sometimes described as one of the most fateful developments in American history. By no means, however, was it inevitable. The framers of the American Constitution could have strengthened their existing government under the Articles of Confederation—as indeed they were instructed to do by the Continental Congress. Many of the framers recognized the need for further centralization of power, yet centralization and the invention of a chief executive were not one and the same.

The Constitutional Convention

Few Americans now appreciate how close we came to adopting a kind of parliamentary system. The Virginia plan, the outline that guided discussions at the Constitutional Convention in Philadelphia, had proposed that the president and federal judges be selected by Congress. Delegates initially looked favorably upon this arrangement. Only after debate and deliberations had gone on for some time did the delegates move away from the idea. Nor can we completely dismiss the rumors about the possibility of Americans importing some kind of monarch. Gossip spread that Prince Henry of Prussia or Frederick, Duke of York might be suitable prospects for establishing a limited monarchy in America. Nonetheless, the notion of three separate and distinct branches gradually won out—the result of prolonged negotiations and extensive compromise.

At Philadelphia the framers recommended both a more centralized national government *and* a relatively independent executive. The creation of the presidency, like the development of the Constitution, was the result of the collective experience and wisdom of the nation. The founders carefully examined their own experiences—both good and bad—under the crown, under royal governors, with their own governors, with General

73

George Washington during the Revolution, and with the successes and failures of the Confederation. They also read about other systems—those of antiquity, and those described in legal commentaries and theoretical treatises. Still, the creation of the national executive involved imagination, vision, and risk taking, moving well beyond the lessons of history.

The framers acted against the backdrop of two explicit fears—that the national government would be ineffective or that it would be tyrannical. The last thing they wanted was the "second coming" of a George III on American soil; antimonarchical sentiment ran deep. They were distressed also by the popular uprisings, lawlessness, and unchecked democracy Massachusetts had endured with Shays' rebellion the year before in 1786. They wanted a more potent national government, yet they were keenly aware that the American people would not accept too much central control, especially if a lot of power were to be concentrated in a single person or office.

Roger Sherman

In fact, however, most framers recognized that the nation's executive would have to enjoy a certain independence. Both experience and a growing body of political thought pointed to a need for some executive discretion and perhaps even a dose of inherent or prerogative power to be lodged in the office of the president. Their challenge was to invent an executive office strong enough to provide effective governance without threatening balanced republican forms of government. "The majority of the delegates brought with them no far-reaching distrust of executive power," writes Charles Thach, "but rather a sobering consciousness that, if their new plan would succeed, it was necessary for them to put forth their efforts to secure a strong, albeit safe, national executive." In effect, the question had become one of whether the Articles of Confederation had pushed too far in the direction of legislative rule. Leaders at Philadelphia thought so, but they doubted most Americans were willing to diminish much of their devotion to republican ideas.

The Convention was divided into three groups on the issue of the executive. A staunch antimonarchy group was composed of older men, like George Mason of Virginia, Roger Sherman of Connecticut, and Hugh Williamson of North Carolina. Suspicious of power, they thought the executive should be subordinate to the legislature. Moreover, they argued that the nation would not accept what was virtually a king, merely because he was an elected one.

A second group favored a strong chief executive, the more

politically controversial position. James Wilson of Pennsylvania, the framer who had the greatest influence on the design of the presidency at the Convention, insisted that despotism could arise not only from a monarch, but also from the military, or the legislature. Thus, power had to be divided and balanced. Gouverneur Morris contended that a strong executive would protect the people against the potential of tyranny of the legislature.

Moderate delegates, caught between these two positions, supported some kind of executive yet they viewed the office as a potential source of danger and wanted its powers limited. One delegate proposed importing a monarch to work under legislative auspices, as the British had done with William of Orange in 1689. John Rutledge wanted to follow the model of most states (including his own South Carolina) and empower Congress to choose the president.

The Convention finally accepted the necessity of an executive, but a series of fundamental matters had still to be discussed. Should there be a plural or a single executive? How independent should the executive be from Congress? Who should choose the executive and for how long a term? What about reelectability? What kind of executive office would conform to republican theory? How much power should be granted the executive? A powerful executive might usurp legislative functions, yet too weak an executive would be devitalized by the strong legislature.

The British crown provided an ever-present model to the framers. Many, wanting to avoid the example of the Confederation which had no viable executive, sought to reproduce the powers of the monarch, restraining them where excessive. The framers also had the precedent of the United States as colonies and as independent entities. Royal governors, succeeded by elected state executives in some of the states, had made the idea of a single, functioning administrator part of America's heritage.

Gouverneur Morris

It was New York that provided the most compelling example in post-colonial America of a single executive head of government with significant power. An important model for the United States Constitution and its separation of powers, the New York constitution of 1777 provided for a popularly elected governor who served a three-year term and whose duties included "taking care that the laws are faithfully executed to the best of his ability." The term was renewable with no limits stipulated. John Jay, Gouverneur Morris, and Robert Livingston—all of whom questioned the political wisdom of the general public—had devised a strengthened executive in New York, not just as a check on the legislature but also as a check on the people and their role in popular democracy.

New York would have been a less valuable example without an effective executive willing and able to use his powers. Governor George Clinton made full use of his powers during his several terms. He exercised independent control over the militia, proposed legislation, threatened to terminate legislative sessions, and vetoed fifty-eight bills in the ten years prior to the Philadelphia Conventon. Clinton's executive leadership plainly provided a model for the framers of the Constitution.

In setting up the Confederation government in the 1780s, Americans had virtually omitted the executive. Allowing their contempt for the British king to dictate their decisions, they created a government incapable for many reasons of performing some of its functions. By 1787, confronted with both this unsuccessful model and less driven by the emotions of the hour, the framers were willing to consider vesting a single individual with powers adequate to the office.

In addition, everyone presumed that George Washington, whose reputation was unequaled in the country, would become that first president. His deft handling of power during his command of the revolutionary forces constituted reassurance to the framers that his performance in office would be properly restrained.

Writings of political theorists also played a role in the thinking of the men at Philadelphia. Most of the delegates had college educations and were widely read. Although practical experience influenced the proceedings most heavily, the general ideas of the Enlightenment—as reflected especially in the writings of Locke, Montesquieu, Blackstone, and the writers of the Scottish Enlightenment—were a part of the political culture on both sides of the Atlantic.

John Locke's influence was especially important. In his *Second Treatise on Government,* Locke asserted that people give up their freedom and enter political society because the state of nature lacks three things: clear settled laws, impartial judges, and the power to carry out the laws and enforce the decrees of judges. Locke outlined specific powers an executive might have: the ability to call together and to end legislative sessions, to certify legislative districts, and to act according to his own discretion when the public good required—even when laws were silent and even sometimes in opposition to the direct

John Locke

letter of the law. This was the doctrine of "prerogative." Locke was saying, in effect, that sometimes an executive might determine that emergency or survival warranted extralegal or illegal action. He maintained that legislatures were too large and too slow to cope with some kinds of emergencies and that executive discretion was therefore essential. Too strict or rigid an adherence to the law could sometimes do severe harm. Further, in Locke's view, "federative powers," which included conducting foreign relations, making war and peace, and entering into treaties and alliances, also required executive discretion. The King of England possessed these powers; Locke interpreted them as a necessary aspect of competent government.

James Madison said Montesquieu was a main source for the theory of separate powers, although several other theorists had advocated similar systems. Montesquieu, who had spent several years studying the British system, was convinced it was the soundest model for a people who wanted to preserve and nourish liberty. He believed power was fairly evenly distributed in England among king, House of Commons, and House of Lords. Montesquieu also believed the executive branch of government was better administered by one than many, the legislative branch better by many than one.

In the end, America's founding politicians moved well beyond the theorists' ideas. The examples of the crown, colonial governments, experience with their new state governments, and Governor Clinton's performance in New York as well as General Washington's military leadership doubtless had more influence on the pragmatic political architects in Philadelphia than any strict reading of any theorist or collection of theorists. After all, they were revolutionaries who had fought and won a bloody war and they were also practical politicians representing specific regions and distinctive interests.

Article II

When the delegates in Philadelphia finished their work, Article II, section 1 of the Constitution read: "The executive power shall be vested in a president of the United States of America." This language is generally interpreted today as giving the president broad powers, including the authority to take emergency actions to protect the lives of citizens and the vital interests of the nation.

In addition, Article II, section 2 stated specifically that the president would be commander in chief of the army, navy, and militia of the several states, when Congress called them into service. He would, like the British king, have the power to grant reprieves and pardons for offenses against the United States. This section also gave the president the authority to conduct foreign affairs: to make treaties and appoint ambassadors (albeit with the consent of the Senate). Further, again with the consent of the Senate, the president was to appoint other executive officials as well as the justices of the Supreme Court. (No mention was made about a president's powers to remove appointed executive branch officials. Presidents would win considerable discretion in this area, but not without prolonged fights with Congress and litigation in the federal courts.)

George Clinton

Presidents were also expected to play a role in the legislative process. The Constitution stipulated that they provide Congress information on the state of the union and recommend to its two houses such measures as they deemed necessary. As was the case in Massachusetts (but not in most states), a president would also have a qualified veto to prevent Congress from overstepping its boundaries and to enable him to influence the actual course of legislation. Congress could, however, overrule the veto by a two-thirds vote of both houses.

The president would provide for continuous administration of national programs, seeing that the laws were faithfully executed. Little did these early Americans realize how many laws would pass and how often Congress would delegate broad discretion to the executive branch.

The Constitution also made the president head of state by designating him to receive ambassadors and other foreign dignitaries. Defenders of the Constitution implied this was common sense and far more convenient than calling Congress into session to perform this chore every time visitors came. Yet this ceremonial or symbolic responsibility in effect turned the president into an exceedingly important spokesperson and symbol-in-chief for the nation.

The considerable responsibilities assigned to the president engendered heated debate during the tense political battles preceding the ratification of the Constitution. The scope of his powers and the fact that the incumbent would have a four-year term and would remain eligible to stand for reelection for an unlimited number of additional terms led opponents to fear this office. Supporters maintained that though this new president would have important responsibilities, the executive would be for the most part subordinate to Congress. The Constitution enabled the president to exercise swift independent action only under exceptional circumstances.

The president would also be subject to impeachment. In one of his many outbursts at the Philadelphia convention, Gouverneur Morris demanded that the new executive not be impeachable. In response, the venerable Benjamin Franklin observed: "Well, he'd either be impeachable or he'd be assassinated." Morris looked at that great source of wisdom and experience and said at once: "My opinion has changed."

The method of selecting this chief executive occupied a great deal of time at the Constitutional Convention. Several delegates, as mentioned earlier, believed the executive should be chosen by Congress, following the example of most of the states. Others objected, however, saying that procedure would make the executive overly dependent on Congress. The delegates also considered selection by the Senate, by state governors, by the people, and by state legislators. There were objections to every proposal.

Eventually, a compromise plan provided for the now famous "electoral college." A president would be elected by this body to which each state might appoint, in any way its state legislature prescribed, as many members as the total of its representatives and senators in Congress. These electors would exercise their own judgment in selecting a virtuous and prudent man to serve as president. The framers had plainly invented an idealized selection process that stressed virtue and underestimated the inevitability of conflict and party competition.

President Washington

The Constitution, as drafted and ratified, was a bold and ingenious document. Yet it did not itself guarantee that the presidency would work and that Americans would enjoy both representative *and* effective government. Much would depend on how George Washington interpreted the Constitution and how his compatriots would respond to his executive leadership.

For more than eight years, Washington had served his country as commander in chief of the Revolutionary Army. He had been granted extraordinary powers and had exercised them wisely. With the war won he resigned and returned, a national hero, to his Mount Vernon farm. During the war he had rebuked officers who had plotted to make him king. "Everyone knew him to be above suspicion and without overweening ambition," historian Marcus Cunliffe writes. "Everyone knew too that with ratification of the new Constitution it would be unthinkable to name any man but him as America's first true president."

Washington reluctantly accepted this new honor. He was fifty-seven years old and his health was not good. He worried about the potentially crushing burdens and obligations of the office; he told friends he was not qualified. Seeking to escape, he asked in vain if he had not already served his country long and well enough. But he was one of the only persons known, respected, and trusted in all the states. Further, he had been a prime mover in bringing about the constitutional changes that had created the new executive. The first election for president was held in January 1789. His choice by the electoral college was unanimous.

Washington knew that he walked "on untrodden ground." "There is scarcely any action the motive of which may not be subjected to a double interpretation," he said. "There is scarcely any part of my conduct which may not hereafter be drawn into precedent." "[My] movements to the chair of Government," he wrote Acting Secretary of War Henry Knox in April 1789, "will be accompanied by feelings not unlike those of a culprit who is going to the place of his execution: so unwilling am I, in the evening of a life nearly consumed in public cares, to quit a peaceful abode for an Ocean of difficulties, without that competency of political skill, abilities and inclination which is necessary to manage the helm." A man of enormous pride, self-esteem, and achievement, Washington knew his limitations. He knew he was not an orator, philosopher, constitutional theorist, or political organizer.

On the other hand he was, and had been for nearly a decade, a national hero, the recipient of lavish praise. Washington not only accepted the deference graciously, he used it as a means of legitimizing both his new office and the new national government he had labored so long to bring into being. No matter how ably Alexander Hamilton and others had explained the Constitution, and the provisions relating to the chief executive, it was now up to Washington to carry out the promise of the office, establishing precedents at every turn. He understood that written constitutions do not implement themselves, that a functioning constitution includes traditions, practices, and interpretations which fill out the written document. Washington may not have been a philosopher, but he had mature political values about the purposes and appropriate processes of the Constitution. Thus, he was committed to the rule of law. Although he was somewhat of a skeptic about the doctrine of separated powers he recognized the primacy of Congress in domestic policy making. He regularly declined to use his veto power even when Congress sent him legislation he disliked. And he held fast to the "Federalist" view that the nation's power and responsibilities must be respected by the states.

As noted, the founders decided to grant the chief executive the additional responsibilities of receiving ambassadors and other foreign dignitaries, making the president head of state and chief symbolic leader as well. President Washington acted out superbly the head of state and symbolic functions Americans now regularly expect of presidents. As a morale builder and national spokesman, he unified the nation, encouraging the integration of disparate states and regions. His reverence for the Constitution and faith in constitutionalism, a crucial American value, set standards for his successors.

President Washington knew his immediate responsibility was as an administrator, and he concentrated efforts on stabilizing the structure of the Republic's new government. Fortunately for Washington, the newly structured two-house Congress did not attempt to regain the dominant role the legislature had played during the Confederation. Speaker of the House James Madison, however, would sometimes contend that the president could not exercise even powers assigned to him by the Constitution without approval of Congress. Secretary of the Treasury Hamilton, Madison's friend, disagreed and insisted that executive power was generally vested in the president. Congress concurred in Hamilton's view and readily conceded to Washington the right to choose his own officials as well as to nominate judges and diplomats. However, unlike modern day presidents, Washington sought scrupulously not to impose his policy views on Congress, and Congress, in turn, allowed him considerable freedom to implement the laws and policies of the new republic.

Washington, for example, assumed the responsibility of creating the cabinet. While he did not regard his department secretaries as a team or council that would act collectively, he did look to his department heads as assistants and advisors. At first there were no regular meetings. He let them run their own departments, reserving his right to make all final decisions. In an effort to promote national unity, he appointed Thomas Jefferson, an Anti-Federalist, as Secretary of State, and Alexander Hamilton, a consummate Federalist, as Secretary of the Treasury. He avoided making the executive branch an arm of any one party even though he was himself a staunch Federalist. Washington served as a balance between the Jeffersonian and Hamilton groups—neither side could do without him if it was to be heard.

Washington's actions as commander in chief laid claim to broad authority. In 1794 Washington called out the militia from Virginia, Maryland, Pennsylvania, and New Jersey and, at least initially, took to the field himself as commander of 13,000 troops headed for western Pennsylvania where "Whiskey Rebels" had refused to pay national excise taxes.

In April of 1793, President Washington issued the Proclamation of Neutrality that stated America was at peace with both Great Britain and France and urged Americans not to get involved in the conflict between those two feuding nations. This decision involved complex and delicate questions both about presidential authority and about foreign policy. Washington consulted his cabinet and acted with determination.

Presidential prerogative as commander in chief, it soon became clear, would naturally extend into areas of foreign policy. Congress generally left major decisions of making and implementing foreign policy to the president. It was his authority to "make" treaties (meaning to negotiate them), to submit them to the Senate, and if the Senate consented, to make the final decision whether to ratify them on behalf of the nation. This procedure has become standard. In 1792, when it looked as if America might go to war with Britain, Congress recognized that the challenge required quick, firm action of a kind the deliberative national legislature itself could not take. It therefore granted Washington the additional power of conducting diplomatic negotiations.

Washington saw his task as consolidating the government, to bring coherence to the particularistic policies the several states had earlier tried to pursue. It fell to him to organize a permanent national government, recruit, nominate, or appoint its officials and reconcile the diverse, competing aspirations the citizens had for their government. In doing so, Washington helped establish the presidency as an effective branch of government.

George Washington

As one of his last major gifts to the nation, President Washington voluntarily left office at the end of his second term. Some contemporaries thought he would stay until his death. Washington believed, however, that the American experiment needed to witness the orderly transfer of power from one president to an elected successor. Only then would we complete the demonstration that a people could rule itself according to its own laws. His decision after two terms to retire from this new center of power and prestige in the nation set a precedent that was followed without formal instruction for more than 144 years and then, after one departure, it was mandated by the Twenty-second Amendment to the Constitution.

Conclusion   The invention and establishment of the American executive took place over a twenty-year period, roughly between 1775 and 1796. The excesses and deficiencies of legislative government caused people to reconsider the executive institutions they had earlier rejected, and to create a chief executive with adequate authority to do the job.

Still, our fundamental ambivalence toward executive power remains. Today we have an even greater recognition of the need for occasional executive discretion and prerogative in crises. During the course of normal business, however, we prefer that the president be bound by instructions from Congress and the letter of the law.

More and more, presidents have been forced to bypass deliberations with the Congress and to become popular or plebiscitary national leaders—rallying the people to their programs. In the absence of effective parties or sympathetic leadership in Congress, many of our presidents continue to enlarge their office. Part of this practice is due to the transformation of the role of the United States in global affairs. Part is also due to our changing economy and the rise of the "Administrative" and "Regulatory State." Not everyone is pleased by this development. Some students of the presidency wish for more self-restraint by presidents or seek additional checks and balances.

The vast growth of the country and its economic reach throughout the globe have had a profound influence on the office of the president. The national executive exercises the indispensable statecraft responsibilities circumstances periodically demand in every society. In doing so, it surely fulfills one of the important goals of the Constitution's framers.

The dynamics of American democracy and the American economy increasingly revolve around the presidency. This result was not exactly intended. Yet the permanently preeminent presidency is the product of forces that continue to roll and events that cannot be undone. Unique, dangerous, yet necessary, the creation of the American presidency was a brilliant gamble and it has served us reasonably well.

The enduring challenge for us at the two-hundred-year mark is to encourage the presidential leadership we need, yet strengthen alternative constitutional processes that will ensure responsible and accountable democratic leadership. We need to be wary about giving the presidency additional political advantages or powers. We are also well-advised to heed the counsel of the late Clinton Rossiter when he wrote that we should be "alert to abuses of those [powers] he already holds, cognizant that the present balance of the Constitution is not a cause for unlimited self-congratulation."

SUGGESTED ADDITIONAL READING

Corwin, Edward S. *The President: Office and Powers* (1957).
Fisher, Louis. *Constitutional Conflicts Between Congress and the President* (1985).
Flexner, James Thomas. *Washington: The Indispensable Man* (1974).
Ketcham, Ralph. *Presidents Above Party: The First American Presidency, 1784-1829* (1984).
Morris, Richard. *Witnesses at the Creation: Hamilton, Madison and Jay and the Constitution* (1985).

Thomas E. Cronin wrote this while serving as Visiting Professor of Politics, Princeton University (1985-86). He is McHugh Distinguished Professor of American Institutions and Leadership at The Colorado College. His writings include *The State of the Presidency* (1980) and *Rethinking The Presidency* (1982).

The Origins of the National Judiciary

Philip B. Kurland

A reading of the Constitution as originally drafted and as it has existed for almost two hundred years quickly reveals that the judicial branch was probably the least well-defined of the three great divisions of national government in terms of its organization and its powers. The provisions of Article III, although listing the various jurisdictional categories, made few of them compulsory on the national courts. Only some original jurisdiction of the Supreme Court was made compulsory. But no constitutional provision established any national courts other than the Supreme Court. The Convention of 1787 could not reach agreement as to whether there should be such national courts. The founders were certainly ambivalent about the utility of a national judiciary and compromised the question by leaving the issue for resolution by Congress.

There can be little doubt that the statesmen no less than the people of the time feared a strong judiciary. But they also recognized that some judicial power had to be vested in central government because the national government could founder without tribunals to resolve questions that could not be left to the partisanship of state courts—this lack had been one of the weaknesses of the Articles of Confederation. Yet history had shown that the judiciary, if it had a great potential for centralization of power, also stood fair to become an engine of repression. Thus, the founders included provisions in the Constitution specifically to limit the authority of the judges. They carefully defined the crime of treason, lest that concept be allowed to grow as inordinately as it had under royal tutelage in the mother country. They also provided for jury trials in the original document. Insistent demands for still more assurance of the supremacy of the jury over the judiciary led to the addition of the Sixth and Seventh Amendments as well. "We, the People," were to safeguard the freedoms of the citizenry from invasion by the judiciary.

Alexander Hamilton

In Anglo-American history, the judiciary had always been the handmaiden of the crown. It enforced the wishes of the king, serving him as a political tool, whether enhancing the royal treasury, or punishing the king's political enemies, or imposing the "king's peace" on the barons and their vassals. Two particularly egregious examples of judicial tyranny remained well-remembered bugaboos for those who had the task of framing a new government—"Bloody Jeffreys," the Chief Justice under James II known for his profligate imposition of the death penalty, and the Star Chamber, a political court completely devoid of judicial temper used by the crown to punish its enemies.

The Declaration of Independence iterates charges against the crown for imposing its despotism, in no small part through the machinations of the royal courts at Westminster and the Vice-Admiralty courts in the colonies themselves. Americans clearly saw that the courts were devices for centralization of power, no less than tools for subordination of the popular will. Concentration of political power was one of the great fears of the constitutional era, but so, too, was the danger of disseminating that power among the people. "Democracy" was as dirty a word at the end of the eighteenth century as "elitism" has become in the twentieth. With the examples of the abuse of judicial power under the crown on the one hand, and the problems of operating without a centralized judicial authority under the Articles of Confederation on the other, there were good reasons for the ambivalence about making provision for a judicial branch in the original Constitution.

In order to overcome resistance to the notion of a judicial branch in the new government, the framers contended that this branch of government would be innocuous, rather than desirable or useful. In a framed passage from *The Federalist* No. 78, Alexander Hamilton argued:

> Whoever attentively considers the different departments of power must perceive, that in a government in which they are separated from each other, the judiciary, from the nature of its functions, will always be the least dangerous to the political rights of the Constitution; because it will be least in capacity to annoy or injure them. The Executive not only dispenses the honors, but holds the sword of the community. The legislature not only commands the purse, but prescribes the rules by which the duties and rights of every citizen are to be regulated. The judiciary, on the contrary, has no influence over either the sword or the purse; no direction either of the strength or of the wealth

of the society; and can take no active resolution whatever. It may truly be said to have neither FORCE nor WILL, but merely judgment; and must ultimately depend upon the aid of the executive arm even for the efficacy of its judgments.

However inaccurate a description of the judicial power of today, such rhetoric sounded good in its own time.

Perhaps Hamilton meant what he said—although *The Federalist* did have the aura of propaganda about it. Perhaps Hamilton's arguments were even valid. But their validity depended on the dubious proposition—dubious even then—that the sole function of a judicial body was to resolve the particular "case" or "controversy" before it on the basis of law that was already existent. When, however, one takes into account the well-known dictum that he who interprets and applies the law is the true law maker and not he who promulgates it, the Hamiltonian argument seems more preachment than substance. If one looks backward from the Hamiltonian argument adopted by Marshall in *McCulloch v. Maryland,* doubts about the candor of *The Federalist* No. 78 are turned into certainties about its sophistical nature.

In any event, in *Marbury v. Madison,* John Marshall announced, in the great tradition of Louis XIV, that "le loi, c'est moi," and this dictum has been accepted by every court since, right down to the Burger Court. "It is emphatically the province and duty of the judicial department to say what the law is," said Marshall. From *Marbury* to date there has been continual debate about the legitimacy of the power of judicial review, the power to declare national statutes to be invalid because they contravene the Constitution. And none has gainsaid Judge Learned Hand's proposition: "There was nothing in the United States Constitution that gave courts any authority to review the decisions of Congress; and it was a plausible—indeed to my mind an unanswerable—argument that [judicial review] invaded that 'Separation of Powers' which, as so many then believed, was the condition of all free government." But then, "there was nothing in the United States Constitution" that provided for the doctrine of "Separation of Powers." Judicial review, like separation of powers, was part of the background against which the Constitution was painted. Failure to include either in the words of the text did not bespeak their rejection.

With all respect to the gallons of ink and forests of paper spent on the subject, the legitimacy of judicial review is not

Learned Hand

now, and has never been, the real issue. The question is what the scope of that power should be. We do know that the authors of the Constitution specifically rejected the concept of a council of revision, that is, a government body, whether judicial in whole or part, which would substitute its judgment for the legislature's as to the desirability of the legislation. If not so broad a discretion, what limits of the judicial power did the founders intend in determining when a law contravened the Constitution and was, therefore, invalid? To say that courts could pass on the question of congressional power is not the same as saying that their discretion is unlimited on this score. The Justices were to measure infringement of the Constitution, not the degree to which their own sensibilities had been violated.

At the same time that Marshall proclaimed the power of judicial review, he announced the limited way in which it could be invoked:

> If two laws conflict with each other, the courts must decide on the operation of each. So if a law be in opposition to the Constitution; if both the law and the Constitution apply to a particular case, so that the court must either decide that case conformably to the law, disregarding the Constitution; or conformably to the Constitution, disregarding the law, the court must determine which of these conflicting rules governs the case. This is of the very essence of judicial duty. If, then, the courts are to regard the Constitution, and the Constitution is superior to any ordinary Act of the Legislature, the Constitution, and not such ordinary Act, must govern the case to which they both apply.

Marshall's argument, here as in other important decisions that he wrote, closely parallels Hamilton's arguments. Neither of them charge the Court with the function of rewriting the Constitution to the taste of the Justices. Both of them justify judicial review of national legislation within the context of deciding a case or controversy properly before the Court for adjudication. There is no suggestion that such decision was to be treated as a general rule of public policy for the governance of other branches of the national government or of the behavior of persons who had not submitted the cause for judgment.

Clearly, however, the power of judicial review did invoke some discretion on the part of the judiciary. Neither the Constitution nor most legislation was so lucidly written that their meanings were obvious to anyone who read them. Thus, when a question arose as to whether a tax on carriages was a

John Marshall

"direct tax" which had to be apportioned to meet the terms of the Constitution, the courts had to decide what a "direct tax" was. This was a judicial problem that had to be resolved before the conflict between the Constitution and the legislation could be said to exist.

There was less doubt about the authority of the national courts to review state legislation. The Supremacy Clause specifically subordinates the actions of state courts as well as state legislatures to the terms of the Constitution, and section 25 of the first Judiciary Act makes specific provision for such judicial review. Section 25 was promulgated by those who were "present at the creation." Even so, our earliest constitutional history records the hard-pressed efforts of the states to negate the provisions of section 25 as invalid. This effort was unavailing, not least for the reason that the Supreme Court had the last word on the subject. As Justice Holmes once said: "I do not think that the United States would come to an end if we lost our power to declare an Act of Congress void. I do think that the Union would be imperilled if we could not make that declaration as to the laws of the several states."

However often the fight has been joined over judicial review during the course of American history, the First Congress faced more pressing difficulties in creating a judicial system from scratch. The system had to serve as a cement and not a solvent of the Union; it had to disperse its course among the countryside and not emulate Westminster by compelling the people to come to the capital for justice; it had to mediate disputes largely without a body of law of its own, for there was little legislation and the common law was not a property of the national judiciary. The First Congress did well; its Judiciary Act has long been admired as a remarkably effective response to practical needs. Some of the original law remains in effect today.

The keystone of the Judiciary Act provided for national courts in addition to the Supreme Court which the Constitution itself created. This national court system, together with judicial review by the Supreme Court of state court action on matters of federal concern, lay at the center of the conception of a national judicial function. No other modern confederation of states has established national courts for trial and intermediate appellate review, not even in nations covering so wide a territorial expanse as do Australia and Canada. The decision of the First Congress to afford such national courts was probably a response to the deficiencies of the Articles of Confederation, which lacked any such system. The plan devised by the First Congress under the leadership of Oliver Ellsworth consisted of three judicial components to be administered by two sets of judges. District courts were to be manned by district judges. Circuit courts were to be presided over by a district court judge and one or two Supreme Court Justices.

Since marine commerce was at the heart of the nation's economic structure, the district courts were given jurisdiction over cases in admiralty, a body of judge-made law common to the United States, England, and compatible with the law of

The Old Royal Exchange Building, New York City, the first temporary home of the Supreme Court

most maritime nations of that era. The protection of internal but interstate commerce was effected by giving jurisdiction to the federal circuit courts when residents of different states were involved in litigation. This tactic protected merchants and creditors from the parochialism of state courts which might diminish their willingness to engage in interstate trade. Again, the applicable law was largely judge-made law in the form of the common law of the state of trial. The circuit courts were also given a modest role of appellate review of district court judgments.

Admiralty and maritime causes, and disputes between citizens of different states, formed the bulk of the national judicial realm, although there was provision too for other areas such as enforcement of national criminal law, which included only federal statutory offenses and not common-law crimes. The Supreme Court exercised appellate review of the judgments of the lower federal courts and the highest state courts.

The burden on Supreme Court Justices, if not on the Supreme Court itself, was inordinate because of the need for the Justices to ride circuit. From the beginning the Justices sought relief from some or all of their circuit-riding duties, which tested their endurance and capacities to the limit, and made the position of a Supreme Court Justice less than attractive to the lawyers of greatest capacity in the new nation. Still, relief from circuit riding was not fully obtained until well into the nineteenth century.

With the advent of the "second American Revolution," when the states'-rights Jeffersonians replaced the nationalists in the executive and legislative branches, the federal judiciary became the bulwark of nationalism. The judges of the federal courts, both in their law-making roles and as administrators of the national grand jury system, took every chance they got to forward the idea of centralized power. The effort of the Jeffersonians to reduce the federal courts' power resulted in several constitutional crises but did not control the courts. Thus, the Federalists retained an imposing nationalist counterforce against the Jeffersonians which helped shape the new nation.

The origins of the national judiciary are to be found in the words of the Constitution and the Judiciary Act of 1789, but they were only adumbrated there. Like the national executive, if not the national legislature, the national judiciary has created itself in its own image. The words of Thomas Reed Powell describing the development of the power of judicial review are equally applicable to the development of the national judicial power generally: "Those of you who recall how Topsy characterized her own genetic process may not be offended if I find a similarity between her origin and that of what we know as [the judicial power]. . . . Like Topsy, it just 'growed.'"

Philip B. Kurland is William R. Kenan, Jr., Distinguished Service Professor in the College and Professor in the Law School at the University of Chicago. He is now at work, with Ralph Lerner, on a collection of documents relating to the Constitution, entitled *The Founders' Constitution.*

III. *National Power:*
Limits and Potential

Liberty and Taxes: The Early National Contest

Thomas P. Slaughter

When eighteenth-century Americans discussed politics, they revealed their British heritage, their Enlightenment sensibilities, their distinctive brand of "Whig" ideology, and their capitalist experiences and values. They conceived of governance as something of a balancing act among the few and the many, the rich and the poor, the powerful and the weak. They imagined a delicate scale with liberty on one side and order on the other. Too much weight on either side, they believed, could bring disarray to the political world—anarchy if the masses ran amok, tyranny if the rulers became corrupted by power.

The Power to Levy Taxes

Politically aware Americans envisioned the various levels of government—town, county, colony or state, and empire or nation—as points on spectrums of representation and authority. The more local political institutions were close to the people, more representative of their interests, and thus more responsive to their needs. Here, at the local level, some believed, was the place for those decisions that most directly affected the lives of common people—the repair of roads, the building of town halls, sanitation, and "internal" taxes (taxes on domestic products, land, and trade). More remote central authority had the virtue of seeing the big picture and thus seemed best qualified to make decisions affecting all in common—national defense, regulation of international commerce, patents, and "external" taxes (taxes or duties on imported goods). All of these governmental responsibilities required the sort of coordination and continuity best achieved by one national decision-making body like the British Empire's parliament or an American congress.

Taxes were, as always, a particularly sensitive matter. Indeed, it was the imposition of an internal stamp tax on the colonies by Parliament in 1765 that first raised the issues of the relationship between taxation and representation, local versus central governance, and liberty and order in irreconcilable ways between Americans and the Empire. "The parliament of Great Britain have no right to level an internal tax upon the colonies," one writer asserted. Another believed that the British legislature's attempt "to establish stamp duties and other internal taxes" threatened to reduce colonists to "the miserable condition of slaves."

For the most part, Americans agreed that they were not represented in Parliament. They shared a vision of the linkage between preservation of liberty and taxation only by their elected representatives, but they disagreed about the precise nature of these relationships and even the definitions of the terms involved. Benjamin Franklin, for example, thought that colonists could be represented in Parliament and then justly taxed by that body. "If you chuse to tax us," he wrote to an English correspondent, "give us members in your Legislature, and let us be one people." Other Americans were less sanguine about Parliament's ability ever to become sufficiently representative for the purposes of taxation. They held a different standard of what it meant to be "represented" in a legislature and a greater suspicion of geographically remote central governments. Stephen Hopkins, for one, thought the colonies were "by distance so separated from Great Britain that they are not and cannot be represented in Parliament."

Implicit disputes such as this would not prevent many Americans from uniting against Great Britain, its remote and unrepresentative government, and the threat posed to their liberty by the Empire's claim to authority over internal taxes. By any standard—either Franklin's or Hopkins'—British taxes and troops assaulted their liberty and property. Ideological fissures first revealed in 1765 would, however, have a profound impact on Americans' ability to balance liberty and order after they secured self-rule in the Revolution.

When it came to debate over the Constitution in 1787, some Americans—now pejoratively termed "Anti-Federalists" by their opponents—had not changed their minds about the relationship between local and central governments or representation and internal taxation. These men were appalled by the similarities between British ambitions in the 1760s and the authority granted by the proposed constitution. They were especially shocked by Article I, section 8, which gave blanket authority over taxation—internal and external—to the national government. "They have the unlimited right to imposts and all kinds of taxes, as well to levy as to collect them," one distraught Anti-Federalist observed. "They have indeed very nearly the same powers claimed by the British Parliament. Can we have so soon forgot our glorious struggle with that power, as to think a moment of surrendering it now?" "When I recollect," another localist lamented, "how lately congress, conventions, legislatures, and people contended in the cause of liberty and carefully weighed the importance of taxation, I can scarcely believe we are serious in proposing to vest the powers of laying and collecting internal taxes in a government so imperfectly organized for such purposes."

To the localists of 1787, the national congress of the proposed constitution was little more fit for the purpose of levying internal taxes than Parliament had been in 1765. They predicted a proliferation of taxes—poll, land, excise, and stamp—and hordes of tax men to collect them, men who would, "like the locusts of old, destroy us." If the people resisted such threats to their liberty and property, which surely they would according to the Anti-Federalists, an "internal war" might result. "Look at the part which speaks of excises,"

Anti-excise cartoon, 1792

Patrick Henry warned, "and you will recollect that those who are to collect excises and duties are to be aided by military force. . . . Suppose an excise-man will demand leave to enter your cellar, or house, by virtue of his office; perhaps he may call on the militia to enable him to go."

Lack of knowledge and sympathy for the conditions and views of many regions, localists believed, would make the proposed congress the wrong institution to enact internal taxes. As in 1765, it seemed unlikely that the whole people could ever be represented adequately in a national legislature for the purposes of internal taxation. The Anti-Federalist standard of representation was different from that of most British politicians and American nationalists. To Anti-Federalists, the legislative branch of the proposed national government appeared to have "but very little democracy in it." The Constitution seemed to its opponents almost to ensure a wave of economic repression and political violence. They believed that the "same force that may be employed to compel obedience to good laws, might and probably would be used to wrest from the people their constitutional liberties."

For Anti-Federal localists, then, the issues and the stakes

had changed little from the 1760s. The constitutional conflict over internal and external taxation had as much, if not more, meaning for some Americans in 1787 as it had in 1765. In both cases many saw the reservation of internal taxation to the colonies/states as crucial to the survival of liberty. In each case they predicted violent conflict and consequent loss of liberty as the likely results of granting the central government authority to assess internal taxes. It made little difference that the supreme authority after 1787 would be managed by elected Americans rather than British politicians over whom they had virtually no influence. The problems of representation remained largely the same. Whether elected or not, men who shared no sympathy for the needs of some regions could not represent all their constituents' interests adequately to tax them. In 1787 as in 1765, localists believed that internal taxing authority must be left to local representatives who lived among their constituents and knew their wants and needs. Under the proposed system this was not possible. Each congressman represented as many as 30,000 people, and districts would grow even larger. A senator from Philadelphia, Boston, or Charleston, for example, could never truly appreciate or represent the unique problems and needs of frontiersmen.

Furthermore, as a matter of logic and political theory, localists strongly resisted the idea that two sovereign governmental bodies could coexist, share concurrent jurisdiction, cooperate, and survive. They believed that sovereignty could be divided but not shared. To give both the central government and the states authority to lay internal taxes was to decree the virtual death of the states. The larger and stronger government would inevitably overwhelm the states with taxes, tax collectors, and if necessary, soldiers to enforce its laws. In the face of such might, state governments would be compelled to repeal tax laws or simply leave an overburdened populace alone and not collect taxes at all. In the end, the states would either fade to shadows or be violently annihilated by a national army. However the end came, the fate of the citizen, the state, and the nation would ultimately be the same. Discontent, resistance, repression, violence, tyranny, and death would be the short and brutal history of the republic.

As subsequent events showed, the localists of 1787 were only partially correct in their predictions. The state governments were not annihilated, nor did they glide out of existence. The national government did not dissolve in a caldron of tyranny and anarchy.

Site of the Whiskey Rebellion on the Monongahela River

The Whiskey Excise

On the other hand, the nationalists' assurances—which localists interpreted as promises—that a direct excise would only be a tax of last resort under the Constitution proved false. One of the earliest fiscal measures of the new congress was the whiskey excise of 1791. Localists were also correct in predicting that passage of internal taxes by a remote central government would bring the nation to the brink of "internal war." The Pennsylvania militia did not invade New England or Virginia to "quell an insurrection occasioned by the most galling oppression," as one Anti-Federalist had predicted. The militias of Pennsylvania, New Jersey, Maryland, and Virginia marched west, however, to suppress a tax revolt on the other side of the Appalachian Mountains in 1794. The Whiskey Rebellion resulted from precisely the sorts of tensions foreseen by localists in 1765 and 1787.

Most members of Congress were ignorant of or unsympathetic to the unique regional economy that made the whiskey excise an untoward burden for trans-Appalachian frontiersmen. Because the lower Mississippi River was periodically closed to American trade by its Spanish possessors, settlers had no option but to carry their meager crops back across the mountains to an eastern city such as Philadelphia, Baltimore, Richmond, or Charleston. The weight and bulk of wheat—the major surplus production of the West—made the journey unprofitable. Distillation of surplus grain into whiskey, however, created a more potable and portable commodity, making it the region's only lucrative product. Indeed, the frontier's entire culture revolved around distilled spirits. Whiskey circulated locally as the primary medium in a fundamentally barter economy. It was a crucial component of wages paid to day-laborers, who refused to work unless liberally rationed liquor. It brought in what very little cash the region accumulated. And it lubricated the social life enjoyed by people with few other luxuries.

The tax on distillation hit hardest at the small and intermittent producer, the farmer who had just enough wheat left over after feeding his family and animals to distill some whiskey for himself, for his laborers, and to barter for other necessaries. He realized no cash from the product, but the tax had to be paid in hard money. With cash so dear and whiskey so important to the delicate balance of his solvency, the tax seemed particularly unjust to the poor and marginal yeoman. Moreover, the government was far away, its services to him were unapparent, and its leaders were inaccessible. The frontiersman refused to pay.

Western farmers used the language and the logic of opposition to internal taxes levied by remote central governments as the rallying cry of resistance. Protestors writing in the public press reminded their readers of the Stamp Act crisis, when "the quick sightedness and spirit of Americans [first] showed themselves." In 1765, some still believed, Americans "made the world sensible that usurped power could neither cheat them by sophistry, nor awe them by force, giving a noble lesson to their posterity ever to watch against governmental encroachments, and to stifle them in their birth." In sum, opponents of the whiskey excise frequently argued during the 1790s that stamp tax resistance was a landmark in defense of liberty because Americans then first displayed their absolute rejection of the authority of remote central governments to levy "internal taxes" on a free people.

The issues of representation and internal taxes were again, as they had been in 1765 and 1787, at the heart of debates over just taxation. According to an anonymous writer, "every judicious politician must anticipate the remark that even the House of Representatives must necessarily be too limited in point of numbers, and in point of information, will possess too little knowledge of the citizens, and too feeble a participation in the particular circumstances of the subjects of taxation" to levy internal taxes justly. At the time the excise law was passed, according to this same author, the local interests of about one-half the people of the nation were not represented. Since some states elected representatives-at-large before results of the first national census were available and since almost all senators were from the East, the needs and views of the vast rural reaches of frontier America were very poorly understood. "If we had not other proof," he argued, "this is sufficient to demonstrate that the federal government never was intended to embrace extensive internal powers; and that the powers of that kind which it possesses, were only intended for emergencies, in which the preservation of the government itself was at risque."

The difference for localists of 1794, compared to those of 1765, was that they lost their battle against the central government. The new constitution, drafted in response to nationalist fears of disorder epitomized by Shays' Rebellion in 1786, was purposefully constructed to insure suppression of resistance to the law. Before the Whiskey Rebellion, however, neither side knew for certain whether the solutions embodied in Articles I, II, and IV would actually work to crush political dissent. President Washington, utilizing his authority as commander-in-chief, was able to quell unrest in a manner only dreamt of by like-minded British authorities in the 1760s and 1770s. Washington marched an army of 12,800 men—approximating in size the force he led in the American Revolution—to make an example of frontier farmers in western Pennsylvania. Those nationalists who, like Alexander Hamilton, had hoped for a test of the document's power, could now rest assured that the Constitution was capable of maintaining order.

But what about liberty? American localists' most nightmarish fears seemed confirmed by the crushing of the Whiskey Rebellion. Additional excises and even a stamp tax assessed under the Federalist administrations, and President Adams' forceful suppression of the "Hot Water War" against federal tax assessors in 1798, all seemed to testify to the unlimited power and desire of the national government to levy internal taxes. Localist fears had not changed, although the threat to liberty once perceived to emanate from London now seemed to reside in the national capital.

But a lost battle is not necessarily a lost war. When the Jeffersonian Republicans emerged victorious in 1800, one widely celebrated consequence was repeal of all the Federalist internal taxes. The "country" party of America's first party system remained loyal to its localist ideological roots and never adopted a peacetime internal tax. Only in war—President Madison's excises during the War of 1812—would the Republicans call upon what they saw as the emergency taxing power of the Constitution. Only for the duration of an extraordinary threat, localists agreed, might an exception be made to their ideological demand that remote central governments refrain from intrusion upon local control over internal taxes. After the three-year emergency had passed, the temporary revenue measures lapsed. Not until the Civil War was an internal tax again adopted, and it is in the 1860s that our modern system of excise stamps on liquor and tobacco products originated.

The power of the federal government to assess peacetime internal taxes was thus irrevocably determined by the Whiskey Rebellion. The ideological question, however, remains to this

GENERAL GEORGE WASHINGTON.
Reviewing the Western army at Fort Cumberland the 18ᵗʰ of octobᵗ 1794

President and Commander-in-Chief George Washington, reviewing troops at Fort Cumberland, Maryland, October 1794, in preparation for quelling the Whiskey Rebellion

day a partisan issue unresolved even by a constitutional amendment authorizing the federal income tax. The battle continues as the federal government destroys thousands of homemade stills each year, machines designed by their owners to evade the national excise on whiskey. Annually, millions of dollars worth of cigarettes are smuggled out of the tobacco-producing states in an effort to avoid stamp taxes. Although the language of internal and external taxes has passed from the scene, newspaper reports of shoot-outs with internal-revenue agents, protest movements, and organized tax resistance on moral and political grounds testify to the modern legacy of this ideological debate that pre-dated the Constitution.

SUGGESTED ADDITIONAL READING

Bernard Bailyn, *The Ideological Origins of the American Revolution* (1967).

Charles A. Beard, *An Economic Interpretation of the Constitution of the United States* (1913).

Merrill Jensen, *The Articles of Confederation* (1948).

Gary B. Nash, *The Urban Crucible: Social Change, Political Consciousness, and the Origins of the American Revolution* (1979).

Herbert J. Storing, *What the Anti-Federalists Were For* (1981).

Gordon S. Wood, *The Creation of the American Republic* (1969).

Alfred F. Young, ed., *The American Revolution: Explorations in the History of American Radicalism* (1976).

Thomas P. Slaughter is an assistant professor of history at Rutgers University, and the author of *The Whiskey Rebellion: Frontier Epilogue to the American Revolution* (Oxford University Press, 1986).

'To Regulate Commerce':
Federal Power Under the Constitution

Charles A. Lofgren

Today the commerce clause of the Constitution stands dramatically revealed as a fountain of vast federal power. Under its authority, for example, Congress has enacted civil rights legislation and may now dictate the wages of state employees. Yet the clause itself merely grants Congress the right "to regulate Commerce with foreign Nations, and among the several States, and with the Indian Tribes." As with several key constitutional provisions, however, the clause's text provides only an inkling of its present meaning and potential. To understand the bold expansion of the commerce power, let us begin by briefly examining its sources.

Commercial problems under the Articles of Confederation **Origins** helped fuel the drive for a new constitution in the 1780s. With the end of the Revolutionary War, Great Britain had limited trade between the newly independent United States and the remaining parts of the Empire, closing altogether the previously important West Indies market to American shipping and most American goods, and putting sometimes prohibitive duties on goods imported into the British Isles. Because the Articles in effect guaranteed each state the right to regulate its own trade, Congress had no power to retaliate. (In actuality, however, smuggling operations helped soften the impact of the British restrictions.)

Another difficulty arose from import taxes that some states placed on goods from abroad. These provided revenues for the states imposing them, but they irritated the citizens of states lacking their own harbor facilities. (By one estimate, Connecticut residents supported a third of New York's public expenses through payment of New York's import duties.) Finally, interstate tariff wars loomed. In the spring of 1787, just before the Constitutional Convention met in Philadelphia,

New York imposed fees on vessels running to and from Connecticut and New Jersey, and in response the latter state slapped a tax on a New York-owned lighthouse located on New Jersey soil. The Confederation Congress held no authority to intervene in either area.

To cope with these difficulties, the Constitution written during the spring and summer of 1787 not unexpectedly included the commerce clause among the provisions of Article I, section 8, defining the major powers of Congress. But what did the clause mean? It evoked almost no debate, emerging when a committee of the Constitutional Convention fleshed out the preliminary Virginia plan. Drafted by James Madison who was then a strong nationalist, the Virginia plan proposed for Congress "to legislate in all cases to which the separate States are incompetent, or in which the harmony of the United States may be interrupted by the exercise of individual [State] Legislation." Some argue that this origin shows the framers intended the clause as a broad grant. However, a comparable provision also appeared in the New Jersey plan—the opposition proposal within the Convention—which envisioned fairly restricted central authority within a strengthened union. Indeed, had many people sensed that the clause threatened the internal authority of the states, the Anti-Federalists would likely have objected; but with only a few exceptions they did not. In the final analysis, probably all we can say with certainty is that Americans in 1787-1788 concluded the clause would at minimum prevent the sort of interstate commercial difficulties they had so recently experienced.

Early Interpretation   What history left murky, Chief Justice John Marshall set on the road to resolution in *Gibbons v. Ogden* (1824). The case arose when Aaron Ogden sought to prevent his former partner, Thomas Gibbons, from running a steamship between New York City and Elizabethtown, New Jersey, in defiance of the monopoly grant Ogden held from the New York legislature. After the New York courts upheld Ogden's claim, Gibbons appealed to the federal Supreme Court. The right to control commerce among the states belonged *exclusively* with Congress, he claimed; in any event, he was exempt from New York's regulations because his boat operated under a federal "coasting license" issued under the Coasting Act which Congress passed in 1793.

In his opinion, Marshall came close to accepting the argument for exclusive congressional power. "The court," he allowed, "is not satisfied it has been refuted." But he finally backed off and instead relied on the supremacy clause of Article VI, which makes federal law supreme over state law. Ogden's monopoly grant, Marshall held, was invalid because it conflicted with the Coasting Act.

As a result, Marshall did not directly answer the question of how far states might go in regulating or interfering with commerce in the *absence* of federal legislation. During most of the nineteenth century, this issue remained a lively one because Congress generally refrained from enacting domestic commercial regulations. (Before the Civil War, a major reason for this reluctance was the South's fear that passage of any federal commercial legislation might open the door to regulation of its "peculiar institution"—slavery.) Marshall's opinion in *Gibbons* nevertheless bristled with language that could be used to support extensive congressional authority at a later day.

To begin, Marshall explained the proper method of interpreting constitutional language. Although the Constitution contained an enumeration of powers, he argued that it nowhere stated those powers had to be construed strictly. He especially attacked narrow readings that "would cripple the government and render it unequal to the objects for which it is declared to be instituted."

He next applied this approach to the commerce clause, asserting that by common sense "commerce" encompassed a wide range of activities. Everyone admitted, moreover, that Congress could regulate all kinds of commercial intercourse with foreign nations, and therefore it held the same authority over commerce among the states, for within the same sentence identical words must have the same meaning. He showed similar acuity in examining the phrase "among the states," noting that "among" means "intermingled with." This reasoning led him to the conclusion absolutely necessary to the sweep the commerce clause has gained in our own day: "Commerce among the states cannot stop at the external boundary line of each state, but may be introduced into the interior."

Of course, the fact of enumeration implied *some* limits, but in reality Marshall's concession in this regard was itself a claim of broad power. Congress' authority did not extend "to those [concerns] which are completely within a particular state, which do not affect other states, and with which it is not necessary to interfere, for the purpose of executing some of the general powers of the government." But what if, for example, it became "necessary to interfere" with an *intra*state activity "for the purpose of executing some of the general powers of the government"? Avoiding a direct answer, Marshall observed: "the power over commerce with foreign nations, and among the several states, is vested in Congress as absolutely as it would be in a single government." As restraints, there remained only "the wisdom and discretion of Congress, their identity with the people, and the influence which their constituents possess at election."

Congress Acts   Not until the emergence of large interstate railways and industries toward the end of the nineteenth century did Congress significantly begin to occupy the area Marshall had sketched in *Gibbons*. The first of two pioneering ventures, the Interstate Commerce Act of 1887, came after the Supreme Court struck down an Illinois law setting rates for the interstate operations of interstate railways operating within the state. Federal action now appeared the only viable approach to a problem that had been receiving increased state and national attention. Even some railway leaders saw benefits in limited national regulation, concluding it might ward off harsher legislation as well as soften the fierce competition that threatened to drive some lines into bankruptcy. Paradoxically contributing to the public outcry against the rail companies, this same competition had pushed the lines to make seemingly unfair rate discriminations between "long hauls," where competition was typically greatest and hence rates lowest, and "short hauls," where particular companies held monopolies and hence could charge higher rates per mile. (The situation resembled the picture confronting today's air traveler.) Also, to attract business, railroads sometimes rebated part of the charges paid by large shippers, putting smaller concerns at a disadvantage and drawing still more public criticism.

In response, Congress mandated that rail charges be "reasonable and just," outlawed rebates and "undue or reasonable preferences" to any person, company, or locality, and created the Interstate Commerce Commission to administer the new act. Indicating some appreciation of the ICC's importance, President Grover Cleveland appointed as its first chairman Thomas M. Cooley, a leading legal scholar of the period and a former member of the Michigan Supreme Court. Soon, however, the ICC found its powers narrowed through several court cases.

Yet the setbacks proved only temporary, for just after the turn of the century Congress rejuvenated the Commission by

Woodcut, 1857

clarifying and expanding its role. In America of the Progressive Era, regulation found support at both state and national levels; cases were prosecuted more effectively than before; and now the courts cooperated in upholding Commission orders. Critics later contended that the ICC quickly became the champion of the carriers it was supposed to regulate, thereby tampering with normal competitive forces and creating serious long-term problems in American transportation. True or not, the ICC became a prototype for a growing number of independent regulatory commissions in the twentieth century. Hanging on the commerce clause as a constitutional "peg," such bodies as the Federal Trade Commission, the Federal Communications Commission, the Securities and Exchange Commission, and the Consumer Products Safety Commission compose an integral part of America's actual framework of government. They also touch the lives of every American.

Congress' second pioneering measure struck off in a different direction. Although industrial expansion and consolidation, typified in the public mind by Standard Oil Company's growth in the 1880s, brought substantial benefits in product development and distribution, it threatened to overwhelm the American dream of individual entrepreneurship. In the 1888 presidential contest, not surprisingly, Republicans and Democrats both endorsed national legislation to control the "trusts," and bipartisan majorities soon passed the Sherman Anti-Trust Act of 1890. Whereas the Interstate Commerce Act aimed in part at slowing competition, the 1890 law sought to restore it by outlawing "every contract, combination in the form of trust or otherwise, or conspiracy, in restraint of trade or commerce, among the several States, or with foreign nations."

But the Supreme Court soon held that the Sherman Act did not outlaw all kinds of "bigness." Quite early, the Supreme Court in *Standard Oil Company v. United States* (1911) came close to endorsing Teddy Roosevelt's notion that there were good trusts and bad trusts. The act had to be interpreted in light of earlier English and American legal doctrines on restraint and monopoly of trade, wrote Chief Justice Edward White. These doctrines, and thus the Act, embodied the common-sense notion that not all the large business combinations were harmful to the public welfare and hence forbidden.

Responding indignantly to White's "rule of reason," Justice John Marshall Harlan retorted that when Congress included "every contract" in the Act's coverage, it meant *every*. Although the Court had ordered the breakup of Standard Oil,

John Marshall Harlan

Harlan parodied White as telling the big corporations: "You may *now* restrain such commerce, provided you are reasonable about it; only take care that the restraint is not undue." But if Harlan had the better of the argument from a literalist's point of view, White better captured the ambivalent American view of business concentration. And recent responses to the dismantling of the American Telephone and Telegraph Company again confirm the "love-hate" relationship of Americans toward the reach of the commerce clause in the form of anti-trust policy.

The Sherman Act led also to a more fundamental issue, one John Marshall had opened in *Gibbons:* As conferred by the Constitution, how far did Congress' commerce power extend? Put differently, what activities did the commerce clause authorize Congress to regulate? The question arose when the American Sugar Refining Company, which already produced

Cooley   Morrison   Bragg   Walker   Schoonmaker

The ICC moving on the animals in Uncle Sam's "Wild West" (East and South) show

nearly two-thirds of the sugar refined in the United States, bought the E. C. Knight Company and three other Pennsylvania-based refineries. Because the purchase gave American Sugar control of all but two percent of the industry's output, the Justice Department sought a judicial order under the Sherman Act to annul the contracts of purchase. In *United States v. E. C. Knight Company* (1895), the Supreme Court denied the government's request, upholding a lower court ruling.

Assuming Congress had meant the term "commerce" within the Sherman Act to convey the same meaning that it carried in the Constitution, Chief Justice Melville Weston Fuller asked if the constitutional meaning of "commerce" embraced "manufacturing." By his reading, it did not: "Commerce succeeds to manufacture, and is not part of it"—where manufacturing left off, commerce began; the two were neatly compartmentalized. Furthermore, to equate them would be fraught with danger, for it would take federal authority into every nook and cranny of American life and hence would destroy "the autonomy of the States" that was so necessary to "our dual form of government." By this reasoning, the commerce clause did not allow regulation of manufacturing, and accordingly the Sherman Act did not apply to the Knight purchase.

Over the next four decades, both in applying the Sherman Act and in testing other federal legislation, the Court admitted that the commerce power allowed *some* regulation of intrastate activities. One approach examined whether the object of regulation, although itself purely local in scope, formed part of a larger "stream of commerce." (Stockyards did and thus came within federal jurisdiction.) Another and more problem-laden test was whether the local activity had a direct or an indirect effect on interstate commerce. If direct (as in the instance of railway safety devices), regulation was permissible; if indirect (as with child labor), it was not. But the line between direct and indirect effects was obscure, to say the least. Its fuzziness gave considerable room to the policy choices of legislators and judges alike.

By the time of Franklin D. Roosevelt's New Deal, the Supreme Court had available a variety of precedents. Some pointed toward a strict interpretation of the commerce power; others offered more latitude. Because FDR's war with the "nine old men" on the Court is a story in itself, suffice it here to say that the justices initially took the narrow view, one that

Roosevelt gloomily labeled "the horse-and-buggy definition of interstate commerce."

Reading the opinions in the early New Deal cases recalls to mind John Marshall's stricture in *Gibbons* against using metaphysical niceties to constrain federal power. As developed by Justice George Sutherland in *Carter v. Carter Coal Company* (1936), the direct-indirect effects test turned out *not* to involve the economic magnitude of a local activity's impact on interstate commerce. Discussing the relation of labor-management strife in coal mines to the nation's commerce, Sutherland explained that "the extent of the effect bears no logical relation to its character. . . . An increase in the greatness of the effect adds to its importance. It does not alter its [indirect] character." Yet *economic* magnitude is precisely the sort of consideration one might expect to enter crucially into a "test" relating to *commerce*. For Sutherland, however, the necessary requirement was practically a direct physical impact on commerce; an undeniable chain of cause-and-effect involving only broad market forces would not do.

Easy though it is to ridicule Sutherland's position, he conveyed a troubling message. His rejection of mere *economic* connections as sufficient to establish federal authority rested on a *political* concern. "The Constitution, in all its provisions," he reaffirmed, quoting from an earlier case, "looks to an indestructible Union, composed of indestructible States." He then added:

> Every journey to a forbidden end begins with the first step; and the danger of such a step by the federal government in the direction of taking over the powers of the states is that the end of the journey may find the states so despoiled of their powers, or— what may amount to the same thing—so relieved of the responsibilities which possession of the powers necessarily enjoins, as to reduce them to little more than geographical subdivisions of the national domain.

Stripped of its judgment about the undesirability of the outcome he foresaw, Sutherland's opinion offered a prediction: If the federal government could regulate a local activity merely because it had a generalized economic relationship to interstate commerce—and perhaps only a slight and even vague relationship—then no area of life would necessarily remain free from federal supervision.

Was Sutherland's prediction accurate?

In the spring of 1937 the Supreme Court reversed itself,

upholding the National Labor Relations Act as a valid exercise of the commerce power even though it regulated labor relations in production or manufacturing. To be sure, in the major case, *National Labor Relations Board v. Jones and Laughlin Steel Corporation* (1937), Chief Justice Charles Evans Hughes emphasized the real and substantial interstate impact of labor strife in a large, far-flung steel company. But another decision applied the NLRA against a small clothing manufacturer, which employed about 800 of the 150,000 workers in the men's clothing industry. If the company were closed immediately, the dissent accurately protested, "the ultimate effect on commerce in clothing obviously would be negligible."

Such concerns now carried little weight, and the future became vividly outlined in *Wickard v. Filburn* (1942). Roscoe C. Filburn owned and operated a small farm near Dayton, Ohio; in 1941, he had grown 23 acres of winter wheat, totaling nearly 12 acres more than he was legally permitted by federal law. These production quotas, established under the New Deal's Agricultural Adjustment Act of 1938, sought to promote agricultural prosperity by limiting production and thus raising prices. Filburn, wishing to avoid a penalty, sued to prevent the Secretary of Agriculture from enforcing the measure. Filburn admitted that he generally sold some of his crop; but he also fed part to his poultry and livestock (some of which were sold), saved a portion for making flour for home consumption, and kept some for the next planting. In any event, counsel for the Secretary never alleged that the amount Filburn would directly market exceeded his quota.

No matter. The Supreme Court accepted the argument that even if farmers like Filburn consumed their wheat on the farm, they still affected commerce, for their home consumption depressed the agricultural economy by relieving them of the need to make purchases in the market. Moreover, although each farmer's share was minuscule, the total effect was great. With *Wickard v. Filburn,* the line between *inter*state and *intra*state commerce all but evaporated.

The Commerce Clause and Civil Rights

Intrastate commerce, although not specifically mentioned in the Constitution, is at least still commerce. In 1964, Congress, with the subsequent endorsement of the Supreme Court, used the commerce clause to support legislation on a subject that most of us think of as quite different—the protection of civil rights. This use of the clause is even more surprising because the Constitution offers other foundations for civil rights legislation. The Thirteenth Amendment, for example, both abolishes slavery and (as sometimes construed) bans practices that constitute "badges of servitude." The Fourteenth Amendment prohibits a state from denying equal protection of the laws. (Racial discrimination, the argument would assert, indicates state action in the form of failure to protect minority rights.)

As early as 1883, however, in his classic dissent in the *Civil Rights Cases,* Justice John Marshall Harlan protested that the just-invalidated Civil Rights Act of 1875 could be justified as a regulation of commerce. Eighty-one years later, Congress accepted Harlan's suggestion when it passed the Civil Rights Act of 1964. Here the commerce power came to underpin legislation in which the economic concern was at best secondary, however laudable the legislation was in its own right.

Relying explicitly on the commerce clause, the public accommodations section of the 1964 act outlawed (among other practices) racial segregation in restaurants that served or offered to serve interstate travelers or obtained a "substantial portion" of their food from interstate sources. While the section also banned discrimination "supported by State action" and thus took a bow toward the Fourteenth Amendment, the Supreme Court nevertheless upheld its public accommodations provisions on commerce grounds.

One case arose when Ollie McClung and his son, Ollie, Jr., the operators of "Ollie's Barbecue" in Birmingham, Alabama, attempted to enjoin Attorney General Nicholas Katzenbach from enforcing the law against them. Their restaurant catered to local business and family groups, it did no advertising, and was situated about a mile from the nearest interstate highway and bus and train stations, and six to eight miles from the nearest airport. To the McClungs' knowledge, they served no interstate travelers, but because they purchased most of their meat from a supplier who obtained it from out-of-state, they clearly fell within the terms of the Act. And because they refused service to blacks, they were just as clearly violating the Act.

In *Katzenbach v. McClung* (1964), Justice Tom Clark briefly reviewed the congressional hearings preceding the Civil Rights Act and found they solidly established that segregated restaurants not only sold less food from interstate sources but hindered both interstate travel and new business opportunities. As in *Wickard v. Filburn,* he observed, the immediate impact of the business in question was nationally insignificant; but combined with the activities "of others similarly situated," it was "far from trivial."

Are There Limits?

As for possible limits to the commerce power, Clark returned to *Gibbons v. Ogden's* exclusion of activities "which are completely within a particular State, which do not affect other States, and with which it is not necessary to interfere, for the purpose of executing some of the general powers of the government." "This rule," Clark declared, "is as good today as it was when Chief Justice Marshall laid it down," but he wisely avoided suggesting any examples of activities that would fall within the rule. Nor did he mention that the Court had last invalidated a congressional commerce regulation in 1936.

Eventually, in *National League of Cities v. Usery* (1976), the Court did overturn an amendment to the federal Fair Labor Standards Act that regulated the wages and hours of state and local employees. Significantly, though, Justice William H. Rehnquist's opinion for the Court did not deny that these employees' wages and hours of work affected interstate commerce. Rather, Rehnquist contended the legislation interfered with the constitutionally essential operations of state governments. But the vote against the FLSA amendments was close—five to four—and in the ensuing years the Court declined to extend the *Usery* ruling. Finally, in *Garcia v. San Antonio Metropolitan Transit Authority* (1985), Justice Harry A. Blackmun changed sides and the Court explicitly overruled its 1976 decision, arguing that the political process adequately protected states from congressional regulation under the commerce clause. Again, however, the vote was five to four, and the dissenters promised that it would take only another one-vote switch to reinstate the judicially enforced *Usery* limits on the commerce power. This area promises to be one of continuing controversy.

With only the power to tax and spend as a near competitor, the commerce clause supports a list of federal activities that ranges about as far as the imagination. From late nineteenth-century bans on transportation of lottery tickets and pornography, it has come to underpin federal attacks on prostitution, tainted foods and dangerous or ineffective drugs, motor vehicle thefts, kidnapping, chaos in the radio spectrum, business "monopolies," labor racketeering, low wages and long hours, agricultural overproduction, racial discrimination, gas guzzling and polluting automobiles, dangerous toys, and improperly shaped toilet seats in the work place—among other economic and social ills.

When you next read that the FCC, say, is investigating the deceptive marketing of cordless telephones, or that the ICC is setting rates on the shipment of yak fat, think about John Marshall. Consider, too, today's complex economy and ask if there remain any limits to Congress' commerce authority.

SUGGESTED ADDITIONAL READING

Paul R. Benson, Jr., *The Supreme Court and the Commerce Clause, 1937-1970* (New York, 1970).

Felix Frankfurter, *The Commerce Clause under Marshall, Taney and Waite* (Chicago, 1964).

Alpheus T. Mason and Gerald Garvey, eds., *American Constitutional History: Essays by Edward S. Corwin* (New York, 1964), ch. 10 ("The Passing of Dual Federalism").

Charles A. Lofgren is Roy P. Crocker Professor of American politics and history at Claremont McKenna College in California; he is completing a book on the "separate-but-equal" case, *Plessy v. Ferguson* (1896), to be published by Oxford University Press.

The Constitution and the Bureaucracy

Martin Shapiro

Americans think of their Constitution as doing a number of basic things. One is to protect the rights of individuals. A second is to set out the basic blueprint of the structure of government. Article I establishes a Congress to wield legislative power. Article II establishes a presidency to wield executive power. Article III creates a Supreme Court which, along with such other courts as Congress shall create, wields the judicial power. The Constitution appears to set out quite a simple, logical, and complete plan for a national government. Yet the Constitution fails to provide for one of the largest and most important institutions of every national government, the bureaucracy. Without a bureaucracy the executive power would be meaningless, for the one man or woman who is president cannot personally "take care that" all the myriad laws of a modern nation "be faithfully executed."

This glaring constitutional omission was in part accidental. The very idea of bureaucracy becomes prevalent only with the writings of Max Weber, over a hundred years after the Constitution was written. The framers knew that the executive could not operate without a body comparable to the servants of the crown in England. Indeed, the Constitution does make one explicit reference to what we would call a bureaucracy: "The President ... may require the Opinion in writing, of the principal Officer in each of the executive Departments. ..." It has nothing more to say, however, largely because people had not yet come to think of the executive's servants as a body of persons with a distinct set of rules, roles, procedures, and values that set them apart from the person who inhabited the presidency or kingship.

Yet the omission of bureaucracy was in part deliberate. The Constitution could easily have said more about the bureaucracy. It does specify how government officers are appointed—some by the president alone and others by the president after an opportunity for the Senate to advise and consent. The Constitution also provides that members of Congress may not hold offices in the executive branch, thus preventing the sort of cabinet government that was emerging in England. The Constitution empowers Congress to establish a post office, an army, and a navy. It could have gone on to specify what executive departments, such as treasury and state, should exist and, like many state constitutions, to provide a detailed organization chart for the whole executive branch. The framers did not undertake this task in part because they felt that the details of government organization should change from time to time in response to changes in the rest of the world. In part, however, they said little in the Constitution because they anticipated that the first president would be George Washington who would surely set the first administration on the right path. Thus the framers deliberately left the evolution of the personnel and organization of the executive branch to be worked out by Congress and the president in the future.

Because the Constitution contains this large hole and because bureaucracies touch the lives of so many Americans, the courts have had to create the constitutional law of bureaucracies. It is not that the courts are ever asked directly what a bureaucracy is or what its role is in our constitutional system. Instead these questions arise in cases that look like they are primarily about the legal or constitutional rights of individuals.

From a 'Spoils System' to the Career Service

Some constitutional litigation involves the intersection of bureaucracies and another institution about which the Constitution is even more silent, the political party. The Jacksonian Democrats developed a theory of bureaucracy in the 1820s, although they did not call it by that name. They argued that if government agencies were staffed by career employees, these governors would become an elite separated in spirit and outlook from the people they governed. The cure was "rotation in office." Each time one political party ousted the other from the control of the presidency or other elected executive post such as governor or mayor, all those appointed by the previous executive should be removed from office and replaced by appointees of the new executive. Thus, everyday citizens would move in and out of government as political fortunes changed. We would not need to worry about keeping the governing bureaucracy under control of the people because the people would be the bureaucracy.

Cartoon by Thomas Nast on civil service reform showing "Mr. Statesman" cutting the tails (salaries) off a mangy dog (civil service "spoils system"). Uncle Sam leans against a poster with civil service reform guidelines, which recommend better salaries and working conditions. Harper's Weekly, April 22, 1876

George Hunt Pendleton

This theory of bureaucracy was also a theory of party finance. As they evolved, European political parties supported themselves in a number of ways. Many, such as the British Labor or French Socialist party, became dues-paying, closed membership clubs. In return for paying dues, a member got a card and a right to vote in party elections. Others, like the British Conservative party, long supported themselves on private wealth. Wealthy families sent one of their sons into politics and provided him an annual income while he pursued his political career. Others yet, like the Communist and Monarchist parties, depended largely on ideological fervor of their partisans to yield many, voluntary, unpaid hours of party work.

American parties have rarely had dues-paying memberships. Neither family support nor ideological commitment has been sufficient to bring out enough party workers to staff election campaigns or to keep the parties alive between elections. In the nineteenth century, American parties instead relied on "rotation in office," or, as it is known less grandly, the "spoils system." With this system, the party simply promises that, while it can pay its workers nothing now, faithful workers will be given government jobs if the party wins the election. These jobs do pay and will continue to pay as long as the party keeps getting elected. Thus, the party is financed partly by the government.

The Jacksonian theory of bureaucracy and party held that government administration really was simple stuff. Any citizen rotated into office to enjoy the spoils that go to election victors could do the job for a while until replaced by a new set of winners. From the earliest days of the Republic, this premise was challenged by those who believed that the business of governing was a highly technical one requiring great experience, impartiality, and expertise. First announced by the Federalists, this theory of bureaucracy as neutral expertise, and thus of the separation of government administration from the hurly burly of democratic politics, reached its high point in the Progressive movement around the turn of the century. The Progressives wanted to replace "rotation in office" with a professional career civil service, appointed on the basis of competitive examinations and shielded by law from political influence. Their greatest victory was the Pendleton Act of 1883 which established such a federal civil service.

The Progressive theory of bureaucracy sought to undermine traditional party supports. The Progressives saw the traditional party machines as the principal enemies of good public administration. The machines were the source of the graft, corruption, and simple incompetence that marred American government. If "rotation in office" were ended, and with it the promise of jobs, the machines could not enlist the precinct captains and ward heelers who were their front line troops. As a result the machines would run down and eventually disappear.

The Supreme Court entered the fray not in the form of direct decisions about whether the Constitution had approved one theory or the other, but indirectly. One of the statutes amending and improving the Pendleton Act was the Hatch Act of 1939 which forbade federal employees from contributing to or participating in party election campaigns. Its basic intent was to protect civil servants from political pressure. If they were forbidden by law from engaging in political activity on behalf of any party, they could not be pressured by the president or those he appointed as secretaries and assistant secretaries of the various government departments to be active on the side of the president's party.

A number of civil servants saw things differently, however, and challenged the Hatch Act as a violation of their constitutional, First Amendment, right to participate in politics. The Supreme Court usually holds that First Amendment rights are not absolute. If the government is limiting speech for a sufficiently compelling reason, it may do so constitutionally. In the course of explaining the compelling government interest that was to be balanced against the individual civil servants' First Amendment rights, the Supreme Court provided a ringing endorsement of the Progressive theory of bureaucracy. The Court held that the government's interest in an expert, neutral, career civil service clearly separated from politics outweighed First Amendment considerations. In upholding the Hatch Act, the Supreme Court read "rotation in office" out of the Constitution.

Carl A. Hatch

Some years later, the Court used the Constitution to abolish the remnants of the "spoils system" that had survived the Progressive era. A number of attorneys employed by Cook County, the county in which Chicago is located, had been appointed to their jobs as prosecutors when one party won a county election. The next time around, the other party won, and in 1971 it sought to replace these prosecutors with its own party faithful. The old prosecutors argued that their First Amendment rights were being abridged—they were being fired from their jobs solely because of their political beliefs. The Supreme Court did not exactly ignore the time-honored place of the "spoils system" in American political life, but it did treat it as irrelevant. Focusing on the First Amendment claim, a majority of the Court confirmed that firing government workers just because of their political views was a violation of their rights to free speech and association.

In order to encourage the acceptance of the civil service concept, new civil service statutes often contained clauses providing for "blanketing in" present employees. Whenever more federal, state and/or local government jobs were brought under civil service designation, workers already on those jobs were allowed to keep them rather than having to compete for them in new examinations. "Blanketing in" was politically essential to the passage of most civil servant legislation. It meant that existing government workers appointed under the "spoils system" would not only cease to oppose civil service laws but would vigorously support them because the new laws would secure their jobs even if the other party won an election. In its Cook County decision, the Supreme Court in effect "blanketed in" every one of the remaining spoils appointees in the United States. The Progressive theory of a bureaucracy of neutral "experts," free from political party control, had become part of the Constitution not as separate clauses but as an interpretation of the First Amendment.

Whose Bureaucracy?   Today, the most important dispute about the constitutional position of the federal bureaucracy is being fought out in cases that appear not to relate to the Constitution at all. In these cases, the parties are not claiming that a particular government action is unconstitutional but only that it is unlawful; not that it violates the Constitution, but only that it violates some statute enacted by Congress. These cases raise the most difficult constitutional question of all about the bureaucracy—to which branch of government does it belong?

The simple schema of the first three articles of the Constitution—Article I which describes Congress, Article II which establishes the presidency, and Article III which provides for the judiciary—would seem to place the executive departments, such as treasury and interior, and the bureaucrats who work in them, squarely under the control of the president who holds not a part of but all of "the executive Power of the United States." Particularly from the time of the New Deal onward, constitutional and political commentators have urged more and more centralized control by the president over an executive branch that was constantly growing in size and complexity. The Nixon presidency, however, brought denunciations of the "imperial presidency" from the same people who had espoused the strong presidency earlier. And the Reagan presidency, with its campaign to cut back on big government, including the big executive branch, has led those who favor more rather than less government activity to re-examine the actual legal status of the executive departments.

When they do so they encounter a very curious phenomenon of American law. In spite of what would seem to be the clear structure of the first three articles of the Constitution, the

Federal postal workers, Washington, D.C., 1890s

130

federal departments are not the servants of the president but the creatures of Congress. Precisely because Article II does not authorize any specific executive departments or provide an organization chart of the executive branch, each federal executive department and agency must be created by a statute enacted by Congress. The agencies not only exist by virtue of such statutes but each and every one of their powers and programs must be authorized by statute and each and every dollar they spend must be appropriated by statute.

It is not that Americans suddenly discovered this legal arrangement. In some sense they knew it all along. In the middle and later 1970s, however, with the presidency in the hands of one party and Congress in that of the other, more observers came to recognize the contradiction between the legal basis of the executive departments as congressional creations and the position of the president as chief executive.

This contradiction is now being discussed in the federal courts. The Reagan administration has inherited hundreds of executive branch programs and regulations that it would like to eliminate, cut back, or redirect. In some cases, the administration believes that a regulation imposes impossible tasks on the companies being regulated, and/or creates costs that far outweigh any possible benefits and/or is based on factual data that is wrong or incomplete and/or misreads the intent of the statute that the regulation is designed to implement. Wielding the powers of the chief executive, administration officials have rescinded some regulations, refused to go forward with others that were in the bureaucratic pipeline when Mr. Reagan took office, and reduced the tempo of enforcement of yet others. The Reagan administration has argued that many of these regulations and styles of enforcement had been adopted by the departments in pursuit of the policy ideas of President Carter and his appointees. That course, Reagan's aides say, was perfectly legitimate, but it is equally legitimate for a newly elected president with different ideas to modify the practices of *his* executive branch to conform to *his* ideas. Those who oppose President Reagan's policies have responded that the regulations and programs that existed when he took office were mandated by Congress and to stop or change them now violates those statutes. Typically, the issue has reached the courts when those who favor retention and extension of the old regulations ask the court to require the agency to enforce the statute. These cases involve the huge body of statutory and case law about the procedures that agencies must use in making, unmaking, and enforcing their own regulations that lawyers call "administrative law."

Because these are complex administrative law cases, few people become aware of the underlying constitutional debate. The debate arises because many congressional statutes not only authorize or empower executive agencies to do things but, at least according to some interpretations, order them to do things. Not just President Reagan, but all presidents, have argued that the president has the authority under Article II to decide just how the laws shall be "faithfully executed" and thus the discretion to decide when, against whom, and under what circumstances the law should be carried out.

Agencies live between the duties imposed upon them by statute and the executive discretion wielded by the president as head of the executive branch. In a common sort of law suit in this area, an environmental group might insist that a particular statute, say the Clean Air Act, imposes a duty on the Environmental Protection Agency (EPA) to achieve clean air now. The agency thus has a duty to formulate the best possible air pollution regulations based on available data and enforce them immediately. The EPA will reply that no statute can ever be read as commanding an agency to make regulations and punish people for violating them before the agency is sure that it knows enough to make a good regulation. Thus the EPA must have discretion to decide when it will make a regulation. Furthermore, the EPA has only so much time, staff, and money to enforce its regulations and never enough to enforce all of them on everybody. Thus it must have discretion to pick and choose its enforcement actions to get the most "bang" for its enforcement "buck." And precisely because these judgments are discretionary, they must be exercised in accord with the policies of the only person who has constitutional authority to control the discretion of the executive branch—the president.

When a court decides whether, in a particular instance, an agency has a statutory duty or, alternatively a measure of discretion, the court is deciding whether the agency belongs to Congress or the president. Depending on the circumstances, the statutory language and the underlying constitutional theory of the judge, individual decisions go one way or the other. Over the years, however, the collective impact of these decisions will move the federal bureaucracy more toward Article I (congressional authority) or more toward Article II (presidential control) and thus determine a fundamental aspect of our constitutional law even though these cases do not overtly raise constitutional questions. This issue, like many constitutional issues, is never totally resolved, but the courts are currently deeply engaged in determining the extent of presidential control of the actions of the executive departments.

Legislative Veto   The Supreme Court has spoken specifically about the constitutionality of congressional control of the bureaucracy in one recent case involving the "legislative veto." In a number of statutes, Congress has delegated to executive agencies the power to make rules and other kinds of decisions, but it retained for itself the right to veto these rules within a specified time. Only after Congress approved the agency action, or refused to disapprove it, did the agency's action become legally binding. These provisions allowed Congress to grant a great deal of discretion to the agencies while at the same time maintaining control over the final decision.

In *Immigration and Naturalization Service v. Chadha* (1983), the Supreme Court held one such veto provision unconstitutional and did so in broad enough language to suggest that most such provisions were invalid. The Court focused not on the constitutional problems of bureaucracy and administration but on the president's veto power. The details of legislative veto clauses varied, but all provided that the congressional veto be exercised by votes and resolutions not subject to presidential veto. The Court held that Congress' action of disapproving an agency decision was itself a legislative action like the passage of a new law. Thus, it was unconstitutional for Congress to take such actions in ways that denied the president his constitutional authority to veto new legislation.

Chadha generally has been interpreted as a pro-president, anti-Congress decision. It does reduce the power of Congress to limit the discretion exercised by the federal bureaucracy. It does not, however, increase presidential control over that bureaucracy. Indeed, it tends simply to grant more autonomy to the bureaucracy. Recent presidents have sought to increase their authority over agency rule-making by executive orders requiring that proposed agency rules be cleared through the Office of Management and Budget, which is part of the president's own staff. These executive orders, and particularly any attempt by the president to prevent a proposed rule from coming into legal effect, raise their own serious constitutional problems.

Although the Constitution does not provide specifically for bureaucracies, courts decide bureaucracy cases under a wide array of constitutional and non-constitutional provisions that do not even use the words. In doing so, the courts shape not only the bureaucracy, but the relationship between Congress and the president. We are used to thinking of that dynamic relationship as a direct struggle between Congress and president over such questions as whether the president has the power to withhold documents from Congress or to send troops into combat without a congressional declaration of war. But there is also a struggle between Congress and president about just how much power each should have over the work of the federal bureaucracy, work that constitutes almost all of the activity of government that actually touches the daily lives of the citizenry. As the courts referee this rivalry, we can expect different constitutional balances to be struck at different times depending on changing political circumstances and changing political theories of Congress and the presidency. The developing constitutional law of the bureaucracy shows that the Constitution can be made to respond to circumstances unforeseen, indeed even to institutions unmentioned, in the original document.

Conclusion

Martin Shapiro received his Ph.D. from the Department of Government at Harvard and has taught there and at a number of campuses of the University of California. He is now a professor of law at Berkeley and has written several books and articles about the Supreme Court.

IV. Forming the American Community

James Madison and the Extended Republic: Theory and Practice in American Politics

Jack N. Rakove

In March 1789, the duly elected members of the First Federal Congress began to assemble in New York City. Like other eighteenth-century legislators, they were a remarkably unpunctual group. Although the new government under the Constitution was supposed to begin operation on March 4, fully five weeks elapsed before both houses of Congress were able to muster a quorum.

In the wake of the intense political maneuvering that had accompanied the ratification of the Constitution and the first federal elections, this delay in the organization of the new government both embarrassed and alarmed its supporters. Many of them were not entirely sure what they wanted the federal government *to do,* but they knew very well what they wanted it *to be:* a collection of enlightened and responsible men who could be counted upon to discharge the public business with a degree of sobriety and wisdom that both the state assemblies and the Continental Congress had seemed sorely to lack. It was this expectation that made the slow convening of the First Congress so painful to witness. Americans wanted to be ruled by governments of law rather than of men but the Federalists who had battled for the Constitution also understood that good laws could be framed and executed only if the right men were in office.

No one had thought more deeply about the problem of how one elected such men to office, and maintained public confidence in their performance, than James Madison, who was about to play as influential a role in the debates of the First Congress as he had at the Constitutional Convention. These issues had been very much on his mind during the months preceding the Convention, which Madison had spent examining both the history and theory of federal government. The results of his research took their first concrete form in a memorandum which he completed only weeks before the Convention met. It was in this working paper, "The Vices of the Political System of the United States," that he first developed the ideas that would receive their classic statement in his Tenth *Federalist,* a document now generally regarded as the cornerstone of American political theory.

'The Mischiefs of Faction'

Madison's concern in both texts was to refute one of the great commonplaces of eighteenth-century political thought: the belief that republican governments could survive only in geographically small, socially homogeneous societies, where a rough equality of condition and similarity of interests would enable the citizens to maintain the virtue upon which all republics rested. Virtue, as contemporaries understood it, meant a willingness to subordinate private interest to public good. In a republic, obedience to law rested on neither the coercive powers of a vigorous monarchy nor the social stability provided by a capable aristocracy. Only the self-restraint of the individual citizen could prevent the descent into anarchy that classical political theory held was the fate of an unruly republic. Since virtue often failed to render men immune to the dangers of passion and self-interest, it seemed wiser to limit the republican form of government to those societies which were relatively simple and homogeneous—where, in other words, the absence of clashing, competing interests would help citizens to preserve the virtue they needed.

Imbued with such assumptions as these, many Americans in the 1780s doubted whether it would be possible to create a government that would be both faithful to republican principles and capable of managing the affairs of a country so large in extent and diverse in interests as the thirteen newly independent United States. Madison's great contribution was to allay such reservations by turning the received wisdom of his age on its head. Since "the latent causes of faction are sown in the nature of man," he argued, clashing interests were inevitable in any society. The great problem was to explain how these divergent interests could best be adjusted and regulated without violating republican principles. One part of his answer—the more familiar part—argued that an extended republic would "cure the mischiefs of faction" more effectively than a small one. The larger and more diverse a society was, Madison argued, the more difficult it would be to organize durable coalitions intent

JA.ˢ MADISON.

52   THE FEDERALIST.

long as it exifts by a conftitutional neceffity for local purpofes, though it fhould be in perfect fubordination to the general authority of the union, it would ftill be, in fact and in theory, an affociation of ftates, or a confederacy. The propofed conftitution, fo far from implying an abolition of the ftate governments, makes them conftituent parts of the national fovereignty by allowing them a direct reprefentation in the fenate, and leaves in their poffeffion certain exclufive and very important portions of fovereign power.—This fully correfponds, in every rational import of the terms, with the idea of a federal government.

In the Lycian confederacy, which confifted of twenty-three CITIES, or republics, the largeft were intitled to *three* votes in the COMMON COUNCIL, thofe of the middle clafs to *two*, and the fmalleft to *one*. The COMMON COUNCIL had the appointment of all the judges and magiftrates of the refpective CITIES. This was certainly the moft delicate fpecies of interference in their internal adminiftration; for if there be any thing that feems exclufively appropriated to the local jurifdictions, it is the appointment of their own officers. Yet Montefquieu, fpeaking of this affociation, fays, "Were I to give a model of an excellent "confederate republic, it would be that of Lycia." Thus we perceive that the diftinctions infifted upon were not within the contemplation of this enlightened civilian, and we fhall be led to conclude, that they are the novel refinements of an erroneous theory.

PUBLIUS.

NUMBER X.
The fame Subject continued.

AMONG the numerous advantages promifed by a well conftructed union, none deferves to be more accurately developed than its tendency to break and control the violence of faction. The friend of popular governments,

THE FEDERALIST.   53

governments, never finds himfelf fo much alarmed for their character and fate, as when he contemplates their propenfity to this dangerous vice. He will not fail therefore to fet a due value on any plan which, without violating the principles to which he is attached, provides a proper cure for it. The inftability, injuftice and confufion introduced into the public councils, have in truth been the mortal difeafes under which popular governments have every where perifhed; as they continue to be the favorite and fruitful topics from which the adverfaries to liberty derive their moft fpecious declamations. The valuable improvements made by the American conftitutions on the popular models, both ancient and modern, cannot certainly be too much admired; but it would be an unwarrantable partiality, to contend that they have as effectually obviated the danger on this fide as was wifhed and expected. Complaints are every where heard from our moft confiderate and virtuous citizens, equally the friends of public and private faith, and of public and perfonal liberty; that our governments are too unftable; that the public good is difregarded in the conflicts of rival parties; and that meafures are too often decided, not according to the rules of juftice, and the rights of the minor party; but by the fuperior force of an interefted and overbearing majority. However anxioufly we may with that thefe complaints had no foundation, the evidence of known facts will not permit us to deny that they are in fome degree true. It will be found indeed, on a candid review of our fituation, that fome of the diftreffes under which we labor, have been erroneoufly charged on the operation of our governments; but it will be found at the fame time, that other caufes will not alone account for many of our heavieft misfortunes; and particularly, for that prevailing and increafing diftruft of public engagements, and alarm for private rights, which are echoed from one end of the continent to the other. Thefe muft be chiefly, if not

E 3   wholly,

The Federalist No. 10 (New York, 1788)

on pursuing their various private interests at the expense of the larger public good.

In pushing his analysis even this far, Madison had already gone a long way toward adding classical political theory to other European legacies the Americans were eager to discard. He had not only suggested that a republic could rest on vice as easily as on virtue, but he had also substituted a recognizably modern image of a fluid and diverse society for the traditional categories of the few and the many, the aristocracy and the democracy. Yet this was not enough. In arguing that "factious majorities" could not exist in a society as diverse and extensive as America, Madison had only posited what would *not* happen; he had not identified the positive principles on which the government would actually operate.

One reading of Madison's theory—usually described as the "pluralist" model—has held that government would somehow constitute an arena within which the various interests of the larger society would be represented, with public policy formed as the outcome of the conflicts and compromises, the push and pull of legislative politics. We now understand that this was not Madison's idea at all. As modern as Madison may have been in understanding the fluidity of society, he still held to an older notion of representation.

In his view, the second great advantage of the extended republic was that it would permit the election to office of more conscientious and capable leaders than the petty politicians and local demagogues who had dominated the state assemblies during the 1780s. Representatives to the new national government would be chosen from constituencies far larger than those which elected state legislators. Within these districts, Madison assumed, politicians of merely local reputation and little talent would cancel each other out; only men possessed of genuine reputation and ability—one suspects Madison was thinking of himself—would be able to command the allegiance of large numbers of voters. Once in office, they would act with a broadmindedness that would elevate the very quality of public life. They would think not in terms of the immediate interests of their constituents, but of the larger public good which was synonymous with the concept of *res publica* itself. The virtue which could no longer be expected to reside in the populace might still be found, he hoped, in its rulers.

It is this aspect of Madison's theory which has, in recent years, commanded the attention of such scholars as the late Douglass Adair, Gordon Wood, and even Garry Wills. Yet with all that has been written about this *idea* of "the filtration of talent," it is striking that we rarely stop to ask whether it bore any correspondence to the reality of early national politics. Madison's theory was, after all, very much a leap of faith, nothing more than a prediction of what he hoped would happen if a vigorous national government replaced the "imbecile" confederation of the 1780s.

Was Madison more nearly right or wrong in hoping that the framing of the Constitution would release new ambitions and draw better men into public life? Of course, it would be extremely difficult to decide whether those who actually gained office were a "better" group of men—better than whom, and in what respect?—or whether they possessed the traits Madison

'The Filtration of Talent'

wanted them to embody. The fact is that for this as for other periods of American history, we know all too little about the range of private motives and public concerns that have worked to bring men (and later women) into public life.

We can, of course, speak confidently about a few prominent individuals who did indeed seem to embody the refined political virtue Madison envisioned. The ninety-odd members of the First Federal Congress included such veteran leaders as Roger Sherman, Richard Henry Lee, Elbridge Gerry, William Paterson, and (perhaps most notably) Madison himself, and it is difficult to deny that a deeply principled commitment to public life was far from being the least important consideration that had led them to seek office under the new regime.

But when one examines the entire roster of membership for this smallest and most celebrated of federal congresses, it also becomes apparent that the process of election was not working only to "extract from the mass of the Society the purest and noblest characters which it contains." Thomas Sumter of South Carolina was elected to the House of Representatives in 1789 not because he had demonstrated any great legislative skills but on the basis of his reputation as a ruthless but daring commander during the vicious warfare that had plagued the Carolina backcountry. Benjamin Contee of Maryland may have hoped that election to Congress would help him stave off the demands of his creditors. If so, he was disappointed: a Philadelphia merchant kept insisting that Contee take a leave from Congress so he could put his affairs in order. Personal considerations of another kind encouraged the young Fisher Ames to accept his friends' urgings to run for the Boston seat in Congress. His father had been a self-educated Yankee almanac-maker whose struggle for prosperity had begun with a bitter legal battle to retain the tavern he had inherited from his first wife. Ames himself knew what it meant to use native intelligence, a Harvard education, and the political connections of a young lawyer to make his way from the status-conscious atmosphere of a small New England town into more elite circles.

Once elected, Ames proved a valuable member of Congress indeed. His success there reminds us that the personal concerns that helped to bring men into public life need not be confused with the sense of responsibility they felt once they were in office. It was entirely possible to pursue election to Congress for reasons of ambition and self-interest, and still act with the kind of political virtue that Madison hoped the

Constitution would foster. Yet when one explores the variety of motives that actually worked to bring men to Congress, it is difficult to resist concluding that his vision was naive. Even in a body as small as the First Congress, there was room for a wide range of ambitions to come into play—and not all of these were consistent with the hopes Madison entertained for the operation of the extended republic.

Political Parties

His theory also proved deficient on other grounds. Madison had designed the extended republic to "cure the mischiefs of faction," but by the mid-1790s, no one could claim that when Congress assembled, its members acted in the disinterested and truly patriotic fashion that Madison had envisioned. Sharp disputes arose over both the financial and the

FROM A CONTEMPORARY PRINT.

FEDERAL HALL, WALL STREET AND TRINITY CHURCH, NEW YORK, IN 1789.

THE FIRST CONGRESS OF THE UNITED STATES OF AMERICA WAS CONVENED IN FEDERAL HALL, IN THE CITY OF NEW YORK, CORNER OF WALL AND NASSAU STREETS, AND WASHINGTON WAS INAUGURATED IN THE BALCONY OF THIS HALL, APRIL 30TH, 1789. BEFORE A LARGE CONCOURSE OF PEOPLE WHOSE JOY WAS INEXPRESSIBLE   WASHINGTON MADE AN ADDRESS TO CONGRESS AND ADDRESSED A FERVENT SUPPLICATION TO ALMIGHTY GOD FOR THE NATION.

James Monroe

foreign policies that Alexander Hamilton had persuaded President Washington to pursue. The divisions within Congress were so severe that Madison himself and Thomas Jefferson undertook the novel task of organizing a genuine political party. In increasing numbers, candidates for both Congress and the state assemblies were running as recognized adherents of Federalist or Republican policies, and, when elected, voting accordingly. The parties became increasingly sectional in character. Madison still resisted the idea that organized parties ought to be a *permanent* part of the American political system; like Jefferson and James Monroe, the two friends who preceded and followed him in the presidency between 1801 and 1825, he hoped that their Democratic-Republican party could wither away as soon as the Federalist menace was finally eliminated. But in accepting the existence of parties even as a temporary and necessary evil, Madison was effectively admitting that legislative politics were being conducted along lines different from those which he and the other framers of the Constitution had hoped to lay down.

Although partisan politics did seem to be on the road to extinction during the presidency of James Monroe (1817-25), with the election of Andrew Jackson and the controversies which his administration witnessed, active political parties were again organized. They now dominated both electoral and legislative politics with a vigor that the earlier struggles of the Federalists and Democratic-Republicans had not attained.

Had the Democratic and Whig parties of the Jacksonian era not been so vigorous, still the framers' vision would have foundered on another shoal. The emergence of militant abolitionism in the 1830s demonstrated that unless the slavery issue could be either resolved or neutralized, the sectional loyalties of Congressmen would always sharply limit their ability to elevate some broad notion of the national interest over more parochial concerns.

Madison's theory of the extended republic had sought to cure the mischiefs of faction within the states by creating a national political arena in which merely local interests could never hold permanent sway. What his theory did not anticipate—or could not avert—was the possibility that "factious majorities" might form within each of the new republic's major regions, each one dedicated to pursuing a vision of the national good that the other could only interpret as deeply threatening to its own vital interests. By the 1850s, Southern spokesmen were convinced that if the authority of the national government were not used to protect the expansion of slavery into the western territories, the "peculiar institution" which was the basis of their civilization would be doomed. Northern Republicans believed with equal fervor that if the national government did not act to halt the extension of slavery, the free institutions and free labor of their own region would be gravely endangered. Two "factious majorities" had coalesced at the regional level within America, and their definitions of the national good were no longer compatible with the preservation of the union. The fact that a greater sense of political virtue and justice lay with the supporters of antislavery does not prevent our recognizing that James Madison's brilliant contribution to American political theory ultimately failed to surmount the central contradiction in American history: the persistence of slavery in a society otherwise committed to liberal ideals.

Yet if the Civil War must always be regarded as the greatest and most tragic failure of the framers' work, the rending of the union in 1861 has not led later generations to re-

Andrew Jackson

ject the Madisonian argument. In fact it has only been in the twentieth century—and not the nineteenth—that the richness and originality of his theory have come to be appreciated. Modern critics of the Constitution may fault Madison and his colleagues for creating a regime with too many checks and balances, a government divided (like Lincoln's union) against itself. But Madison's theory of the extended republic remains central to the American science of politics, for at least two reasons. He was convinced, in the first place, that a vigorous national government could protect individual liberty, a belief which the history of the struggle for civil rights in our own time amply supports. Second, and perhaps more important, Madison understood that republican government could, indeed had to be, reconciled with a realistic theory of human nature. Rather than conclude that evidence of enduring human frailty justified a resort to less popular forms of government, he and his colleagues struggled to create a government by consent that would work even if electors and the elected proved less virtuous than one might hope. From the perspective of the twentieth century, the novelty of their achievement may be difficult to perceive. But in the founders' time, it was a revolution indeed.

SUGGESTED ADDITIONAL READING

Gordon S. Wood, *The Creation of the American Republic, 1776-1787* (1969).

Richard Hofstadter, *The Idea of a Party System* (1970).

Daniel P. Jordan, *Political Leadership in Jefferson's Virginia* (1983).

Jack N. Rakove is associate professor of history at Stanford University and the author of *The Beginnings of National Politics: An Interpretive History of the Continental Congress* (Alfred A. Knopf, 1979).

Education for a Republic: Federal Influence on Public Schooling in the Nation's First Century

David Tyack and Thomas James

Today, as people argue over federal aid to public education, we tend to view the first century of the American nation as an era when public schools were entirely a grassroots affair. Compared to the bureaucratic school systems of the present, the schools of the past looked like community institutions, quite unconnected with federal policy or national politics. But the story of federal influence on the creation of public or "common" schools is more complex, and its implications for education more profound, than we often realize.

An eighteenth-century schoolroom

Starting with an eastern span of thirteen states at the time of the Constitution, the nation grew during its first century into a union of states that reached across a continent. The states shared, as Article IV, section 4 of the Constitution said they must, "a Republican form of Government." Only Congress could create new states from the territories springing up in the vast new regions of West and South. Congress had the duty of ensuring that each territory aspiring to statehood did establish through its own constitution just such a "Republican form of Government." In the negotiations over statehood between territorial assemblies and Congress, it became clear over time that political leaders both in the nation's capital and in the new states assumed that education was an essential feature of a republican government based upon the consent of the people. Thus in the United States, national and state governments played complementary roles in the spread of the American common school.

Land Grants and Schools in the Wilderness

Even before the federal constitution was ratified, the story of the federal government's involvement with schools began with the Ordinance of 1785, which was passed by the congress established under the Articles of Confederation. The ordinance specified how property lines in the western territory should "be measured with a chain ... plainly marked by chaps on the trees, and exactly described on a plat, whereon shall be noted ... all mines, salt-springs, salt-licks, and mill-seats." The document stipulated that land should be divided into townships, each six miles square and subdivided into 36 lots each a mile square. In businesslike fashion, it established the terms of the deed between the United States and citizens buying lands from the public domain. One clause linked the congressional ordinance explicitly to schooling: "There shall be reserved the lot No. 16, of every township, for the maintenance of public schools, within the said township." The intention of the framers was that the land would be sold to settlers and the income from the sales would be used to support the school.

Two years later, the Confederation Congress passed the Ordinance of 1787. This measure went further than its predecessor by setting the rules for governing the territory northwest of the Ohio River. The ordinance stipulated a plan for a governor, general assembly, and courts for each territory to be created from that immense wilderness. It established the procedure whereby each might become a state. Between the existing states of the Confederation and the new ones, the ordinance proclaimed a compact that prohibited slavery and guaranteed religious freedom and basic legal rights like those later embodied in the Bill of Rights. Laying down fundamental conditions for building new states, the ordinance also included a sentence asserting that "religion, morality and knowledge, being necessary to good government and the happiness of mankind, schools and the means of education shall forever be encouraged."

During the first century of the new nation, Congress granted more than 77 million acres of the public domain as an endowment for the support of public schools. In times of pressing national debt, congressional leaders were eager to sell the western lands owned by the federal government; land speculators persuaded Congress to include subsidies for schools as an inducement to attract settlers.

The tracts ceded to states for the support of public schools grew steadily over the years. In 1841, Congress passed an act that granted 500,000 acres to eight states, later increased to make grants to a total of nineteen states, to be used for "internal improvements." A majority of these states devoted all or part of the income from these lands to the schools. In 1848, Congress approved the policy of reserving two lots, 16 and 36, for the support of schools when it established the territorial government of Oregon. In 1850, California was the first state to receive both lots, amounting to 5.5 percent of the public domain in the state. The desert states of Utah, Arizona, and New Mexico—where much of the land had little value—each received four sections per township for the support of public schools.

The federal government also granted money, such as distributions of surplus federal revenue and reimbursements for war expenses, to the states. Though Congress rarely prescribed that such funds be used only for schools, education constituted one of the largest expenses of state and local governments, and so they used federal monies for this purpose. Moreover, Congress awarded a certain percentage of proceeds from the sale of U.S. lands within the borders of the new state; the amount ranged from 3 to 10 percent, with most states receiving 5 percent. Twelve states, all of them west of the Mississippi except Wisconsin, decreed in their constitutions that income from this fund should flow to the common school fund.

On the surface, the legal and constitutional framework of the new nation gave federal authorities little say over the financing and governance of public schools. In the beginning,

Students plow in front of Old Main at Pennsylvania State University, one of the first land grant colleges, in 1859

land endowments for schools had more to do with expediency in selling land and settling communities than with a principled and fixed educational policy. But as time went on, leaders writing constitutions in the new territories came to regard the grants as fundamental to statehood. Many of these leaders hoped that the federal largesse might one day provide full support for the common schools. In some territories the income from federal lands granted to the states and then leased or sold to settlers constituted the only source of state funding. In nearly every state, the availability of the land grants served to generate revenue for public institutions.

The dark side of the story is that vast sums were lost through corruption or mismanagement. States like Ohio, Indiana, and Illinois found it difficult to realize profits from the lands for use in establishing public schools. Learning from experience, Congress and state constitutions began to specify prices and conditions of sale for the lands sold to support schools. The states created supposedly inviolate common school funds to be allocated to local districts. To receive this money, local educators were expected to comply with state regulations about the length of the school term and teacher qualifications.

The gradual evolution toward state control of federal land grants was more the result of pragmatic experience than the outcome of deliberate educational policy. Partly because of a strong commitment to states' rights in the period before the Civil War, Congress stopped short of trying to control the management of education grants, even when states were abusing the terms under which they received the grants. In Illinois, for example, the legislature diverted the funds intended for schools to other purposes. State officials refused to make the required reports to the U.S. Treasury. In retaliation, the federal government refused to make payments. Congress resolved the dispute by repealing the requirement that states make reports.

As years went by, state constitutions in the West became specific about such bureaucratic matters. The educational provisions that regulated land grants expanded along with other language controlling the establishment of schools. Indirectly, the federal government provided leverage to states for centralizing control over schools. By the end of the nineteenth century, Congress itself began to set the terms for the sale of lands to support schools in the enabling acts of new states. It went so far as to require several new states—Montana, North Dakota, South Dakota, and Washington—to establish free, non-sectarian public school systems as a condition for admission to the union and receipt of the land grants.

After the mid-century, congressional grants became more generous and controls over the disposition of land more strict. Citizens in the northwestern states, profiting from the mistakes of governments to the east, creatively conserved and used the funds from land sales for the public good instead of private gain. In states west of the Mississippi, roughly 10 percent of the school budgets came from the sale of public land granted for school purposes. This was far less than a full subsidy of public education, but it was also far from negligible.

The procedure of drafting a constitution and then gaining congressional approval for statehood prompted the citizens of the territories to think systematically about public schools. The act of constructing a frame of government, and of recognizing the place of education in that structure, gave leaders the opportunity to make choices among the policies that had been tried in other states. The newer states could borrow from the experiences of the older ones. In this way, citizens shaped and reinterpreted a living constitutional tradition, embodied in the federal and original state constitutions.

The organization of American education grew more complex as public institutions and the society as a whole expanded in the nineteenth century. Constitutional provisions on schools reflected this growing complexity. In the earlier documents, idealistic preambles and brief treatments of federal land grants seemed enough when settlers were building only log schools in the wilds of the Midwest. By contrast, when territorial assemblies in the sparsely populated far Northwest states created constitutions, they wrote elaborate new bureaucratic structures into their educational provisions. They were trying to reflect the best examples of institution-building in their time.

Although more attuned to administrative detail than leaders in the early years, these educational policy makers also continued to reflect the ideology that had fueled nearly a century of effort to create common schools as an essential feature of American government. In 1874, a group of seventy-seven college presidents and city and state superintendents of schools issued a statement that described this process of institutional development:

> As a consequence of the perpetual migration from the older sections of the country to the unoccupied Territories, there are new states in all degrees of formation, and their institutions present earlier phases of realization of the distinctive type that are presented in the mature growth of the system as it exists in the thickly-settled and older States. Thus States are to be found with little or no provision for education, but they are rudimentary forms of the American State, and are adopting, as rapidly as immigration allows them to do so, the type of educational institutions already defined as the result of American political and social ideas.

While the educational provisions of constitutions of the original states changed but little, new states aspired to incorporate the most up-to-date public school systems. They wanted to show themselves to be enlightened and civilized as they joined the union of states. Accordingly, they wrote more and more elaborate provisions for education into their state constitutions.

They codified the institutional structures that had developed through statutory law in the older states, such as state boards of education, county and state superintendents, and teacher-training institutions. Turning against earlier traditions of religious instruction, many prohibited sectarian instruction in public schools and any public aid to schools affiliated with religious groups. Some constitutional conventions in the South after the Civil War mandated compulsory school attendance in their constitutions, even though their states had only recently established a common school system. An expanding nation composed of dozens of newly added states became a country in which the new states could copy from the old and the old were challenged to innovate to match the progress achieved by younger peers.

Like the land ordinances of the 1780s, state constitutions in the nineteenth century became much more than documents designed to attract new residents and win statehood. They were strategies for achieving organized social life—a political system, a rule of law, a structure of governance, and adequate financial incentives for creating institutions such as public schools. Similar to the town and city plats of the developers, but for an entire system of government, these documents promised that the state on the periphery would one day match the ideal of statehood most admired by its predecessors. Reflecting upon this process during the California constitutional convention of 1849, a delegate quoted the view of Robert J. Walker, U.S. Secretary of the Treasury, who argued:

> Each state is deeply interested in the welfare of every other; for the representatives of the whole regulate by their votes the measures of the Union, which must be the more happy and prosperous in proportion as its councils are guided by more enlightened views, resulting from the more universal diffusion of light, knowledge, and education.

In this process of forming new states, Congress played a subdued role, setting the terms for territorial government, shaping the requirements for admission in the enabling acts, approving the new constitutions, then granting vast amounts of federal land to stimulate improvements, including public schools, in the fledgling societies on the frontier.

Nowhere is the perceived importance of schooling more apparent than in the language used to describe it in state constitutions. A striking feature of the educational clauses in

Political Ideology and Public Schooling

nineteenth-century state constitutions is their idealistic tone. With the exception of language in the declarations of rights, no other sections contained so much exhortation to virtue. None of the other parts of government received such broad justifications phrased in the political discourse of the eighteenth century. Sections on the legislative branch did not extol the virtues of representative government, nor those on the judiciary the glories of justice. Clauses on suffrage, militia, corporations, revenue, and divisions of the executive branch were plain and businesslike. In contrast, the high-flown justifications of the common school declared public education to be a shared value. It was a fundamental guarantee built into government. Like

Teachers and pupils in front of school building, Hecla, Montana, 1893

those other guarantees embedded in the declarations of rights, it was a common good above the squabbles of political party or sect.

The Ohio constitution of 1802 reflected this belief by including a provision for schooling in the declaration of rights itself. Such idealism about education entered into the debates of constitutional conventions with an intensity that often reconciled extreme political differences. To mark a moment of concord between jousting Whigs and Democrats in the Illinois constitutional convention of 1847, a delegate said, "As the soul rises into immortality when the body falls into decay and perishes, so does the cause of education rise in splendor and grandeur above all party schemes and factions."

In ascribing such importance to public schooling, the framers of state constitutions were consciously developing a connection between education and democracy. A resonant political argument, this connection went back to the rhetoric of the nation's founding fathers. "The business of education has acquired a new complexion by the independence of our country," wrote Benjamin Rush, a Pennsylvanian who signed the Declaration of Independence and served as an articulate spokesman for republican ideas, in 1786. "The form of government we have assumed," he continued, "has created a new class of duties to every American." Rush thought it necessary to establish "nurseries of wise and good men," a system of education from common schools through colleges, to ensure the survival of the republic.

Thomas Jefferson had frequently given voice to such sentiments, as when he wrote to his friend George Wythe, "Preach, my dear Sir, a crusade against ignorance; establish & improve the law for educating the common people." On another occasion, Jefferson had written, "I know no safe depository of the ultimate powers of the society but the people themselves; and if we think them not enlightened enough to exercise their control with a wholesome discretion, the remedy is not to take it from them, but to inform their discretion by education." John Adams, James Madison, and other central actors in the creation of the new republic had made similar pleas for an expanded commitment to learning as a safeguard for the republic. "In proportion as the structure of government gives force to public opinion," said George Washington in his Farewell Address as president of the United States, "it is essential that public opinion should be enlightened."

Reflecting this ideological connection between schooling

and the great political experiment of democratic nationhood, at least 17 states adopted language about schooling in their constitutions that closely resembled that of the Ordinance of 1787 and the Massachusetts constitution of 1780, the latter written by John Adams. In part, this copying was an obligatory bow towards their patron, Congress, acknowledging the purpose of the public lands granted to new states for schools. North Dakota's constitution put the underlying principle in these words in 1889:

John Adams

> A high degree of intelligence, patriotism, integrity and morality on the part of every voter in a government by the people being necessary in order to insure the continuance of that government and the prosperity and happiness of the people, the legislative assembly shall make provision for the establishment and maintenance of a system of public schools which shall be open to all children of the State of North Dakota and free from sectarian control. This legislative requirement shall be irrevocable without the consent of the United States and the people of North Dakota.

The last clause indicates that the delegates recognized not only a state interest in education but a national one as well. Like the Bill of Rights, the common school was becoming "irrevocable," an inalienable guarantee of the republican form of government. Both the Florida Reconstruction constitution of 1868 and Washington's constitution of 1889 declared it the "paramount duty of the state" to educate all children.

Education as stimulus to "internal improvement" was a theme that complemented the political and moral argument for schooling. In 1837, the Michigan constitution instructed the legislature to "encourage, by all suitable means, the promotion of intellectual, scientifical, and agricultural improvement." Iowa, one of many states that copied Michigan's language, added "moral" to the list of "improvements" in its constitution of 1846, a change that appeared in subsequent clauses in California, Kansas, West Virginia, and Nevada. Many legislators in Congress and in the states regarded public schools, like roads and canals and railroads, as part of the infrastructure needed for economic development and the settlement of new regions.

The civic, economic, moral, and intellectual benefits of schooling merged together easily into the belief in education as a common good. Supporting this conception was a web of ideological assumptions. One was the conviction that in a government depending on the will of the people, the citizens must be properly educated so that they could, in turn, influence their government in an orderly way. As the Committee on Public Lands in the U.S. House of Representatives argued in a report on land grants in 1826:

> The foundation of our political institutions, it is well known, rests in the will of the People, and the safety of the whole superstructure, its temple and altar, daily and hourly depend upon the discreet exercise of this will. How then is this will to be corrected, chastened, subdued? By education—that education, the first rudiments of which can be acquired only in common schools.

For school leaders it seemed natural and not at all paradoxical that a government by the people must also restrain the people. John D. Pierce, Michigan's first state superintendent of public instruction, expressed this view in a way that was typical of the educational thought of the nineteenth century:

> However unpretending and simple in form, our government is nonetheless effective and perfect. It proceeds from the people— is supported by the people—and depends upon the people—and at the same time restrains and controls the people more effectually than the most rigid systems of despotism. But how is this political fabric to be preserved? Only by the general diffusion of knowledge. Children of every name and age must be taught the qualifications and duties of American citizens, and learn in early life the art of self-control—they must be educated. And to accomplish this object, our chief dependence must necessarily be the free school system.

A related assumption was that educated leaders would perceive the common good, and that when they did not, they could be influenced by citizens who were educated to recognize their rights and responsibilities. Justice Joseph Story, one of the nation's greatest legal minds in the nineteenth century, told a group of New England educators that "the American republic, above all others, demands from every citizen unceasing vigilance and exertion, since we have deliberately dispensed with every guard against danger or ruin, except the intelligence and virtue of the people themselves." Such assumptions about democracy and education gave rise to widespread agreement on the fundamental necessity of enlightened schooling for the survival of the republic, even among people who otherwise disagreed vehemently over many other issues. Democrats, Whigs, and Republicans each had their own reasons for distrusting government and its actions, but each party, in its own formulation, looked to public education as a means of strengthening a republican form of government by creating upright individual citizens.

In 1822 an advocate of such a link between republicanism and education, Governor Dewitt Clinton of New York, argued that "the first duty of a state is to render its citizens virtuous by intellectual instruction and moral discipline, by enlightening their minds, purifying their hearts, and teaching them their rights and their obligations." Many leaders who sought to curb the powers of state governments and to limit their provision of social services were nonetheless willing to support vigorous public school systems partly because they believed that self-regulation by strong individuals was a substitute for external regulation by a strong state. In 1848 the Maine superintendent of common schools, echoing the education clause of the state constitution, instructed school committees to ask prospective teachers: "What method or methods would you adopt in order to inculcate the principles of morality, justice, truth, humanity, industry, and temperance?" A speaker for the American Institute of Instruction in 1878 challenged his fellow educators to make sure that the schools were living up to their republican responsibilities:

> If you wish the public schools to become strongly entrenched in the hearts of the people, especially in the hearts of the tax-payers, let such measures be taken as shall show beyond a doubt that the schools are really protecting, defending and preserving the Constitution and the government, and that they are really making the government safe.

Dewitt Clinton

The hope that a common education might exist above politics and sectarian strife was—and is—no more than a vision. Laden with political idealism, sometimes this vision illuminated and sometimes it obscured the problems of a pluralistic, unequal society. Public education was and always will be inherently political. The high rhetoric of the constitutions advocated a basis of universal public learning for sustaining the political community of a new nation. Yet, leaders were often willing, perhaps unwittingly as much as purposefully, to use new constructs of the public interest and the common good to favor some people's interests more than those of others.

Nevertheless, in public education Americans of different political persuasions attempted to keep alive the dream of an electorate that sought the common good because it was educated to do so. Herein lay the appeal of a system of common schools that would somehow exist above politics, nonpartisan and nonsectarian. For many founders of the nation and the states it was a deeply held commitment, a motive to action. And it was for this reason, seeing the importance of education to the formation of democratic governments across the nation, that the federal government played a role in stimulating and shaping the creation of common schools. Once embedded in political ideology and the legal structure of new states, those schools spread rapidly in the new nation. Over and over again—in constitutional debates and educational provisions, in the speeches of politicians and school leaders, in the textbooks children read in school, in sermons and newspaper editorials—people expressed the conviction that common schooling was a bulwark of the republic. Acting upon this belief in complex ways as the nation expanded in the nineteenth century, national, state, and local leaders worked together to create systems of education. They believed, with Thomas Jefferson, that their survival as a political community depended upon it: "If a nation expects to be ignorant and free, in a state of civilization, it expects what never was and never will be."

SUGGESTED ADDITIONAL READING

Lawrence A. Cremin, *American Education: The National Experience, 1783-1876* (1980).

Carl F. Kaestle, *Pillars of the Republic: Common Schools and American Society, 1780-1860* (1983).

David Tyack and Elisabeth Hansot, *Managers of Virtue: Public School Leadership in America, 1820-1980* (1982).

David Tyack is Vida Jacks Professor of Education and professor of history at Stanford University, author of *The One Best System* (1974), and co-author with Robert Lowe and Elisabeth Hansot of *Public Schools in Hard Times* (1984).

Thomas James is associate director of the Education Studies Program, Wesleyan University, and the co-author with David Tyack and Aaron Benavot of *Law and the Shaping of Public Education: Explorations in Political History* (1986).

Weevils in the Wheat: Free Blacks and the Constitution, 1787-1860

James Oliver Horton

Standing before an Iowa religious convention in the 1850s, Sojourner Truth, women's rights advocate and antislavery speaker, delighted her audience with her analysis of the American Constitution. With a dry wit that was her trademark on the abolitionist circuit, this former slave, the first black woman antislavery speaker in the nation, compared the Constitution to the midwestern wheat which during the 1850s was suffering from the boll weevil blight. From a distance the countryside looked deceptively beautiful but on a closer look one might see the ravages of the blight. The Constitution was much the same, said Sojourner—"I feel for my rights, but there ain't any there." As weevils besieged the wheat, prejudice and bigotry threatened to undermine constitutional guarantees. As Sojourner saw it, American civil rights and liberties were endangered. The Constitution had "a little weevil in it."

In the generations between the Revolution and the Civil War, black people struggled with the weevils in interpretations of the Constitution which denied them citizenship rights. Most blacks believed that their citizenship was protected by the Constitution and by the ideals expressed in the Declaration of Independence. The founding fathers did not specifically mention race as they set out the self-evident truths by which they justified national independence. Although they certainly did not include slaves among those referred to as "the people," they were ambiguous on the status of the free people of color.

Black Citizenship

There were several early indications that the federal government did not consider free blacks full citizens. Despite their significant presence in the American Revolutionary forces, the post-war national militia excluded blacks and early naturalization laws limited the process to white aliens. In the first two decades of the nineteenth century, blacks could not

I Sell the Shadow to Support the Substance.

SOJOURNER TRUTH.

carry the federal mail or hold elective office in the District of Columbia.

Nor did the Constitution protect free blacks from limitations imposed by the individual states. From 1819, when Maine joined the union, until after the Civil War, every new state denied the vote to free blacks and many did not allow them to serve on juries or even to testify in court cases involving whites. Constitutional protections did not prevent states like Ohio, Illinois, Indiana, and Oregon or the territory of Michigan from barring free blacks or from requiring substantial bonds as a prerequisite to their emigration. The Northwest Ordinance, adopted by Congress in 1787, forbade slavery in this northcentral region, but it did not assure the civil rights of free blacks in the area. Even in states like Massachusetts and Pennsylvania, which did not restrict black emigration, there was serious discussion of such action. Save for two votes in its constitutional convention of 1850, California would have barred blacks. Clearly weevils abounded.

The question of black citizenship was further complicated by the fact that although many states obviously precluded it, others did not. Before 1820, free black men in Massachusetts, New Jersey, Pennsylvania, New York, Maine, Vermont, Connecticut, Rhode Island, and New Hampshire voted on an equal basis with white men. Ironically, they lost that right in New Jersey, Connecticut, and Pennsylvania before the Civil War. In New York, black voters had to meet property ownership requirements that were removed for whites during the democratic reforms of the Jacksonian era. Yet Afro-American political participation in states where it was allowed lent legitimacy to the claim of free black citizenship.

Several federal actions also seemed to imply that, on occasion, the Constitution protected blacks. A few blacks received passports to travel abroad under the aegis of the United States during the 1840s and 1850s. At times the federal government also moved to safeguard the rights of free blacks at home as well. In response to the contentions of slaveholders that free blacks had a dangerous effect on slaves, in 1822 the South Carolina legislature passed the Colored Seamen's Act requiring the imprisonment of all free black seamen for the time that their ships remained in South Carolina ports. Moreover, the ship's captain had to pay the cost of the seaman's imprisonment, an amount he often deducted from the seaman's wages. If the captain refused, the seaman was sold into temporary slavery to compensate local authorities. Other southern states adopted similar laws. Since the sea offered a major source of employment for thousands of blacks before the Civil War, this provision posed a major threat to the free black community. In response to protests by free blacks and northern white reformers, a congressional committee investigated these policies and determined that they violated the Constitution. The committee did not express an opinion on the question of black citizenship, however. In 1823 the Supreme Court supported congressional judgment by declaring such laws unconstitutional. (Despite this ruling, several southern jurisdictions continued the practice until the Civil War.)

Although officials interpreted the Constitution inconsistently as it applied to free blacks, Afro-Americans insisted on their fundamental right to its protections. They had stood with other patriots against "British tyranny" and when Thomas Paine, Samuel Adams, and other white patriots declared that Americans would never be slaves, blacks agreed wholeheartedly. Throughout the Revolution, as five thousand of them served in the cause of American liberty, blacks continued their call for the abolition of slavery. A group of nineteen "natives of Africa freeborn" in Portsmouth, New Hampshire, reminded white patriots that "public and private tyranny and slavery are alike detestable" and that "the God of nature gave [blacks] life and freedom, upon terms of the most perfect equality with other men."

Thomas Paine

Afro-Americans drew allies from the ranks of Quakers, who had opposed slavery for a generation before the Revolution, and from more recent converts, who saw an inconsistency between emerging American principles and American slavery. Abigail Adams wrote to her husband John of her discomfort with Afro-American bondage. "It has always seemed a most iniquitous scheme to me," she wrote, "to fight ourselves for what we are daily robbing and plundering from those who have as good a right to freedom as we have." Abigail Adams did not stand alone in her opposition to slavery. In northern states where the institution was less economically important than in the rich plantation areas of the South, the antislavery movement grew during the post-Revolutionary period, attracting such notables as Benjamin Franklin of Pennsylvania, John Jay, Alexander Hamilton, and Aaron Burr of New York, and Moses Brown of Rhode Island.

Blacks and their white allies used the language of the Constitution to prod the conscience of the nation. This strategy succeeded in the North because slaveholders there had less economic and political power. In the South, such arguments moved a few masters to individual acts of emancipation but found little legislative support. By 1804 slavery, which had been practiced in all thirteen colonies, was abolished or set on the road to abolition by gradual emancipation plans in all northern states, isolating that institution in the South. There it remained until uprooted by civil war.

The legal position of southern free blacks during the antebellum years was a complicated one. Living in the midst of slavery, free blacks in the South were an enigma to the slaveholding society. They were always viewed as suspect and potentially dangerous to the institutions of slavery. The liberty extended to southern free blacks was minimal and did not include the right of protest. So precarious was their freedom that on the eve of the Civil War, South Carolina seriously debated enslaving its free blacks. Nowhere in the North did blacks face that kind of official action.

In the North, blacks were especially equipped to demand their rights from the new government. During the colonial period slaveholding in that region was on a small scale. Except for the great plantation-like estates of the Hudson valley in New York and the Narragansett region of Rhode Island slaveholdings averaged about two slaves each. Under these circumstances newly imported Africans were often isolated from one another but they came into regular contact with whites. Unlike slaves on the large plantations of the South who maintained a variety of African traditions well into the nineteenth century and beyond, northern slaves made a more rapid transition from African to Afro-American, quickly learning the language and the customs of their captors. Northern blacks did not forget African cultures and traditions; rather, they modified and combined them with those of Europe. Northern Afro-American culture became a practical blend of Western culture and the many different cultures of Africa.

Thus northern blacks on the eve of the Revolution knew well the rhetoric and the ideals of American liberty, and they used the instruments of democracy to communicate their requests to governmental authority. Time and again, slaves petitioned the courts and the legislatures for their freedom. Astutely they appealed to American political and religious ideals in their message. "We expect great things," wrote one group of slaves to the Massachusetts General Court, "from men who have made such a noble stand against the designs of their fellow men to enslave them." Throughout the northern states slaves pressed for their freedom during the 1770s and 1780s using the language of America's independence movement. Their message was simple. Slaves asked no more from the new nation, "this free and Christian country," than slaveholders had demanded from the Old World—freedom.

Northern blacks also used this tactic in their campaign for civil rights after they won freedom. For two years, between 1778 and 1780, John and Paul Cuffe, two free black ship merchants of West Port, Massachusetts, refused to pay their land taxes so long as their home state did not allow blacks to vote. In the state courts and at local town meetings they argued in strong language calculated for effect. They would not submit

to "taxation without representation." Their action encouraged the state to redraft the 1778 version of its constitution which contained no bill of rights and restricted voting by race. The final constitution, adopted in 1780, did not limit black voting and was later interpreted as prohibiting slavery.

Black Organizations

Throughout the nineteenth century, free blacks continued to employ the language of the Revolution and the structure of democracy in the formation of their community institutions and in the strategy of their antislavery and civil rights protests. As northern blacks emerged from slavery, they established many mutual aid and benefit societies. Long before the federal government provided aid to the poor, Afro-Americans depended upon these organizations during times of crisis and economic hardship. For a people restricted by racial discrimination to the least reliable and lowest paying jobs, the work of these organizations proved indispensable in providing aid to widows and dependent children, workman's compensation and unemployment insurance, and basic charity services. Although state and local governments sometimes aided needy whites, they often ignored blacks or gave them diminished benefits. Usually, blacks relied on their own communities or on the support of progressive whites who were committed to the abolition of slavery and to the improvement of the condition and the welfare of the "free people of color." In Philadelphia and New York, for example, Quakers operated schools and charity agencies for blacks.

These groups were established on the democratic model. They set forth their principles and purposes in organizational constitutions or similar documents in words reminiscent of the Constitution. "We, the African Members" began the *Laws of the African Society* founded in Boston in 1796. "We, the Subscribers . . . , do form ourselves into an Association, for the benevolent purpose of raising funds . . . to aid and assist the widows and orphans of deceased members . . ." read the *Constitution of the New York African Clarkson Association* in 1825. The opening of the *Constitution and By-Laws of the Brotherly Union Society* in Philadelphia in 1833 contained similar language. These documents were divided into "articles" and often prefaced by "preambles." They provided for democratic functions including the election of officers (presidents, vice presidents, secretaries, and treasurers) and for policy decided by majority vote of the membership.

Black Voters

Afro-American community organization extended to political associations. Like other Americans of the period, blacks sought ways to consolidate and exercise political influence. Such influence was slight but it did exist in the early years of the nineteenth century in states where blacks held the franchise. Afro-American voters were not overwhelming in numbers but in some cases they could affect the outcome of important elections because of their strategic location. In New York City, for example, one opponent of suffrage for blacks lamented that "the votes of three hundred Negroes in the city . . . decided the election [1813] in favor of the Federal party, and also decided the political character of the legislature of this state." He no doubt exaggerated the impact of the black vote, but his point remained.

Aware of the important role Federalist party members had played in the antislavery campaigns of the late eighteenth and early nineteenth century, free blacks organized to support the party at the polls. The Federalist party, as a result of its unpopular stance in opposition to the War of 1812, lost power and passed from the political scene before the 1820s. Black voters, left with little support against growing Democratic opposition to their political rights, shifted their allegiance to the Whig Party and later the Liberty Party, Free Soil Party, and finally the Republican Party on the eve of the Civil War. Sophisticated in the ways of democratic politics, blacks operated through a variety of groups, striking political alliances where possible, in the expression of their collective will as American citizens.

The courting of black votes by Whigs and Free Soilers in Providence, Rhode Island, during the 1848 presidential election exemplified the recognition of the strategic positioning of black voters in that state. The Whig candidacy of Zachary Taylor, a Kentucky slaveholder, for president strained traditional Afro-American support for that party. The choice offered by the Free Soil party proved no less complicated. Although the free soilers sought to prevent the spread of slavery to the western territories, a policy enthusiastically endorsed by blacks, their presidential candidate was former Democratic President Martin Van Buren, of New York, who had strong ties to the slaveholding South and in the past had supported slavery in Washington, D.C.

Afro-Americans organized on both sides. Frederick Douglass, powerful abolitionist and former slave, lent his prestige to the Free Soil campaign, urging that Van Buren's promise to

Zachary Taylor

support the abolition of slavery in the District of Columbia in the future be taken as a sign of his conversion to "free soil" principles. Conversely, many local Providence black leaders and several black newspapers encouraged Afro-Americans to stay with the Whigs. At election time, the Whigs carried the day with Taylor receiving almost all the city's black vote which accounted for at least one third of the Whig victory margin in the county of Providence. Thus, politicians and parties at all levels recognized black citizenship when blacks' political participation brought them rewards. Unfortunately, such recognition was rare.

Assertions of Afro-American citizenship faced a severe challenge from the activities of the American Colonization Society. Founded in 1816, this group sought to encourage the colonization in western Africa of free blacks and slaves subsequently freed. The most liberal colonizationists hoped that if they could assure southern masters that free blacks would be settled outside the country, more would consent to manumit their slaves. Other colonizationists saw the plan as an opportunity to rid the nation of troublesome free blacks. Although colonization never attracted wide support among free blacks, some expressed a willingness to emigrate to Africa. Early in the nineteenth century, ship merchant Paul Cuffe advocated African emigration and even transported a group of 38 blacks to the West African colony of Sierra Leone in 1815. Cuffe's efforts encouraged such white colonizationists as Henry Clay, Daniel Webster, Supreme Court Justice Bushrod Washington, Francis Scott Key, and others to establish their society a year later.

Colonizationism

Despite the interest of many blacks in Providence, Philadelphia, and Boston, most free blacks disapproved of colonization. In several mass meetings before 1820, Philadelphia blacks took the lead in protesting the plans of the new society. The colonizationists' acquisition of territory in West Africa which became the society's colony of Liberia in 1822 heightened the interests of many southern free blacks but nearly all northern blacks remained opposed. So strong was the opposition among northern blacks that when John Russwurm, cofounder of *Freedom's Journal,* the nation's first black newspaper (New York City, 1827), became a supporter of colonization the resultant hostility forced him to leave the paper.

Black opposition to the American Colonization Society had complex sources. It included great suspicion of the motives

Daniel Webster

Frederick Douglass

of an organization which counted some of the most prominent slaveholders in the country among its membership. Blacks feared the unstated motive behind colonization plans—to remove free blacks from the nation, thus silencing the most vocal opponents of slavery and making slaveholdings more secure. Beyond these suspicions, blacks also resented the notion, implicit in the colonization program, that they had no right to American citizenship. "This is our home," declared a speaker at a Philadelphia meeting, "and this is our country. Beneath its sod lie the bones of our fathers; for it some of them fought, bled, and died. Here we were born, and here we will die."

The Colonization Society portrayed its aims as enlightened philanthropy which realistically addressed the nation's race problem. Supporters of colonization believed it impossible that blacks could find acceptance as fellow citizens by white Americans and saw African colonization as the only humane alternative. Afro-Americans disagreed—"Our condition can be best improved in this our own country and native soil, the United States of America," wrote a black abolitionist in the pages of the *Liberator* in 1831. Most free blacks argued that they would never willingly relinquish rights for which they paid dearly in the Revolution and again in the War of 1812.

In their anticolonizationist struggle, which continued throughout the pre-Civil War years, free blacks constantly appealed to the Constitution and the Revolutionary ideals which they insisted guaranteed their freedom and civil rights. Beginning in the early 1830s, Afro-Americans met in national conventions to discuss and organize a response to the growing influence of the "Slave Power" and to colonizationist plans. On September 20, 1830, approximately thirty delegates representing five states met in Philadelphia's Bethel Church for five days to propose strategies for dealing with the problems of black America. In the first line of the convention proceedings, these delegates proclaimed a commitment to the spirit of the Declaration of Independence. The next year, delegates resolved that the Declaration and the Preamble of the Constitution be read at the opening of each convention. They asserted: "Truths contained in the former document are incontrovertible and . . . the latter guarantees in letter and spirit to every freeman born in this country all the rights and immunities of citizenship."

'Slaveholder's Document'

Although this commitment to the Constitution and the Declaration was sorely tested, it never broke, though revered Afro-American leaders and white allies challenged the notion that these documents protected black rights and opposed human bondage. The Constitution endorsed the apprehension and return of fugitive slaves to masters even when slaves managed to escape into free states or territories. It had also allowed the continuance of the African slave trade to American dealers until 1808. Indeed, the adoption of the Constitution had hinged upon a series of compromises which granted additional national representation to slave owners according to the extent of their slave holdings. The Constitution itself, not simply the actions of proslavery national officials, sustained slavery.

By the 1830s, white abolitionist editor William Lloyd Garrison moved to this position and took a radical stand against the Constitution. On several public occasions, he denounced and burned copies of it as a "slaveholder's document." Some blacks, following Garrison's lead, also attacked the Constitution as proslavery. Until the late 1840s, Frederick Douglass disdained it "as a most foul and bloody conspiracy against the rights of three millions of enslaved and imbruted men." Douglass supported Garrison's antipolitical stand, reasoning that "until the government and the Constitution were replaced by institutions which would better answer the ends of justice, no true friend of liberty in the United States could [in good conscience] vote or hold office."

At the American Anti-Slavery Society's meeting in New York in 1844, black delegate Thomas Van Renslear called on blacks to "have nothing to do with the government [of the

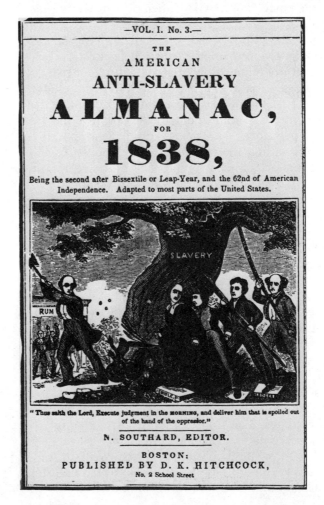

United States]; and as regards the Constitution, ... have nothing to do with that instrument." Other blacks in Massachusetts again challenged the government on the grounds of "taxation without representation." In defiant language one black Bostonian urged his fellows to exert economic pressure in the fight for civil rights: "Let every colored man, called upon to pay taxes to any institution in which he is deprived or denied its privileges and advantages, withhold his taxes, though it may cost imprisonment or confiscation. Let our motto be—No privileges, no pay." By the end of the 1840s, a growing number of blacks agreed. "The government does not protect my rights, and I will not support such a government," said black abolitionist Charles Lenox Remond in 1847. "Show me a Constitution which protects the rights of all men and I'll sustain that."

Despite such pronouncements by Garrisonian abolitionists, most free blacks continued to assert their rights as citizens under the Constitution. When in 1837 Pennsylvania considered a state constitution which deprived blacks of the right to vote, Afro-Americans argued in petitions to the legislature that they were citizens both of the state and the nation. Afro-American citizens of Pennsylvania reminded the leaders of their state that "among all the rights of a Republic none are so sacred, and among all the safeguards of the liberties of freemen none are so powerful, as the right of suffrage." To deprive black people of that right after all they had done for the state and the nation, they charged, was an affront to democratic principles and an "insult and mockery to the Almighty Creator of all things and Judge of all men." These appeals did not succeed in preventing the disenfranchisement of blacks in the state, but the claim that such discrimination was a violation of the federal Constitution and an insult to God's plan for human development became the standard argument echoed throughout the 1840s.

In 1843 the state convention of Afro-Americans in Michigan passed a resolution to that effect, but there also were dissenting delegates. A year later New York blacks convened a state gathering to argue in similar tones for the extension of the vote to Afro-Americans in that state. At the end of the decade, black Ohioans used the appeal to God and the principles of the founding fathers to bolster their drive for an extension of civil rights in their state. In all these actions minority voices argued the inappropriateness of such appeals and that the Constitution offered no protection for their race.

The debate among blacks continued into the 1850s, but during that pre-Civil War decade most came to believe that interpretations of the Constitution as not protecting black rights perverted its Revolutionary ideals. In the spring of 1850, Afro-American abolitionist Henry Bibb addressed a meeting of Boston blacks denouncing the failure of the federal government to fulfill its obligation to all Americans. He called upon his listeners to participate in the move to "correct the public sentiment [and] get the Constitution and the people right." Even Douglass reversed his anti-Constitution position during these years, focusing his condemnation not on that document but on those who, for their own purposes, would subvert it. The Bible is not a "bad book" simply because it was used for evil, he said. "The slaveholders of the South, and many of their wicked allies in the North, claim the Bible for slavery; shall we therefore fling the Bible away as a pro-slavery book?" He believed not—"It would be as reasonable to do so as it would be to fling away the Constitution."

Eve of Civil War   Yet even as most blacks argued for this stand during the 1850s, Afro-American protests became more strident after Congress passed the fugitive slave law of 1850. The new law not only made the retrieval of fugitive slaves easier but, because one captured as a runaway could not testify in his or her own defense, it also endangered the liberty of free blacks. Angry and discouraged with the prospects of ever forcing whites to recognize their citizenship rights, a sizable minority of blacks again turned to the notion of African colonization.

The emergence of Liberia as an independent nation in 1848 renewed Afro-American interest in African emigration. The leadership of militant blacks like Dr. Martin R. Delany of Pittsburgh replaced the moderate to conservative white leadership of the earlier American Colonization Society making the possibility more acceptable. Starting in 1850, several black organizations like the Liberian Agricultural and Emigration Society (1851) and the African Civilization Society (1858) attracted a considerable following. Yet emigration continued as a distinctly minority position. Most blacks elected, as Dr. John Rock of Boston explained, to "remain in this country and try to make it worth living in." On the eve of the Civil War, blacks continued to debate the wisdom of leaving the American land of their birth for the African land of "their opportunity." Most held fast to their rights as Americans.

The events of the late 1850s, however, made claims of black citizenship constitutionally moot. In *Dred Scott v. Sanford* (1857), the Supreme Court held that Scott remained a slave even though he had lived for a number of years, with his master's consent, outside a slave state. The court had, seven years earlier, rendered a similar judgment in the case of *Strader v. Graham* (1850). More disheartening, however, was Chief Justice Roger B. Taney's conclusion that Afro-Americans, slave or free, were not citizens of the United States and were not entitled to the protections of the Constitution. Although like opinions had been expressed by members of the federal government, never before had the highest court made such a clear statement on the matter.

Blacks debated the *Dred Scott* ruling until the outbreak of the Civil War. Some considered it "illegal." Others asked what else might be expected from a court which represented "pro-slavery doughfaces" and "Democratic slave-breeders." That blacks continued to vote in five New England states and in New York (with property requirement restrictions) further complicated the issue as did the support they received in their denunciation of the court decision from white allies, many of them state or federal government officials.

By the mid-1860s, this debate had become a constitutional dead letter, as the Civil War changed the mood of the Congress and ultimately changed the wording of the Constitution. First in the Civil Rights Act of 1866 and then in the Fourteenth Amendment, ratified in 1868, black citizenship was finally guaranteed. Although, as would soon become clear, these guarantees did not ensure the protection of their constitutional rights, blacks were at last irrefutably American citizens. For most black Americans, these acts provided the formal constitutional recognition of a status they had never doubted was their due.

Throughout the antebellum period, blacks drew upon America's most cherished ideals in their struggle against slavery and for civil rights. They argued for the fair application of constitutional rights irrespective of color. They demanded no more and determined to accept no less. Within the American context, the concept of racial equality seemed a radical one. Yet most blacks willingly pressed their demands within the moderate bounds of the American constitutional framework. They accepted movement in evolutionary steps towards equality through the popularly sanctioned routes of education, hard work, and respectability. They resented having to "prove" their fitness for citizenship, but most consented to do that required of them, but of no other native-born American.

Most Afro-Americans maintained a reverence for America's promise as set forth in its statement of purpose. Although there may have been disagreement on whether the Constitution protected black rights, blacks always insisted on their right to citizenship by virtue of their birth, their commitment to the ideals of the American Revolution, and their service in the struggle to achieve and protect American freedom. A century later, the struggle to achieve the reality of America's promise continues.

SUGGESTED ADDITIONAL READING

Curry, Leonard P., *The Free Black in Urban America, 1800-1850: The Shadow of the Dream* (1981).

Cottrol, Robert J., *The Afro-Yankees: Providence's Black Community in the Antebellum Era* (1982).

Dick, Robert C., *Black Protest: Issues and Tactics* (1974).

Franklin, John Hope, *From Slavery to Freedom: A History of Negro Americans* (1979).

Finkelman, Paul, *An Imperfect Union: Slavery, Federalism, and Comity* (1981).

Horton, James Oliver and Lois E. Horton, *Black Bostonians: Family Life and Community Struggle in the Antebellum North* (1979).

Litwack, Leon F., *North of Slavery: The Negro in the Free States, 1790-1860* (1961).

Sweet, Leonard I., *Black Images of America, 1784-1870* (1976).

The author is indebted to Paul Ruden, Joseph McLaughlin, Paul Finkelman, and Spencer Crew who read and offered valuable advice on this manuscript at various stages of its preparation.

James Oliver Horton is associate professor of history and American civilization, George Washington University; Director of the Afro-American Communities Project at the National Museum of American History of the Smithsonian Institution; co-author with Lois E. Horton of *Black Bostonians: Family Life and Community Struggle in an Antebellum City* (N.Y., 1979) and co-editor with Steven J. Diner of pilot volumes for *City of Magnificent Intentions: A History of the District of Columbia* (Washington, D.C., 1983). He is currently writing a history of free blacks in the antebellum North.

The Meaning of
American Citizenship

Rogers M. Smith

What does it mean to say, "I am an American citizen"?
The law supplies dry technical answers: the statement means
that one falls under a constitutional or statutory category
conferring full membership in the American polity. The chief
ones are, with minor exceptions, birth within the United States,
which confers citizenship under the Fourteenth Amendment,
plus birth to American parents overseas, and naturalization,
categories regulated by federal statutes.

Yet in saying these words, most Americans surely mean to
express more than their juridicial status under national law.
They are professing their sense of belonging to a unique nation,
with a heritage of great deeds and tragic flaws, a shining set of
ideals, vast resources, and a singularly commanding and
demanding position in today's world. For many the sentence is
also a revelation of their sense of self, of who, for better or
worse, they feel themselves to be at the deepest emotional level.
It has, then, much more than a merely legal meaning. It is at
bottom a statement of political and personal identity that
evokes complex, powerful, and often contradictory ideas and
sentiments, for Americans and non-Americans alike.

But while the laws regulating American citizenship have
never captured all the rich significance of the status, neither
have they been immune to these broader political and personal
meanings. Because being a United States citizen has stood for
different things to different Americans at different times, the
constitutional provisions, legislative statutes, and judicial decisions governing civic membership have blended several distinguishable and evolving conceptions of what American citizenship means.

"Blended" may be a deceptively soothing word. America's
changing citizenship laws have been produced by recurring,
often bitter contests between partisans of rival notions of

177

American civic identity—a historical drama that is entering a momentous new phase in our own time. To over-simplify for clarity, there have been three basic conceptions or "ideal types" of American citizenship that the nation's laws have always combined, though in strikingly different mixtures. Scholars have termed these conceptions "liberal," "republican," and "nativist."

Concepts of Citizenship

The "liberal" conception derives from the emancipating spirit of the eighteenth-century Enlightenment and from the political experience of the middle classes in England and America, who fought in that era against restrictive feudal economic and political prerogatives and against intolerant religious and intellectual orthodoxies. The liberal citizen believes that all persons should have freedom from any imposed political status, religious creed, or economic position, and equal opportunities for the pursuits they find most meaningful—political activism or private family life, spiritual perfection or material enrichment. In the great revolutionary and constitutional documents of eighteenth- and nineteenth-century America, these beliefs were presented as rationally discoverable natural or divine rights to "life, liberty, and property" or "the pursuit of happiness." In the twentieth century, liberals no longer hold their truths to be self-evident, and so they stress even more the right of all to pursue their preferred beliefs in a fruitful plurality of communities and associations. But in both its older absolutist and its modern relativistic phases, the liberal tradition has conceived of citizenship, in America and in all nations, as properly a matter of choice, not inheritance or prescription, and as involving at root only a duty to abide by the laws of regimes in which human rights are honored and a multitude of private and public activities flourish.

The republican conception reflects the new form of government and of civic life that formed the goal of many leading seventeenth- and eighteenth-century revolutionaries in England and America, who often signed their writings with names of their Roman republican heroes, such as Cato, Cicero, and Publius. Republican citizens are convinced that they cannot be truly free, and cannot have dignity, unless they participate actively in the political divisions that shape the common life of their people. They value popular, or republican, institutions that promote extensive democratic participation; small, relatively homogeneous political communities, in which citizens feel themselves to be a great civic family; and a public morality of civic virtue, of services and sacrifices on behalf of the common good—even if this means the abandonment of many personal aspirations and "liberal" private pursuits.

The nativist conception was not so visible until the late nineteenth and early twentieth centuries, when the nationality the American revolutionaries created came to seem natural to later generations, and to be threatened by new immigrants and other social changes. Yet from early on, Americans often identified membership in their political community not with freedom for personal liberal callings or republican self-governance, but with a whole array of particular cultural origins, customs, and traits—with northern European, if not English, ancestry; with Christianity, especially Protestantism, and its message for the world; with the white race; with male leadership and female domesticity; and with all the customary economic and social arrangements that came to be seen as the true, traditional "American way of life." In the first *Federalist* paper, John Jay described Americans as a providentially guided "band of brethren," "descended from the same ancestors, speaking the same language, professing the same religion, attached to the same principles of government, very similar in their manners and customs"—an account by a wealthy Anglo-Saxon Protestant that ignored the considerable ethnic, regional, and religious diversity Americans already displayed.

But while nativism has often been cruelly narrow-minded, at its heart are genuine feelings of affection, belonging, and

Americanism poster

Harper's Weekly, November 20, 1869

loyalty that Americans might today express as love for their land of "baseball, hot dogs, apple pie, and Chevrolet." These are feelings born of deep human needs to affirm one's origins, needs captured memorably by Sir Walter Scott: "Breathes there a man with soul so dead/Who never to himself has said/This is my own, my native land!" It is questionable whether any country's laws of membership can or should be so liberal as to leave no place for such nationalistic sentiments. They have, in any case, always had great influence on America's citizenship provisions.

In their unmixed, archetypical forms, these three conceptions are in tension. For a pure liberal, the republican and nativist concepts are too intolerant of human variety and privacy. For a pure republican, the liberal conception licenses selfish egoism, while nativists are patriotic enough, but may not value political participation enough. Nativists believe that only their conception really captures who they are; so while they may cherish liberal ideals and republican institutions because they are American, they will not allow them to shield "un-American" trends that endanger the particular communal order they take as definitive of their very identity.

None of these conceptions has ever won exclusive sway in American law. From the founding to the present, they have waxed and waned, always exerting some discernible influence. Painting broadly, we can describe three eras in which particular combinations have been especially predominant in the nation's governing policies, laws, and judicial decisions.

The first era, from the birth of the nation through roughly the 1880s, was the period in which the three were best harmonized. It can nonetheless be termed the era of "liberal republican" citizenship, for these two elements were most pronounced. During the American Revolution, liberals, republicans, and incipient nativists were united by the belief that the cause of liberty required throwing off English monarchy and establishing an American republic dedicated to securing inalienable human rights. That liberal goal argued for open immigration and easy naturalization policies which would make America an "Asylum" for the "oppressed and persecuted of all Nations and Religions," as George Washington urged repeatedly in the 1780s. Liberal policies basically prevailed for the first third of the nation's history—but only when tailored to nativist and, particularly, republican concerns.

'Liberal Republican' Citizenship

Thomas Jefferson, for example, originally feared extensive immigration of the unrepublican offspring of Europe, who would make the American public "a heterogeneous, incoherent, distracted mass," incapable of self-government. While he later decided that the young republic needed new population to fill the Western agrarian lands that would preserve rustic republican virtues, he always urged the prompt "amalgamation" of newcomers into the pre-existing society. Similarly, in the early nineteenth century nativists proclaimed the Anglo-Saxon race peculiarly suited for liberty and self-government. But so long as the nation clearly needed more inhabitants, citizens of English stock were confident that they could bestow their innate virtues on other European peoples by assimilating them into the mold of that purified new Anglo-Saxon creation, the American.

Even so, republican and nativist concerns did produce major restrictions on eligibility for citizenship. Both the unreconstructed feudal elite of Europe and the "uncivilized" non-European masses were excluded. Under federal law, naturalization was available only to those who surrendered their unrepublican aristocratic titles, and only to whites. Applicants also had to spend a period in residence, usually five years, to imbibe republicanism, and then swear allegiance to the principles of the Constitution. The states, as the chief repositories of republican powers of self-government, were constitutionally entitled to maintain an exclusive and homogeneous body of citizens if they so chose, and most denied rights of citizenship to blacks and to those most worthy of the title, "Native Americans." Women were disfranchised citizens, confined to the role of "republican mothers," which meant they were to teach civic virtue to their sons. Even so, in the years when the national experiment in republican government required rapid population growth, American citizenship was easier to obtain than virtually any in the world. Once the Civil War extended the liberal rights of the Declaration of Independence, and citizenship, to American blacks, persons of African descent (but not other non-whites) were also made eligible for naturalization.

But as the West started to fill, and immigration increased and diversified during the nineteenth century, both republican and nativist tenets were invoked to justify new, restrictive citizenship laws. The cosmopolitan belief that American membership should be available to all who professed liberal principles did not persuade those who found their community identity threatened by the alien newcomers, now from southern and eastern Europe and China, who were transforming America's urban vistas.

'Republican Nativism'   In the 1840s and 1850s, the nativist "Know-Nothings" urged exclusion of the foreign-born and Catholics from public office and a requirement of 21 years of residence prior to naturalization. Their efforts failed, but they made familiar an alliance of republican and nativist arguments that would be used to defend every restrictive policy thereafter. Free republican institutions, they insisted, required intelligent citizens, accustomed to self-government, and united by the fraternal feelings bred by a common faith and customs. Republicans and nativists further contended that those born to different races and raised under despotic governments and religions generally lacked the ability and upbringing to grasp the principles of free government, and to exercise political power responsibly. Certain groups must therefore be denied access to full American citizenship if the republic and its unique Christian civilization were to be saved. In the late nineteenth century, the nation's of-

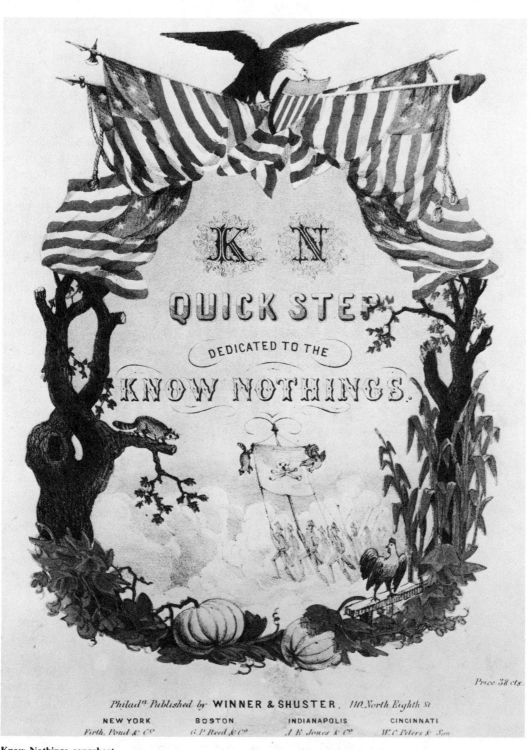

Know-Nothings songsheet

ficials repeatedly recited these claims as they instituted new limits on immigration and naturalization and created legal categories of second-class citizenship. Thus commenced a harsh era of "republican nativism" that would reach its nadir in the 1920s and extend through the Second World War, leaving shameful legacies that seem almost ineradicable.

The treatment of Asian immigrants provides an example of "republican nativism" in action. For a variety of motives, economic, political, and xenophobic, the Chinese were portrayed as habituated to despotism, dishonesty, and disease: even crusading journalist Horace Greeley claimed their "heathenish propensities" would mean the end of "republicanism and democracy." In the 1880s and 1890s, immigration of Chinese labor was first partly curtailed, then banned entirely. The U.S. Supreme Court upheld these anti-Asian views when it confirmed the new immigration restrictions in the famous *Chinese Exclusion Case* of 1889. The Court contended in nativist fashion that "differences of race" which made assimilation "impossible" meant that the Chinese were a danger to American morals, institutions, indeed "the preservation of our civilization." Beginning in the early twentieth century, Japanese applicants for naturalization also began to be rejected on the ground that they were non-white, a position the Supreme Court eventually affirmed in 1922.

Similarly, after America's burgeoning nationalism turned to aggressive imperialism during the Spanish-American war, the Filipino and Hispanic inhabitants of the nation's new Pacific and Caribbean colonies were denied full citizenship because the different "religion, customs, laws, and modes of thought" of "alien races" made it impossible to rule them according to "Anglo-Saxon principles" of "free government" (as the Supreme Court held in regard to Puerto Ricans in 1901). The flagging liberal legacy of belief in human equality was of little help in opposing the prejudices of these years, for this was the heyday of "Social Darwinism," and the thesis of the inferiority of non-white races claimed to be more "scientific" than the old ideals of the Declaration of Independence and the egalitarian abolitionists.

Prodded by Henry Cabot Lodge and the handful of Boston bluebloods who comprised the Immigration Restriction League, the nation also repeatedly considered, and in 1917 adopted, a literacy test for immigrants that was chiefly aimed at excluding southern Europeans. Further, it added more ideological requirements for naturalization designed to ban the newest threats to republican government, Europe's radical socialists and anarchists. These restrictive developments culminated in the landmark immigration and naturalization laws of 1921 and 1924. They created the patently racist national quota system, which limited European immigrants to 3 percent of the number of foreign-born of each nationality present in the United States at the time of the 1910 census, thereby favoring northern Europeans, and banned completely all those ineligible for naturalization, including virtually all Asians.

The menace of foreigners to republican institutions was a constant refrain of the supporters of these measures, but republican arguments continued to serve in another important way to further nativist ends during this era. The constitutional traditions of federalism and states' rights, originally generated by republicanism's advocacy of small, self-governing, homogeneous political communities, retained great vitality at least up to the New Deal. Thus even after more egalitarian principles were enshrined in the Constitution via the equal protection clause of the Fourteenth Amendment, traditionalists could still

Chinese immigrants to the United States

argue that the states must be permitted to decide for themselves who should exercise political power and on what terms. The federal judiciary repeatedly invoked deference to the states' republican powers of self-determination to justify acquiescing in direct and indirect denials of political and civil equality to women and blacks. The pattern was evident as early as *Bradwell v. State* (1872), where the Supreme Court upheld Illinois' refusal to permit a qualified woman to practice law. Justice Joseph Bradley wrote a notorious concurrence in the case that drew on the arsenal of nativist justifications for ethnic discriminations. Bradley argued, in parallel fashion, that "nature" and the "divine ordinance" supported permanent legal relegation of women to the "domestic sphere." The majority of the Court, however, relied on the republican contention that the practice of law, like the ballot, was a privilege of state citizenship, which states could bestow in any way they thought beneficial. This republican "states' rights" argument subsequently served as a chief justification for innumerable state actions that effectively disfranchised and segregated blacks in the late nineteenth and early twentieth centuries, making a mockery of the constitutionally equal citizenship.

The Revival of 'Liberal' Citizenship

But beginning in the Progressive era, the more cosmopolitan, liberal conception of American citizenship was revived in somewhat altered form. President Woodrow Wilson articulated it deftly in a 1915 address to newly naturalized citizens, who had just sworn allegiance to the United States. Wilson told the new Americans that they had vowed loyalty "to no one," only to "a great ideal, to a great body of principles, to a great hope of the human race." He urged them to think of America, but to "think first of humanity," so as not to divide people into nationalistic "jealous camps."

The true prophet of the new liberal conception of citizenship generated by Progressive thought was, however, Horace Kallen, a Jewish philosopher influenced by the pragmatism of William James and John Dewey. Like Dewey, Kallen was disgusted by the harsh Americanization movement of World War I, which included public and private efforts to strip recent immigrants of "alien" characteristics virtually overnight. He argued in opposition that the true ideal of American identity was "cultural pluralism": the United States should be a "federal republic" in form, but a "democracy of nationalities" in fact, a commonwealth of numerous organic communities that would cooperate voluntarily in the "enterprise of self-

Judge in chambers swearing in a new citizen, New York City, 1916

realization" within culturally distinctive, but mutually respect-
ful, ancestral groups. Kallen thus added to Wilson's emphasis
on shared liberal ideals the contention that needs for a "native"
community should be met by memberships in smaller
ethnocultural bodies. This did not mean that Kallen's interpretation of American citizenship was less cosmopolitan than
Wilson's. For Kallen, that citizenship was "no more than
citizenship in any land with free institutions" that permitted
heterogeneity while encouraging cultural cross-fertilization. In
his important 1924 summary of his views, *Culture and Democracy in the United States,* Kallen wrote that the enlightened
citizen, educated by the experience of diversity, would be
"essentially a citizen of the world."

Wilson's liberalism, and its elaboration in Kallen's cultural pluralism, did not forestall the inflamed xenophobia of
World War I and the post-war period. In fact, Wilson himself
came to urge repressive measures against native dissidents and
aliens alike, to safeguard "morale" for the war effort. The chief
monuments of the nation's rising nativism, the bigoted immigration laws of the 1920s and the second-class citizenship
accorded blacks, women, and other minorities, continued to
predominate in American law and public policy through the
Depression and the Second World War. But in the wake of that

conflict with racist totalitarian regimes, liberal egalitarian forces gained new vigor in American life.

In the 1950s, most leaders of ethnic groups, immigrant organizations, and social reform movements came to accept some form of cultural pluralism, of equality among autonomous but cooperative ethnocultural groups, as the proper ideal for American life. Slowly, they gained successes in re-shaping American laws and policies to accord with this modern liberal conception. In 1952, Congress passed the McCarran-Walter Act, which finally abolished all overt racial requirements for naturalization, though the national quota system was largely maintained, and as part of the Cold War, federal powers to deport ideologically undesirable aliens were increased. Shortly thereafter, the Supreme Court struck down racial segregation, and later in the decade Congress adopted tentative legislation on behalf of black voting rights.

The 1960s marked the real ascendancy of the liberal notion of "cultural pluralism" as the dominant conception of civic identity in American public law. The historic 1964 Civil Rights Act promoted social equality for blacks and also for other minorities and women; the Voting Rights Act of 1965

Japanese agricultural workers packing broccoli, March 1937

furthered their political equality, and the 1965 Immigration and Naturalization Act at last terminated the discriminatory national quota system. New governmental programs were created to address the special needs of ethnocultural minorities, such as educational curricula more attuned to the nation's varied cultural heritage, bilingual ballots and governmental publications, and federally sponsored affirmative action programs in hiring and school admission policies. In the early 1970s, many of these initiatives were extended, by legislative amendments and by judicial decisions that broadened remedies against discrimination for all citizens and that provided almost equal protection to aliens as well.

Those measures could not, however, succeed in erasing the marks past policies had left on American institutions, social practices, and popular beliefs. Efforts to do so, moreover, increasingly encountered resistance. The tense struggle over desegregation, especially in northern cities, remains an ongoing national dilemma. Affirmative action measures, and the spread of representative quotas, explicit or implicit, within political parties and governmental administrative proceedings, have produced mounting acrimony. Concerns about the social changes that might result from the Equal Rights Amendment grew so strong that it was defeated, at least for the present.

The return to more open immigration since 1965 has led to an unprecedented influx of Asian and, especially, Spanish-speaking newcomers, heavily concentrated in a few regions, where they sometimes constitute local majorities. In consequence, many are again expressing fears that native American citizens are losing jobs to aliens, and that our political institutions and expanded social programs are being rendered unworkable by strangers in the land who cannot or will not participate in them responsibly. Recent controversies over bilingualism, refugee policies, amnesty for illegal aliens and education for their children, all reveal that the sorts of anxieties many Americans experienced prior to the closing of the immigration doors in the 1920s have not disappeared, but only slumbered in the intervening years. Their re-awakening has already had an impact on the actions of legislators, judges, and immigration officials, who show signs of a new hardening toward the claims of aliens, refugees, and domestic ethnic minorities. The Supreme Court has recently broadened the range of public employments that states may limit to citizens; the Immigration and Naturalization Service has resurrected near-punitive confinement for refugees awaiting processing;

and federal officials have stopped advocating affirmative action programs and sweeping desegregation measures.

To be sure, few in public life today would defend the explicitly racist and chauvinistic nativism that pervaded American public discourse in the first quarter of this century. But immigration, ethnic, and racial questions are once again visibly central to America's public life; and so it is impossible to avoid the fear that the nation will see heightening ethnic conflicts in the years ahead. These consequences of the post-war move toward public policies promoting "cultural pluralism" raise anew some disturbing and unsolved questions. Can Americans hope to meet their needs for a sense of meaningful civic identity and national community if citizenship in the United States rests only on the cosmopolitan ideal of shared commitment to liberal principles, and so means no more than membership in any land with free institutions? Or must liberal policies always prove counterproductive, thrusting people back into their more communitarian subgroups, and generating not tolerance and openness but bitter ethnocultural rivalries? Will these quarrels, in turn, generate a disaffected citizenry that limits its political participation to agitation on behalf of special group interests, leaving more remote than ever the republican ideal of a vigorous public actively cooperating for the common good? Can feelings of allegiance to one's roots, the fuel of American nativism, be made to serve a healthy patriotism, or must they generate parochial perspectives that can only produce bigotry in a society that is now ineradicably heterogeneous?

These painful and perplexing issues will probably continue to be addressed in American law through some combination of liberal, republican, and nativist views. Whether any new combination can be found that will seem legitimate, meaningful, and satisfying to Americans is a further question, however—one that the nation will be unable to avoid as it ponders the significance American citizenship should be given in public policies and adjudication during the American Constitution's third century.

Milton Gordon, *Assimilation in American Life* (1964).

Louis Hartz, *The Liberal Tradition in America* (1955).

John Higham, *Strangers in the Land: Patterns of American Nativism, 1860-1925* (1966).

James Kettner, *The Development of American Citizenship, 1608-1870* (1978).

J. G. A. Pocock, *The Machiavellian Moment* (1975).

Rogers M. Smith is assistant professor of political science at Yale University and the author of *Liberalism and American Constitutional Law* (Harvard University Press, 1985). He is currently writing on the concept of citizenship in the American constitutional tradition.

V. Civil Rights and Civil Liberties

The Meaning of a
Free Press

Paul L. Murphy

On the facade of the *Chicago Tribune* building, chiseled in the marble, is a statement by Chief Justice Charles Evans Hughes. Taken from a 1931 Supreme Court case, *Near v. Minnesota,* it reads:

> The administration of government has become more complex, the opportunities for malfeasance and corruption have multiplied, crime has grown to most serious proportions, and the danger of its protection by unfaithful officials and of the impairment of the fundamental security of life and property by criminal alliances and official neglect, emphasize the need of a vigilant and courageous press especially in great cities. The fact that liberty of the press may be abused by miscreant purveyors of scandal does not make any less necessary the immunity of the press from prior restraint in dealing with official misconduct.

The case which produced this vitally important ruling also generated a massive body of argumentation on both sides as to the true meaning of freedom of the press, its history as a concept and instrument in American development, and its role in and relation to the Constitution and constitutional government. The case illustrates both the Constitution's ability to meet new challenges, and its conservative nature: the classical values incorporated in the document proved equal to a modern confrontation. The process of judicial interpretation emphasizes the character of the Constitution as a living document, but one whose modern application comes from its history and the history of the nation. It also illustrates the propensity of modern justices to translate terms like "freedom of the press" from legal abstraction to operational reality. Further, the case itself raised a specific, crucial constitutional issue with which Americans still wrestle. How much does the public, through the media, have a right to know about the actions of its governing officials, the policies they intend to follow, the methods they plan to use in that pursuit, and the degree to which they indulge their own human venality? It also raises questions as to the proper use of press freedom, and the responsibility of both government officals and media decision makers to the public and to the general welfare of the nation.

The *Near* case involved a Minnesota law enacted in 1925 to shut down an unscrupulous Duluth newspaper which was critical of public authorities for their alleged connections with crime and corruption. The statute was also used against a sleazy Minneapolis publication, the *Saturday Press,* which, too, asserted links between local officials and the underworld. Flamboyant, but still reasonably accurate, its revelations had led to two gangland attacks on one of the publishers, the second of which was fatal. The local county attorney and future governor, Floyd B. Olson, asked a judge to close down this "malicious, scandalous, and defamatory publication." The judge quickly obliged and the newspaper was suppressed under a temporary injunction after the Minnesota Supreme Court

Charles Evans Hughes

upheld the constitutionality of the "gag law." The plight of the
Saturday Press had attracted the attention of both the liberal
American Civil Liberties Union, and the conservative Chicago
publisher, Robert R. McCormick. His lawyers helped convince
the United States Supreme Court that the case was an
important test of the First Amendment, and that it should be
the occasion for applying the traditional and historic concept of
"no prior restraint" to state laws inhibiting the dispersal of
information which the public had a right to know.

Charles Evans Hughes, who considered his role in the
Near case a highpoint of his career, wrote the majority opinion.
His now classic statement on prior censorship, which he read
from the bench with great feeling, set forth a general principle
which still largely defines freedom of the American press, a
principle cited frequently in subsequent rulings including the
famous Pentagon Papers case in the late years of the Vietnam
War. But possibly more importantly, the ruling stiffened the
backbones of countless editors and publishers and helped stave
off periodic attempts by politicians, judges, and prosecutors to
muzzle the journalistic watchdog.

The Bicentennial of the adoption of the Constitution is an
appropriate time to examine the founding fathers' perception of
what freedom of the press was supposed to mean. Did they
have in mind the establishment of the constitutional right of a
newspaper to publish without prior restraint and a conception
of the newspaper's role as a herald to expose political corruption and public malfeasance? While conclusive answers are
impossible, a look at the history casts some light on the subject.

Control of a New Medium

From the invention of the printing press and the ability of
a writer to distribute ideas to a general audience, a concern
evolved as to the proper use of that process. Prevailing
doctrines of spiritual and temporal sovereignty made it inevitable that control over the new medium of expression would be
gathered firmly in the hands of the ruling authorities. In
England, printing first developed under royal sponsorship and
soon became a monopoly granted by the crown. The crown
retained, however, the right to restrain in advance the publication of material considered threatening or unwarranted. The
government initially used its authority against certain religious
works "with divers heresies and erroneous opinions." But once
the crown began the process of censorship by curtailing one
segment of the press, the whole field became open to official
suppression. In 1566, the Star Chamber issued a decree

limiting printers to publication of only the most innocuous material, a restriction enforced with increasing severity under the early Stuart rulers of the seventeenth century. To this control, the authorities added over the years further royal proclamations, Star Chamber decrees, and parliamentary enactments, constantly increasing the complexity of the regulations and further shackling the art and business of publication.

Resistance to the crown on this matter arose early. Although opponents of these practices did not question the propriety of punishing seditious libels, they did object to "prior punishment." The licensing power allowed authorities to place a prior restraint on a publication's issuance; anything published without a license was criminal. During the period of the English Civil War, when Parliament assumed control over printing, some Puritan leaders demanded that publication still be subjected to prior restraint. Strong objection ensued. Parliamentary leaders, convinced that there was a "definite, discernable, and discoverable truth in religious doctrine, the presentation of which could not fail to convince the unbeliever," began talking in a vocabulary strikingly similar to the modern view of the importance of the truth being tested in the "marketplace of ideas." As the poet John Milton wrote at the time:

> And though all the winds of doctrin were let loose to play upon the earth, so Truth be in the field, we do injuriously by licencing and prohibiting to misdoubt her strength. Let her and Falshood grapple; who ever knew Truth put to the wors in a free and open encounter?

Milton was also a pragmatist. As he wrote his friend Samuel Hartlib, "the art of Printing will so spread knowledge that the common people, knowing their own rights and liberties will not be governed by way of oppression." Thus, the importance of the press' effect on the relationship between the government and the people was recognized early.

In time, Puritans, including Milton, quickly saw that "Truth is not always victorious even where given a free field," and that control of the press to suppress erroneous opinions could be useful. Hence, early attention arose as to what unlicensed words might be found mischievous and libelous and the problem of seeking a balance between freedom and legitimate restraint was sharpened in public argumentation. Generally, cautious restraint won. Toleration for intolerant views had few adherents. "No opinions contrary to human society, or to those moral rules which are necessary to the preservation of civil society, are to be tolerated by the magistrate" wrote the Englishman, John Locke, in his 1689 *Letter Concerning Toleration*. But for Locke, the proper form of punishment was not prior governmental censorship. A system of prior restraint was cumbersome and unpopular, and when the English Licensing Laws expired in 1695 they were not extended.

Thereafter, freedom of the press from licensing came to be recognized in England as a common law or natural right. That law was summarized by the English jurist, Sir William Blackstone, in a now famous passage:

> The liberty of the press is indeed essential to the nature of a free state; but this consists in laying no *previous* restraint upon publication, and not in freedom from censure for criminal matter when published. Every freeman has an undoubted right to lay what sentiments he pleases before the public; to forbid this is to destroy the freedom of the press; but if he publishes what is improper, mischievous, or illegal, he must take the consequences of his own temerity.

The governmental method for controlling the press in England evolved from the prior censorship of Milton's day to the subsequent punishment of Blackstone's.

Eighteenth-century liberals, less secular and more political, came to view freedom of the press in far more modern terms. The popular pamphlets known as *Cato's Letters,* published in England, were widely read in the American colonies as an esteemed source of political ideas. The most famous of the *Letters* were those on freedom of speech, and *Reflections upon Libelling,* one of three essays on libel law and freedom of the press. It was "Cato" from whom the founding fathers derived certain of their First Amendment ideas, and it was "Cato" who redefined the proper relationship between government and the press, affording a basis for the evolution of a free press in America.

In "Cato's" view, freedom from illegitimate authority was vital. Freedom of expression constituted a primary value. Governments could rightly limit these freedoms only when their use might directly hurt or abrogate the rights of another. "Cato" argued that free government and free expression would prosper or die together. Moreover, because government officials are agents of the people's interests, they should be subject to popular criticism and should welcome having their activities openly examined. "Only the wicked Governors of Men dread what is said of them," "Cato" contended, and it is only they who fear a free press. While the press should be pressured to correct its errors, the government should not seek in most cases to punish them when they occurred. In Cato's view, libels rarely provoked causeless discontent against the government. Libels were the inevitable result of a free press, an evil arising out of a much greater good that brought advantages to society which far outweighed potential harm. "Cato" was aware, however, of his own need for protection at a time in England when his views were decidedly premature. Thus, he asserted that libels against the government should be punishable, while truthfulness about public people and measures should constitute a legitimate defense against a criminal libel charge.

Cato's Letters were the high water mark of libertarian theory until the close of the eighteenth century. In fact American libertarian theory, neither original nor independent, was at its best little more than an imitation of "Cato." But as British repression became increasingly heavy and objectionable, Americans more and more discussed this vital area and the role of the press.

A 'Sacred' Free Press   In 1765, at a time when the colonists were outraged over the Stamp Act, John Adams wrote a *Dissertation on the Canon and Feudal Law* in which he expressed the view that he knew of no "means of information . . . more sacred . . . than . . . a free press." A free press, he went on to argue, was an instrument the mass of the people might take to compensate for some of the disadvantages they labored under in their struggle with the executive. More specifically, Adams maintained, it offered a remedy for the people's most chronic ailment, disunity. Newspapers could play a special part in welding together a united populace by disseminating knowledge of the constitution and of how their rulers related to it. Without such knowledge, subjects would not know when their rights were invaded, nor have a common principle on which to act. The press could also arouse the people to action. "Inconsideration" no less than ignorance had brought ruin on mankind, and people are not persuaded without the utmost difficulty to attend to facts and evidence. The position clearly suggests the importance of the press' role as well as the nature of its responsibility.

This view set eighteenth-century America on a different course from that taken by Britain. The power to control the press through the courts diminished more rapidly in the colonies than in the mother country. Colonial juries had more

John Adams

immediate reason to balk at collaborating with crown officials and convicting printers of seditious libel. Although executive officials would not formally renounce the right to prosecute for libel, they could no longer bend the judicial machinery to their will.

The lower houses of the assemblies, however, did not so readily surrender their power. While championing the liberty of the press against royal officials, the colonial assemblies refused to have such a weapon turned against themselves and suppressed dissent without a qualm. It was these alleged bastions of the people's liberties that persecuted the press, later especially the pro-British loyalist press, and harassed authors and publishers for breaches of privilege. Further, they usually had considerable popular support for their acts. These facts suggest that the revolutionary period was a testing ground for the extent to which Americans were committed to a free press in modern terms.

The picture was mixed, but the circumstances were unique since, as Richard Buel has pointed out, a classical power struggle was then going on between the crown and the people, and between authority and liberty. Concessions to English "truth" as opposed to American "truth" were a dangerous luxury to many Americans, at a time when mustering a shaky public opinion behind the revolution was essential to national, and some feared personal, survival.

Once war broke out, the states lost little time in censoring newspapers critical of the patriot cause. Many enacted treason and sedition statutes and took jurisdiction over numerous matters of opinion. A loyalist point of view was not to be expressed, at least not until victory was securely at hand, and even then many had doubts. Congress alone showed restraint in controlling the press during the war. Three times it was asked to act against presses allegedly violating Congress' privileges, and each time it invoked the precedent of freedom of the press to excuse its inaction.

But if the practice was flawed, the broader concept was still ingrained in American values and many American hearts. Section 12 of the Virginia Bill of Rights of 1776, a segment of the new Virginia Constitution which became a model for the other new states and eventually for the federal Bill of Rights, had claimed the freedom of the press as "one of the great bulwarks of liberty [which] can never be restrained but by despotic governments." Four years later, John Adams emphasized that "the liberty of the press is essential to the security of the state. It ought not, therefore, to be restrained in this Commonwealth [of Massachusetts]."

The meaning of "liberty of the press," although vitally important, had no precise boundaries. Neither the Articles of Confederation nor the Constitution defined the proper relationship between government and the press. Given its importance to many citizens, this gap seems inexplicable. The best wisdom suggests that the term meant no prior restraint. But attempts to move beyond Blackstone and spell out more precisely the law and theory of freedom of expression went unfulfilled.

Practical episodes afford a window into the post-revolutionary mind on this subject. When Eleazer Oswald, a Philadelphia printer, was successfully prosecuted for libel, his

We have the heart-felt pleasure to inform our fellow citizens that the Fœderal Convention adjourned yesterday, having completed the object of their deliberations— And we hear that Major W. Jackson, the secretary of that honorable body, leaves this city for New-York, this morning, in order to lay the great result of their proceedings before the United States in Congress.

A correspondent expresses his concern, that any proposition should have been made in the general assembly, for opening and prolonging the time for officers and soldiers to draw their donation lands, beyond the time allowed by law; he fears it will make many delay their application, on account of the advance they must make for the surveying fees—and at last be shut out; for certainly the measure will never be adopted by the legislature, as the same principle would unquestionably go to open again the door to the accounts for depreciation, and other numerous claims upon the public, which are barred and excluded by this state, and by the United States.

A Mezzotinto Print of His Excellency GENERAL WASHINGTON, done by CHARLES WILSON PEALE of Philadelphia, from a portrait which he has painted since the sitting of the Convention. is now completed: the likeness is esteemed the best that has been executed in a print.——This is one of an intended series of prints, to be taken from Mr. Peale's collection of portraits of illustrious persons, distinguished in the late revolution. Those of His Excellency Doctor Franklin and the honorable the Marquis de la Fayette, have been already published.

The price of these prints, in a neat oval frame, (the inner frame gilt) is two dollars each, or one dollar for the print only: and a large allowance will be made to those who purchase to sell again.—Apply to Charles W. Peale, at the corner of Third and Lombard streets, Philadelphia.

˙˳˙ The printers in the several states, who are desirous of encouraging the fine arts in America, are requested to publish this as an article of intelligence; which will oblige the numerous friends of the General.

The states of Holland and West Friesland have, in answer to the baron de Thulemeyer, minister to the king of Prussia, declared, that they, as sovereign of the province, always should act for the good of their country, and make no alterations in any of their resolutions, by paying regard to the threats or intreaties of any foreign power whatsoever.

By private letters from Holland, dated July 22, 1787, we are informed, " that propositions are presented to different towns and provinces to re-establish the old constitution so far that the sovereigns in every province shall chuse officers for the sea and land services and never to set an upper admiral or general over them, but state deputies will be appointed with the secret orders of the sovereign in the fleets and in the armies— and the government in the several towns to be chosen by the votes of the citizens and the Gildens, which are the societies of tradesmen of every denomination. At the same time there shall be a general congress to rectify the abuses crept from time to time into the different parts of government, when without partiality the offspring of ancient families will be chosen, if they by their abilities and good conduct deserve it; and others for their capacities though of foreign extraction, provided they have had their residence in the country the time which the law requires, will with equal impartiality be elected. Thus the states will without mediation of foreigners, settle their differences by their sea and land forces, with their command of money, which is very properly called the nerves of a long war, and the successful means of inducing every German to engage with spirit in the service of those patriots, who will set them the example in fighting in the glorious cause of liberty, as his Britannic majesty and ministers experienced in the late war when they were paid and hired to serve tyranny and oppression, but afterwards shewed their fond love for liberty by their desertion and flying at once from English service and German slavery. Thus will the republic of Netherland (for their prosperity has always been envied by nations and kings) settle their own affairs, and establish their liberty and independence on a solid foundation.

˙ ˙ The American Philosophical Society will hold

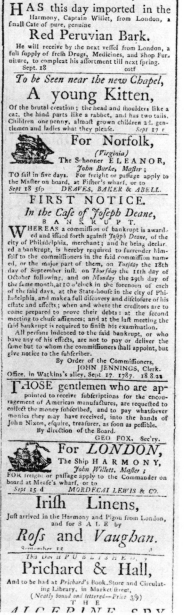

Philadelphia newspaper account of the adjournment of the Constitutional Convention

supporters in the Pennsylvania legislature aided his attempt to impeach justices of the state supreme court who convicted him. Although they were unsuccessful, their actions produced considerable public debate regarding the permissible limits of a free press and the precise meaning of the free press clause in Pennsylvania's Bill of Rights. The Oswald case also made other state courts sensitive to violations of civil rights and led to a number of rulings protecting the press from interference. On the other hand, when Thomas Jefferson proposed a new constitution for Virginia in 1783, he wanted the press exempted from prior restraints but specifically liable for punishment for false publications. This ambivalence implies that once independence was achieved and American leaders occupied positions of power, they saw less value in the press as a safeguard against arbitrary power than they had when British authorities ruled. American statesmen resented critics who suggested that they might misuse their offices.

When the Constitutional Convention met in May 1787, protection of a free press was not high on the agenda. It was not until August 20, near the end of the famous meeting, that Charles Pinckney submitted a proposal for a bill of rights. The press provision was among its thirteen propositions and simply stated: "The liberty of the Press shall be inviolably preserved." This language had little appeal to the other founding fathers. Many did not want a bill of rights because they believed that provisions to safeguard individual liberties, originally created to protect subjects from rulers claiming absolute powers, had no place in a constitution founded on the will of the people. Such attempts to stipulate basic principles of liberty failed to win a majority.

Nevertheless, the framers supported, even assumed, the existence of a free press. They took painstaking efforts in drafting the original body of the Constitution to set up a representative political process. Representation implied citizen participation, which further implied intelligent participation, which meant the ability to communicate freely and take part in the political process. Thus, as James Madison stated: "a popular government without popular information, or the means of acquiring it, is but a prologue to a farce or a tragedy; and a people who mean to be their own governors must arm themselves with the power which knowledge gives." But such ambiguous reassurance was inadequate, and when the Constitution came before the states for ratification, citizens voiced protests about the absence of a bill of rights.

The Constitution's advocates resisted. Alexander Hamilton argued that there was no way to secure a concept such as freedom of the press by words. Freedom of the press, he said, "must altogether depend on public opinion, and on the general spirit of the people and of the government." James Madison agreed that those rights which were solely dependent upon majority public opinion could be snuffed out whenever that opinion changed. In Virginia, he contended, "I have seen the bill of rights violated in every instance where it has been opposed to a popular current."

Nevertheless, Madison advocated action. Experience quickly reinforced his belief that when it came to the rights and liberties of individual dissenters, a democratic majority could be as repressive as a king, and thus the majority must have its power over certain rights clearly limited. This view was widely shared, and the Virginia representatives when they ratified the Constitution insisted on their position that "liberty of conscience and of the press cannot be cancelled, abridged, restrained, or modified, by any authority of the United States." The implication of the statement was clear—the Constitution should forbid not only Congress, but the executive and the judiciary from limiting the guarantees later placed in the First Amendment.

But Madison wanted more. Possibly anticipating a situation such as the one in *Near v. Minnesota,* and clearly responding to the repressive behavior of some of the states during the Confederation period, he advocated an amendment which he considered the most valuable in the whole list. It stated that "no State shall violate the equal right of conscience, [or of the] freedom of the press . . . because it is proper that every Government should be disarmed of power which trench upon those particular rights." "I cannot see any reason," he said "against obtaining even a double security on these points. . . . It must be admitted, on all hands, that the State Governments are as liable to attach these invaluable privileges as the General Government is, and therefore ought to be as cautiously guarded against."

Madison's proposal was not adopted. The ultimate language on press in the freedom in the First Amendment read, simply, "Congress shall make no law . . . abridging the freedom . . . of the press." Such wording begged the definition which would have been desirable, even though the Amendment initially appeared strong enough to support Madison's general

'Congress Shall Make No Law . . .'

view that, in this new American democracy, the power of censorship should be exercised by the people over the government and not the government over the people.

As to whether the drafters had in mind the constitutional right of a newspaper to publish without prior restraint and a conception of a newspaper's role as a herald to expose political corruption and public malfeasance, the record is also tantalizingly incomplete. The prior restraint point seems clearer. As Hughes wrote in *Near:*

> The fact that for approximately one hundred and fifty years there has been almost an entire absence of attempts to impose previous restraints upon publications relating to the malfeasance of public officers is significant of the deep-seated conviction that such restraint would violate constitutional right. Public officers, whose character and conduct remain open to debate and free discussion in the press, find their remedies for false accusations in actions under libel laws providing for redress and punishment, and not in proceedings to restrain the publications of newspapers and periodicals. The general principle that the constitutional guarantee of liberty of the press gives immunity from previous restraints has been approved in many decisions under the provision of state constitutions.

Regarding the limits of public criticism and exposure of officials, Hughes quoted Madison. Pointing out that statesman's role as a leading spirit in the preparation of the First Amendment, the Chief Justice stated:

> Some degree of abuse is inseparable from the proper use of everything, and in no instance is this more true than in that of the press. It has accordingly been decided by the practice of the states that it is better to leave a few of its noxious branches to their luxuriant growth than, by pruning them away, to injure the vigour of those yielding the proper fruits.

Hughes understood Madison in another way as well, and his *Near* opinion finally concretized the Virginian's desired safeguard in protecting press freedom from the states. Following a path which had been begun six years earlier in *Gitlow v. New York* (1925), Hughes incorporated freedom of the press from state action in the term "liberty" in the "due process" clause of the Fourteenth Amendment, and held the Minnesota "gag law" to be void. The question, Hughes said, was "whether a statute authorizing such proceedings in restraint of publication is consistent with the conception of the liberty of the press as historically conceived and guaranteed." His answer was resoundingly negative.

One vital question remains which even *Near* did not solve. Hughes had made clear, in a frequently overlooked portion of his opinion, that the First Amendment was not absolute. But what, if any, information should be exempted from its protection, particularly under claims of national security, a term which itself is capable of governmental abuse? This area still remains troublingly unresolved. It is especially a concern when definition is in the hands of officials who might seek to use their powers in dubious ways by blacking out public information and crippling the legitimate censorial role which the American public has come to feel is its birthright and obligation as participants in maintaining a free society.

SUGGESTED ADDITIONAL READING

Bernard Bailyn and John B. Hench, *The Press and the American Revolution* (1980).

Fred Friendly, *Minnesota Rag: The Dramatic Story of the Landmark Supreme Court Case That Gave New Meaning to Freedom of the Press* (1981).

Leonard Levy, *Freedom of the Press from Zenger to Jefferson* (1966).

Richard L. Perry and John C. Cooper, *Sources of Our Liberties* (1952).

Paul L. Murphy is professor of history and American studies at the University of Minnesota, Minneapolis and the author of *The Meaning of Freedom of Speech* (Greenwood Press, 1972) and *The Constitution in Crisis Times* (Harper & Row, 1972).

Retrieving Self-Evident Truths: The Fourteenth Amendment

Howard N. Meyer

In 1983, when Congress established a Commission on the Bicentennial of the Constitution, it observed that the document set forth the "inalienable rights, and the timeless principles of individual liberty and responsibility, and equality before the law." This was not always so. The concepts of "inalienable rights" and "equality" were indeed proclaimed by the Declaration of Independence of July 4, 1776, but they were not in the Constitution of September 17, 1787. The Constitution's Preamble announced a purpose to "secure the Blessings of Liberty," but the six Articles that followed gave little specific security. In 1791, the newly ratified Bill of Rights began to close the gap between the Declaration and the Constitution. However, the establishment of liberty on a national scale, and the very idea of equality before the law, did not achieve constitutional status until the Fourteenth Amendment was ratified in 1868, the product of an agonizing civil war.

Abraham Lincoln, in his speech at Gettysburg in 1863, made the clearest call for the changes wrought by the Fourteenth Amendment. Recalling the establishment of a new nation in 1776, "conceived in Liberty" and dedicated to equality, he pointed to the "unfinished work" we had to do: to see to it that the nation "shall have a new birth of freedom." Because of its eloquence and brevity, the Gettysburg address has been memorized and recited by innumerable school children, and often quoted by politicians of every party. But rarely does anyone think about when and how the "new birth" Lincoln called for took place.

Lincoln took the self-evident truths of the Declaration of Independence seriously. In debating with Stephen Douglas, he said he had never embraced a political idea that did not spring from the Declaration. In his notable Cooper Union speech, he

'All Men Are Created Equal'

209

said that the Union of the States into a Nation dated not from the Constitution, but from 1776. Lincoln had defended Jefferson's generation for failure to take action in their own days to see to the equality they had pledged:

> The assertion that 'all men are created equal' was of no practical use in effecting our separation from Great Britain; and it was placed in the Declaration not for that, but *for future use.* [emphasis added]

The lasting promise of the Declaration, Lincoln had said on another occasion, was that "in due time the weight would be lifted from the shoulders of all men, and that all should have an equal chance." The key to that idea was in the words: "in due time."

From the very outset of their movement some thirty years before, all who advocated the abolition of slavery included in their pronouncements the "created equal" passage of the Declaration. Some denounced the Constitution as a betrayal, a "covenant with death," to use William Lloyd Garrison's phrase. Pragmatism motivated others to assert that the Bill of Rights of 1791 had implanted the ideas of 1776 into the document of 1787. James G. Birney, the Liberty Party candidate for president in 1844, argued that the Fifth Amendment forbidding deprivation of liberty without "due process of law" had ended constitutional sanction for slavery—or at least given Congress the power to abolish it.

Unfortunately, an 1833 Supreme Court decision (*Barron v. Baltimore*) stood in the way. The Court used this case, which did not involve slavery, to rule that the Fifth Amendment (and the rest of the Bill of Rights) were limitations on the federal government only. Thus, the states could disregard the "due process" clause and the other rights, privileges, and immunities mentioned in the first ten amendments to the Constitution. The Bill of Rights, therefore, did not touch the question of slavery, or its repressive consequences.

Neither that Court decision, nor propaganda mounted in slavery's defense, nor fear that abolitionism was a danger to the Union, could affect the status of the Declaration of Independence as a powerful symbol of nationhood. The Declaration was recited annually at Fourth of July celebrations. The "unalienable rights" were reiterated in many state constitutions. The egalitarian sentiments of the Declaration were taken seriously enough to be included in the platform of the newly formed Republican Party in 1856, and repeated when Lincoln first ran in 1860.

After his election, Lincoln, in attempting to preserve the Union without bloodshed, disregarded that part of the platform. In his first Inaugural Address, he went so far as to tell the seceding states and their sympathizers that he would support a constitutional amendment insulating slavery from abolition by future constitutional change. That proposed Thirteenth (!) Amendment had already been sent by Congress to the states and three had already ratified it. The two-thirds vote achieved in each House to submit it for ratification illustrated the fragility of the adherence to "the proposition that all men are created equal." But despite the effort to accommodate the slave states, all attempts at peaceful settlement of the secession crisis failed, "and the war came . . . ," as Lincoln said in his second Inaugural speech. By that time, March of 1865, a new Thirteenth Amendment, now for total abolition, was well on its way; in April, Lincoln was assassinated by a Confederate sympathizer. In the eulogy he was selected to give the assassi-

Charles Sumner

nated president, Charles Sumner, the abolitionist senator from Massachusetts, traced Lincoln's dedication to the Declaration throughout his career. Sumner, who had been isolated in the Senate when he joined that body but who was now one of its leaders, announced as the war drew to a close: "We shall insist upon the Declaration of Independence as the foundation of the new state governments."

A Rapid Reversal of Opinion   The nation had undergone perhaps the most rapid reversal of "grass roots" public opinion in our history. Abolition sentiment spread as the conflict went on; support for equality began to develop after scores of black regiments were allowed to join the Union Army and they helped to turn the tide. As the war waned and the institution of slavery crumbled, new tragedies brought about even stronger sentiment for the ideas of 1776 than that which had made abolition inevitable. Lincoln's assassination, which inflamed antislavery feeling still more, also installed a new president in the White House who seemed intent on reversing the outcome of the war.

During the long congressional recess, from the death of Lincoln in April until December of 1865, events moved rapidly. President Andrew Johnson rapidly restored former Confederates to power in their home states. While doing so, he required of them no safeguards for ex-slaves or former Union sympathizers, or even for the black Union veterans who had returned to their homes in the South. The effect was devastating. In the words of one of his own emissaries, former Union general and future statesman Carl Schurz, by December 1865, southern blacks, no longer the slaves of individuals, were becoming "the slaves of society."

Disclosure of Johnson's policies and news of their effect persuaded many that the mere outlawing of slavery was not enough additional affirmative steps were needed to remedy its results and to insure against the return of bondage in another guise. But the president vetoed or sabotaged the civil rights laws enacted by the thirty-ninth Congress in 1865 and 1866. Congressional response was decisive and in tune with public reaction. It included further legislation and the preparation and submission to the states of the Fourteenth Amendment.

Although President Johnson's policies were rejected in the 1866 mid-term elections, he did not accept the verdict. He campaigned to defeat ratification of the Fourteenth Amendment, but he succeeded only in delaying it. In response,

Congress produced the Fifteenth Amendment to enfranchise former slaves.

Convenient shorthand is available to identify the Thirteenth and Fifteenth Amendments: "abolition" for one and "voting rights" for the other. The Fourteenth cannot be so easily summed up. "Equal Justice Under Law" may do, if read with separate emphasis on the first two words, since the Fourteenth deals with both equality and justice. In the view of its framers, the Fourteenth Amendment in its first section was designed to give constitutional force to the human rights principles of the Declaration of Independence:

'Equal Justice Under Law'

> All persons born or naturalized in the United States, and subject to the jurisdiction thereof, are citizens of the United States and of the State wherein they reside. No State shall make or enforce any law which shall abridge the privileges and immunities of citizens of the United States; nor shall any State deprive any person of life, liberty, or property, without due process of law; nor deny to any person within its jurisdiction the equal protection of the laws.

The fifth section gives to Congress the power of enforcement "by appropriate legislation."*

In its opening sentence, the first section of the Fourteenth Amendment aimed to undo the ruling in the ill-famed *Dred Scott* decision of 1857. That case had held that persons of African ancestry were not eligible for United States citizenship. Now a new definition remedied the omission in the 1787 charter that made such exclusion possible. It did more: it created a definite *national* citizenship, specified as prior to the connection with the state of residence. (The earlier view was that state citizenship was source, not product, of U.S. citizenship.) Now there was to be mutuality of relation directly between each person and the federal government.

Citizenship is a two-way connection embracing not only loyalty to the society from which it stems, but society's

Dred Scott

---

* Only the provisions of the first section, and the power of Congress under the fifth are of active contemporary concern. The second clause, drafted three years before it was thought possible to forbid completely the denial of suffrage to black males, provided that states that cut their electorate by barring the vote to some portion of their male population should have the number of representatives curtailed in proportion. This law was never enforced, and it became moot when the voting rights laws of the 1960s went into effect. The third and fourth clauses dealt with disqualification of and amnesty for rebels and war debts and became obsolete in the course of time.

Andrew Johnson

obligation equally to protect its citizens and to defend their rights. In the words of the Declaration of 1776, "to secure these rights, Governments are instituted among men": the new and explicit definition of national citizenship was aimed at making possible the fulfillment of that obligation. The equality of national citizens was expressly extended to *all* "persons" in the phrase (in the second sentence of the first section of the Fourteenth Amendment) that forbade "any state" to "deny to any person within its jurisdiction the equal protection of the laws." The "self-evident" truth of the Declaration, "that all men are created equal," was thus at last to be recognized by the Constitution.

The members of the congressional Joint Committee on Reconstruction had lived through years of pre-war state and local proslavery repression that had been immune from federal intervention. After they learned from their own official investigation and other sources that similar conditions persisted or were revived in parts of the nation reconstructed according to the ideas of Andrew Johnson, they wanted to secure federal power to act. They did not confine the new amendment's content to words pledging only equality of citizenship and personhood. They added language forbidding "any law which shall abridge the privileges and immunities of citizens" and they prohibited action by any state that would "deprive any person of life, liberty, or property, without due process of law."

These quoted phrases were not novel.** They were not made up on the spot as the Committee on Reconstruction was hammering out the Fourteenth Amendment. They are traceable to decades of debate and discussion, in print and from platform, initiated by the groups that sought to utilize or amend the Constitution to deal with slavery and the evils that it brought. Their leaders were concerned with the rights of the entire population, whether black or white, whether residing in slave state or free. Their interest ranged over the entire spectrum of rights that had been impaired in consequence of slavery: rights of free association and free speech, protection against unreasonable search and seizure, unlawful interrogation, cruel and unusual punishment. The expressions "privileges and immunities" and "due process of law" used by antislavery activists stymied by the ruling in *Barron v. Baltimore* seemed the best shorthand to employ when they had a chance to put words in the Constitution to repudiate that decision. This language would place the nation's reconstructed basic law in full accord with the Declaration of Independence, to achieve justice as well as equality. They concluded that one could not survive without the other.

** Their genesis, and how they came to be used in the Fourteenth Amendment, was traced most authoritatively by two scholars, Jacobus tenBroek and Howard Jay Graham. The latter's magisterial essays were collected in book form in a 1968 edition, *Everyman's Constitution*, marking the Centennial of the ratification of the Amendment.

Frustrated Objectives

These hopes of the "founding fathers" of the Fourteenth Amendment were not to be realized in their lifetime. They were to recede even further from realization for two more generations. One by one, their objectives were frustrated by a series of decisions of the Supreme Court that began with the *Slaughterhouse* cases of 1873, in which the Court ruled that the clause in the Fourteenth Amendment that prohibited states from abridging the privileges and immunities of citizens of the United States did not include the protection of ordinary civil liberties such as freedom of speech and press, religion, etc. Historian Charles Warren wrote of the ruling:

> It came as a tremendous shock and disappointment; for [the] intent in framing the language of the Amendment was directly contrary to the narrow construction now placed upon it by the Court.

The result: with few exceptions, the ideals of equality before the law, federal protective power, and national insurance of local compliance with the Bill of Rights went down together. There was one great exception: property could not be taken without "just compensation." Trivial exceptions, such as affirmation of the right to a jury selected without racial bars, were voiced but failed to receive effective enforcement. The Fifteenth Amendment's voting right guarantee was treated similarly. The Court's decisions reflected the national mood. The majority of the population viewed the reconciliation of sectional differences in the aftermath of the war as more important than respect for the rights newly incorporated in the Constitution.

Freed from constitutional restraint by the Court's decisions, much of the country reinstituted its caste system, reinforced by a rigidly imposed structure of segregation. By 1915, half a century after the end of the Civil War, the Fourteenth Amendment had been nullified as a bulwark of liberty, equality, and justice. The "new birth of freedom" for which President Lincoln had called, and for which, as he had said, so many had died, had been indefinitely postponed. But the presence of the words of the Fourteenth Amendment in the Constitution remained a guiding star, an objective for which many continued to strive.

Included among those who resisted the annulment of the Fourteenth Amendment was one staunch and determined Supreme Court justice, John Marshall Harlan of Kentucky, who sat on the Court from 1877 to 1911. His vigorous defense of every principle expressed in the Amendment gave heart to those who were to renew the struggle in the twentieth century. As much as any other justice in the Court's history, Harlan, in his dissenting opinions, appealed "to the brooding spirit of the law, to the intelligence of a future day," as he affirmed federal interest in the responsibility of the state governments to secure the civil liberties of their citizens, and to treat their citizens equally.

The "future day" that Justice Harlan must have hoped for as he wrote his magnificent dissents did come—but not overnight. The invigoration of the Amendment was a halting process, punctuated by more than one step backward. It began during the tenure of Edward D. White, a Confederate veteran who became Chief Justice in 1910 after sixteen years on the Court. It continued during the incumbency of every successor; it was the product of persistent efforts over half a century, beginning as we entered one world war and culminating in the aftermath of the second.

The dramatic renaissance of the Fourteenth Amendment began in 1917 under Chief Justice White with a Supreme Court decision invalidating an ordinance that extended segregation to the ownership of homes (*Buchanan v. Warley*). It continued under Chief Justice William Howard Taft in *Gitlow v. New York* (1925) which involved the prosecution of dissenters in the aftermath of World War I and which placed the states under the obligation to ensure the right of free speech.

Dramatic Renaissance

In the 1930s, a pair of cases arose from prosecutions in Scottsboro, Alabama, that established additional responsibilities for state governments in protecting civil liberties. Under the direction of Chief Justice Charles Evans Hughes, in 1932 (*Powell v. Alabama*) the Court extended the Sixth Amendment's right of counsel for criminal defendants to state capital prosecutions. In 1935, the Court forbade the racially motivated exclusion of persons from jury service (*Norris v. Alabama*). The practice had been barred by statute since 1875 but the law had not been enforced. A 1923 decision (*Moore v. Dempsey*) required states to guarantee a degree of due process, by invalidating a trial in which the jury had been coerced by threat of mob violence.

The effects of the renaissance whose beginnings have been described here have been pervasive, but not unanimously welcomed. Some have argued that the developments were "judge-made" law, twentieth-century modifications of the Con-

Thomas Nast cartoon, *Harper's Weekly*, September 1, 1866

stitution. Greater familiarity with constitutional history, its seamy side as well as its nobler aspects, would compel recognition that there has been a restoration of rights rather than the "creation of new rights."

There is urgent unfinished business: many injustices spring from long-standing disregard of the command of the Constitution. As the late Judge Kenneth Keating observed during the Centennial of the Fourteenth Amendment: "Our difficulties are not caused by the recent Supreme Court decisions, but by the fact that those decisions and the principles which they embody did not come decades earlier." From this lag arises a question that does not lend itself to an easy answer: to what extent is differential treatment warranted for remedial purposes?

The "affirmative action" controversy cannot be lightly resolved. But equitable answers conforming to constitutional mandates must take account of the history of their nullification. At an 1854 women's rights convention, abolitionist Thomas Wentworth Higginson argued that those "cramped, dwarfed and crippled" by oppression deserved "more than mere negative duty. . . . By as much as we have helped to wrong them, we have got to help right them."

It is possible to suggest that the long-postponed "new birth of freedom" had arrived approximately at the period of the relatively unobserved Centennial of the ratification of the Fourteenth Amendment in 1968. Birth is a beginning, not an achieving, and there is in a dynamic and ever-changing society always more to seek in order to fulfill the objects for which, according to the Declaration of Independence, governments are instituted among men.

The commemoration of the Constitution's two-hundredth birthday should surely include consideration of the extent to which it has been humanized by the Fourteenth and its sister amendments. The changes they have wrought in the relationship between the federal government, the states, and the people have created virtually a "Second Constitution."

In 1887, at the Centennial of the Constitution, journalist E. L. Godkin observed that the heroes of 1865 had completed what had been left unfinished in 1787, and the "next centennial" celebration would be focused as much on the one date as on the other. At the very least, we should reserve some time and attention for the framers of the Fourteenth Amendment, the founding fathers of 1866.

SUGGESTED ADDITIONAL READING

Richard C. Cortner, *The Supreme Court and the Second Bill of Rights* (1981).

La Wanda Cox and John H. Cox, *Politics, Principle, and Prejudice, 1865-1866: Dilemma of Reconstruction America* (1963).

Harold M. Hyman and William M. Wiecek, *Equal Justice Under Law: Constitutional Development, 1835-1875* (1982).

Eric L. McKitrick, *Andrew Johnson and Reconstruction* (1960).

Howard N. Meyer is an attorney and former special assistant to two attorneys general. He is the author of *The Amendment that Refused to Die* (Beacon Press, 1978) as well as biographies of Ulysses Grant and Thomas Wentworth Higginson.

Winning in the Courts: Interest Groups and Constitutional Change

Frank J. Sorauf

In 1924 the Congress proposed and sent to the states a constitutional amendment that would have authorized it to regulate, even outlaw, goods in interstate commerce made by child labor. By 1930 only five states had ratified it. Even with the impetus of the Depression and Franklin Roosevelt's victories in 1932 and 1936, only twenty-eight of the forty-eight states, eight short of the necessary thirty-six, had ratified it by the late 1930s. A powerful coalition of liberals, organized labor, women's groups, and urban reformers could not break through the social, religious, and economic conservatism that resisted the amendment in much of the country.

The child labor amendment had been born in frustration. Congress twice passed legislation to abolish the movement of child-made goods in interstate commerce, and twice the Supreme Court had struck down the statutes, once as an unlawful use of Congress' commerce power and once as an improper use of its power to tax (*Hammer v. Dagenhart*, 1918; *Bailey v. Drexel*, 1922). The second of those decisions, in fact, came only two years before the proposing of the amendment. But the movement that was strong enough twice to pass legislation and then see a constitutional amendment through a less than reformist Congress could not muster the national strength and the extraordinary majorities necessary to amend the Constitution.

In the end, though, it made little difference. The Supreme Court taketh away, but the Supreme Court giveth back. As a part of the Fair Labor Standards Act of 1938, the Congress once again outlawed the movement of goods made by children. Three years later the Court upheld the entire statute, conferring on the Congress the very powers that a national movement of impressive strength and persistence could not (*U.S. v. Darby* 1941). Included in the opinion of the majority in *Darby* was,

221

moreover, a renunciation of the very decision that had led to the amendment in the first place:

> The conclusion is inescapable that *Hammer v. Dagenhart* was a departure from the principles which have prevailed in the interpretation of the Commerce Clause both before and since the decision and that such vitality as a precedent, as it then had, has long since been exhausted. It should be and now is overruled.

Observers of constitutional politics could draw only some very familiar conclusions. Given the difficulty of the process of formal amendment, constitutional change falls largely to the Supreme Court. Moreover, in the Court one doesn't need mass movements or extraordinary majorities, but merely a suitable case, sympathetic justices, and a bit of strategic skill or luck.

Such lessons have not been lost on American interest groups. They have pursued the goals of constitutional change in the courts with increasing vigor and effectiveness in the last forty years. The trend has been especially marked among groups fighting for individual rights or equality of treatment. The National Association for the Advancement of Colored People (NAACP) and the American Civil Liberties Union (ACLU) have indeed come to symbolize the rise of group litigation for constitutional goals.

Finding the Right Question for the Answer

Two key words—"cases" and "controversies"—dot the convoluted phrases in Article III of the Constitution.

> The judicial power shall extend to all cases, in law and equity, arising under this Constitution, the laws of the United States, and treaties made, or which shall be made, under their authority; to all cases affecting ambassadors, other public ministers and consuls; . . . to controversies to which the United States shall be a party; to controversies between two or more states. . . .

The Supreme Court has always interpreted them to mean that it and the other federal courts would decide only genuinely adversary cases in which the parties had real and opposing interests. In other words, there must be, as the titles of cases suggest, someone against someone else—thus, no opinions about "possible" legality or constitutionality, no hypothetical questions, no answers to "let's suppose" questions. The federal courts, therefore, decide constitutional issues only when they are embedded in conflicts which the combatants bring to them.

If there is no legitimate "case," of course, an issue never comes to the Supreme Court. The Court never settled the

THE LABOR HERALD

Official Organ of The Trade Union Educational League

SUPREME COURT

JULY   99   25 CENTS

The Labor Herald, July 1922, on the Supreme Court decision striking down legislation prohibiting child labor

constitutionality of the Alien and Sedition Acts because the Jeffersonians repealed them before a conviction under them could reach the Supreme Court. Other issues have come tardily to the Court. The Supreme Court had no occasion to rule on the constitutionality of the 1940 Smith Act—which made it a crime to urge, advocate, or teach the overthrow of the United

States—until leaders of the American Communist party were convicted under the statute and appealed their conviction to the Court in 1951.

So, while the Supreme Court provides the constitutional answers, it is the litigants who ask the questions. In a real sense they control the Court's agenda, for while the justices can pick among the cases they are asked to decide, they cannot reach beyond them. For this reason the Court is often described as a passive body, the prisoner of both the issues and the factual settings others bring to it.

In setting the judicial agenda, litigating groups have two tasks: to convince the Court to take the case, and then to convince it to decide it "favorably." The first of the tasks is often more difficult, for the Supreme Court, in exercising its enormous discretion to pick and choose its cases, takes fewer than one in ten of those cases pressed upon it. Some of those cases—those on "appeal"—must be heard and decided, but in its much larger "certiorari" jurisdiction, federal statutes permit the Court to take what cases it wishes. (It is, therefore, very often pure bluster for disappointed litigants to threaten to "take this case all the way to the Supreme Court.")

The "case" then is the vehicle of litigating groups, and their relationship to it differs widely. At the maximum, a group may have organized all aspects of a case from the beginning—picking plaintiffs, providing lawyers, setting strategies, and paying costs. The NAACP, for example, sponsored all five desegregation cases that reached the Supreme Court in 1962 as *Brown v. Board of Education of Topeka.* But at the other extreme, a group may do no more than enter an existing case with a brief as a friend of the court, an "amicus curiae." (In Allan Bakke's celebrated challenge to the constitutionality of affirmative action programs, a record total of 116 organizations filed fifty-eight amicus briefs; *University of California v. Bakke,* 1978.) In between those two extremes lies an almost infinite variety of litigating roles. A group may "adopt" an existing case for its appeal to the Supreme Court in order to assure the best possible legal argument, for example, or it may advise the lawyers and plaintiffs in a case without assuming full responsibility for it.

While entry into a case as an amicus curiae permits the group only a written legal argument, the more extensive roles allow it to set the higher strategies of litigation. Full and early sponsorship of a case often permits the group to choose between federal and state courts, to select the plaintiffs in the case, to frame the facts and recruit expert testimony, to decide on the direction of the legal argument, and to provide the legal and organizational talent to carry the enterprise forward. In short, the greater the role in the case, the greater the opportunity for the strategic play and interaction with the courts.

Consider the NAACP and the Supreme Court as they approached the deciding of the desegregation cases between 1952 and 1955. The Court had already signalled its impatience with segregation by construing the prevailing "separate but equal" doctrine very literally. Texas had created a separate law school for blacks, but the Court found, not surprisingly, that it lacked the reputation, quality of faculty, and influential alumni (!) of the established law school at the University of Texas (*Sweatt v. Painter,* 1950). So, if the separate schools were not equal, integration was the alternative. Yet the "separate but equal" doctrine (*Plessy v. Ferguson,* 1896) still stood, and it was that nineteenth-century doctrine itself that was anathema to the NAACP.

The Warren Court, 1965

It was easy for the NAACP to seize the moment. It had brought that Texas case to the Court, just as it had brought a similar test of Oklahoma's segregated graduate study. Its New York legal staff, headed by Thurgood Marshall, and its network of cooperating attorneys in the states were in touch with local NAACP chapters and local controversies over black elementary and secondary education. Its desegregation cases in Kansas, Delaware, Virginia, South Carolina, and the District of Columbia were simply the next leg of a journey well under way. Those five cases, moreover, bore the unmistakable marks of NAACP sponsorship. The arguments of the lawyers in charge of each case had been sharpened in the usual NAACP rehearsals at the Howard Law School. All cases also used the same expert testimony to show the effect of segregation on the self-esteem of black children. (The experts, though, did differ from case to case; the best known of them, Kenneth Clark, testified in only two of the five cases.)

At the same time, however, the NAACP was able to present the Supreme Court with a useful diversity of findings and arguments. Three of the cases depicted distinctly inferior black schools, but the trial judge in the Kansas case found the separate school systems substantially equal. In the D.C. case the black plaintiffs had not even bothered to allege any disparities, preferring the more aggressive argument that segregation per se was unconstitutional. In these latter two cases, in other words, relief for the black plaintiffs was possible only if the Supreme Court were to overturn the "separate but equal" doctrine, which it did.

The Group Role: How Strong the Trend?

Once set of cases, no matter how celebrated, does not make a trend or movement. Just how common is group participation in constitutional litigation, and when indeed did it begin? Certainly it began well before the American public became aware of it. Clement Vose, for example, has described the work of the National Consumers' League in defending wage and hour legislation in American courts as early as 1907. (The group strategy then was the reverse of today's; legislatures were willing to pass maximum hour and minimum wage laws, but such legislation needed the most persuasive defense to survive challenges in more conservative courts.) It was, in fact, Florence Kelley and Josephine Goldmark of the League who recruited the Boston attorney Louis Brandeis (Miss Goldmark's brother-in-law) to argue the cause of the state legislation. With him they fashioned the detailed, factual brief that came to bear his name. After Brandeis' appointment to the Supreme Court, the resourceful Kelley and Goldmark found a young Felix Frankfurter to take up some of his work.

Whatever the past of group litigation, there is every reason to think it has increased over the last generation or two. Examining all noncommercial cases that came to the Supreme Court from 1928 to 1980, Karen O'Connor and Lee Epstein find that the percentage of cases with amicus curiae briefs has risen sharply from less than two percent of the cases between 1928 and 1940 to more than 53 percent from 1970 to 1980. That latter percentage, however, masks variations in the rates of amici in specific kinds of noncommercial cases. They are at two-thirds or above for cases of race or sex discrimination, for example, but only 37 percent in criminal cases.

As useful as those data are, they leave some questions unanswered. They don't specify the rate of amicus participation in commercial cases; by the accounts of all observers, it is far lower. They also don't separate constitutional litigation from the total load of the Court; observers, though, would expect amici to be more common in cases hinging on the Constitution. Finally, these data on amici record the growth of only the least important of group roles.

Florence Kelley

For a fuller picture of group involvement one focuses on a single area of constitutional litigation, the establishment of religion clause, for example. Between 1951 and 1971, a total of sixty-seven cases raising constitutional issues of the separation of church and state reached the U.S. Supreme Court, the federal courts of appeal, or the highest courts of the states. Twelve of them involved publicly supported bus rides for pupils of religious schools, and ten resulted from prayer or Bible-reading in the public schools. Others grew out of a wide variety of disputes—tax exemptions for religious property, public support for religious schools and hospitals, and a cross in a public park among them.

As that total of sixty-seven cases suggests, the fifties and sixties were the period in which the meaning of the "no establishment" clause was first developed systematically. By the most generous count, the Supreme Court had decided only four church-state cases in the 160 years before 1950. In just the next two decades, it decided ten.

Stationed in the middle of this swirl of constitutional litigation were three national groups: the American Civil Liberties Union (ACLU), the American Jewish Congress (AJC), and Americans United for Separation of Church and State (AU). The first came to separationism from secular humanism, the second from reform Judaism, and the third from conservative Protestantism. Individually or in alliance they participated in fifty-one of the sixty-seven cases (76 percent), and at least one had a role in all ten cases that the Supreme Court decided.

Despite the different sources of their separationism, the three groups divided only once in these sixty-seven cases—a case on tax exemptions for property owned by religious groups. The ACLU opposed all such exemptions, but AU favored them if the property was used for religious purposes; the AJC was divided internally and therefore silent. Both AU and the AJC drew membership support from religious congregations; the ACLU did not. In truth, differences over the meaning of separation did surface in another issue: the hiring of Roman Catholic nuns as teachers in public schools. AU opposed it per se; the other two groups opposed it only if the nuns engaged in religious teaching or proselyting. Their differences were at least one reason why the issue was never brought to the Supreme Court.

Cooperation among the three groups was much more seriously impeded by their conflicting goals for constitutional litigation. For the AJC they were scrupulously legal: favorable judicial precedents and thus influence over the direction of constitutional development. The national organization of the ACLU agreed; its litigation guide explained:

> The ACLU cannot take every case where there is a civil liberties question being raised. Rather, it should direct its efforts to cases which have some reasonable promise of having broad impact on other cases. Thus, it is always appropriate to take a case which offers the possibility of establishing new civil liberties precedents which will control other cases.

But local ACLU affiliates and the local chapters of AU frequently wanted to press litigation for sheer vindication of their separationist position. Moreover, litigation often offered organization-building possibilities. Local publicity and fund-raising benefited from participation in a deeply felt crusade in the courts. The result was litigation and appeals of litigation that the AJC considered reckless and even irresponsible.

Despite different goals and philosophies, the three separationist groups worked cooperatively in many cases and shared a collective wisdom about strategies in them. They certainly agreed on the wisdom of entering a case as soon as possible. In these sixty-seven cases, one or more of the groups were sponsors—"present at the creation," as it were—in twenty and something more than amici in another twenty-one. They preferred plaintiffs who came to their separationist position from religious conviction, who were stable members of the community, and who preferred anonymity to publicity. Increasingly they came to prefer bringing their cases in federal courts, because they usually provided a speedier and less costly route to the Supreme Court than state courts and because their judges were more sympathetic to separationist arguments and more willing to let the plaintiffs build a full factual record.

The most challenging moments for these three groups—for all litigating groups—involved the grander strategies. Ought an issue to be taken to the Supreme Court in the first place? To risk losing a case is to risk a greater loss: an unfavorable precedent that decides other cases. What ought a group to do about an unfavorable precedent, such as the Court's decision from the 1940s permitting public funding for transportation to religious schools? Attack it or work around it? Despite some reservation from AU, the groups chose the latter course, attacking bus rides instead in those states—

"UNION IS STRENGTH."

DISTRIBUTION OF THE SECTARIAN FUND.

SECTARIAN BITTERNESS.

OUR COMMON SCHOOLS AS THEY ARE AND AS THEY MAY BE.—[SEE PAGE 141.]

Thomas Nast cartoon, Harper's Weekly, February 26, 1870

Wisconsin, Oregon, and Hawaii, for instance—where the state constitutions erected higher walls of separation.

Such strategy touches also the pacing, timing, and sequencing of issues. In the words of a short-lived agreement among the ACLU, AU, and AJC:

> It would be desirable if the next case to come to the Supreme Court dealing with aid to sectarian schools showed a substantially higher degree of aid than busses down the road to full aid. Our best chance of turning it away from that road is to pose an issue requiring a large step or none.

The most skillful litigation groups, in other words, play something of a constitutional chess game, trying always to limit the options or force the moves of the Court.

However, not even three purposeful, national groups can control an entire universe of constitutional litigation. Some cases emerge and are decided too rapidly for group intervention. The challenge of the Louisiana Teachers Association to the state's aid to parochial schools in 1970 was filed on September 8 in a local court, removed to the state supreme court, and then argued before that court on September 25. More often, local groups or individuals begin ill-conceived litigation and cannot be talked out of it. The litigation of Madalyn Murray O'Hair is a series of cases in point. Her earthy and combative style, her desire not to have co-plaintiffs, her ties to organized atheism, and her insistence on dominating her cases all made her an unacceptable collaborator. (She also considered the ACLU, AU, and AJC unacceptable allies.) Moreover, the quality of the legal work and the records of fact in her cases were at best unpredictable.

There is, of course, another side to all this church-state litigation: the groups that seek some form of government support for religion (the "accommodationists"). Since the Roman Catholic church operated the vast majority of religious schools in the country, the chief organization on the "other" side was the arm of the Catholic bishops, the U.S. Catholic Conference. However, the structure of church-state litigation inevitably cast some hapless school board, legislature, or other public authority in the role of defendant, rather than the Catholic Conference or another "accommodationist" group. The Catholic Conference had to create a place for itself in the cases as a codefendant, an intervening defendant, or an informal partner or advisor to the defendants. It is rarely easy, in other words, to translate adversarial group conflict into adversarial litigation.

The Ingredients of Group Success

How is it that group litigation of constitutional issues has flourished? In part because the Supreme Court has blessed it. As the NAACP worked for enforcement of the desegregation decision in the South, a number of states retaliated. Virginia charged the organization's lawyers under old laws making barratry (the exciting or encouraging of litigation) a crime. In the final resolution of the case, the U.S. Supreme Court ruled that the activities of the NAACP were forms of political activity protected by the First Amendment and thus not subject to Virginia's law (*NAACP v. Button,* 1963). Wrote Justice Brennan:

> In the context of NAACP objectives, litigation is not a technique of resolving private differences; it is a means for achieving the lawful objectives of equal treatment by all government, federal, state, and local, for the members of the Negro community in this country. It is thus a form of political expression. Groups which find themselves unable to achieve their objectives through the ballot frequently turn to the courts.

Although the 1963 decision came well after the growth of litigating groups, it protected their gains.

Group litigation flourishes also because the groups are good at it. Not many plaintiffs command the legal expertise and experience that Thurgood Marshall and Leo Pfeffer exemplify. Pfeffer, of the American Jewish Congress, was not only the most experienced advocate in church-state law, but a major scholar in the field as well. Interest groups as well have the persistence, the memory, and the long-range view that enable them to see beyond the immediate case or incident. They also have the resources for litigation. It is not that they are wealthy. They are not, but their resources are at the disposal of constitutional litigation, and those of most wealthy Americans are not. To take a major case to the Supreme Court may require a cash outlay well into six figures. The central question is not whether a litigant is able to pay, but whether he, she, or it is willing to pay.

Perhaps the greatest asset of the litigating group is the trust of the courts, born both of respect and of need. Since groups develop better records of fact and make better legal arguments than do individual plaintiffs, the courts depend greatly on them, especially in constitutional cases. That fact probably accounts to a great extent for the success of litigating groups in getting their cases into the Supreme Court. Courts also know that groups will pay attention to the cues they give. When some justices of the Supreme Court became convinced that they had erred in permitting local school districts to force young Jehovah's Witnesses to salute the flag and indicated so in a footnote in a later case (*Jones v. Opelika,* 1942) they must surely have been confident that lawyers for the Witnesses would read the footnote and act on it.

The group role in constitutional litigation continues to expand. In part its growth reflects the increasing mobilization of interests, the explosion of group politics, in American political life. In part, too, it reflects the expanding agenda of American politics. Issues such as those of the environment, equality for women, abortion, and freedom of sexual preference have only lately become dominant, and each has brought new groups into litigation. As a consequence, group activity enjoys a support and respectability it never did in earlier decades. The Ford Foundation, for instance, has made substantial grants to several groups litigating cases on women's rights.

Group Litigation in the Eighties

Explanations for the growth of the group role, however, cannot ignore the increasing willingness of the courts themselves to be agents of constitutional change. That willingness, even eagerness, to seize and decide controversial issues, to use the judicial power actively, inevitably encourages constitutional litigation. Judicial "activism" means easier access to the courts and a greater likelihood that judges will address the policy concerns of litigants. Innovating judges thus attract innovating litigants.

Group litigation today is expanding in another significant way. It combines the more conventional litigating of constitutional questions with litigation based on legislation. The 1970s especially saw the growth of rights and statuses in congressional legislation. So, while women's groups continue to legislate under the "equal protection" clause of the Fourteenth Amendment, they also litigate under the sections of the Civil Rights Act forbidding discrimination because of sex. Groups such as the environmentalists, moreover, have virtually no constitutional bases for their claims; of necessity they are largely limited to litigating statutory issues.

In their pursuit of constitutional goals, some groups succeed and some do not. Their litigation, however, does have an important and inevitable consequence beyond their individual goals: it alters the very judicial process it seeks to influence. Litigating groups have helped create public expectations that courts should and will be active, unabashed agents of constitutional change. They fuel the very judicial activism they reflect. Their skill in litigating also increases the pace of litigation, bringing one difficult question after another to the courts, especially to the U.S. Supreme Court. By bringing the courts more often into policy disputes, they leave them more and more vulnerable to the displeasure of losers in the disputes. In short, now that the struggle and competition among groups over public policy has come to the courts, neither the groups nor the courts will ever be the same again. Nor will the Constitution.

SUGGESTED ADDITIONAL READING

Richard C. Cortner, *The Supreme Court and the Second Bill of Rights* (1981).

Richard Kluger, *Simple Justice: The History of Brown v. Board of Education and Black America's Struggle for Equality* (1976).

Michael Meltsner, *Cruel and Unusual: The Supreme Court and Capital Punishment* (1973).

Karen O'Connor, *Women's Organizations' Use of the Courts* (1980).

Frank J. Sorauf, *The Wall of Separation: The Constitutional Politics of Church and State* (1976).

Clement E. Vose, *Caucasians Only* (1959).

Clement E. Vose, *Constitutional Change* (1972).

Frank J. Sorauf is professor of political science at the University of Minnesota. In addition to his work on the judicial process he writes on political parties and campaign finance.

VI. War Powers
and the Presidency

235

War Powers of the President and Congress: Who Decides Whether America Fights?

W. Taylor Reveley III

How does the Constitution divide control over war and peace between the president and Congress? That question has troubled Americans from George Washington's administration to Ronald Reagan's. Controversy today over Lebanon, Grenada, and Nicaragua replays hundreds of similar arguments in times past. The president and Congress have struggled for almost two hundred years over the war powers. They have quarreled, for instance, about the extent to which the Constitution gives each branch control over remaining neutral in the wars of other nations, stationing our troops on foreign soil, deciding when to send American forces into combat, setting military strategy and tactics, and making peace.

War power developments of the last twenty years have been unusually important. Spurred by the combination of Vietnam and Watergate, Congress took two unprecedented steps in the early 1970s. For the first time in American history, Congress used its appropriations power to force the president to withdraw from a major conflict. The final legislation, passed in 1974, banned the use of federal funds for any "military or paramilitary operations" "in," "over," or "off the shores of" the whole of Vietnam, Laos, and Cambodia. Also, despite Richard Nixon's bitter veto, Congress adopted the War Powers Resolution of 1973, which established procedure for how the president and Congress are to go about deciding whether to fight. No such procedures had previously existed. The constitutionality of some of them remains unclear.

Not unclear is that the United States needs to improve the ways in which it decides when and how to use its military abroad. That need existed in 1789. It is even more acute today

237

because of the radical change since 1789 in our capacity and will to use force abroad and in the potential consequences of doing so. With this background, we turn to the origins of the war powers in the text of the Constitution, its framers' and ratifiers' debates, and events during Washington's presidency.

The Allocation of War Powers

The text of the Constitution is not very helpful in resolving most disputes about the war powers. Many of its crucial provisions are vague. What are the implications, for example, of Congress' power "to make rules for the government and regulation" (Article I, section 8, clause 14) of the military and of the president's "executive power" (Article II)? The Constitution also gives certain prerogatives to the president and others to Congress that can be read as conflicting. Competition is most intense between "Congress shall have power to declare war" (Article I, section 8, clause 11) and "the president shall be commander in chief of the army and navy of the United States" (Article II, section 2, clause 1). In addition to ill-defined, often competitive provisions, there are numerous gaps in the Constitution's war power provisions. It says nothing directly, for instance, about which branch controls deploying ships on the high seas, stationing troops on foreign soil, or declaring neutrality in other nations' struggles.

The debates of the Constitution's framers and ratifiers do help clarify some uncertainties. But these men did not spend much time on questions of war and peace. When they did, they emphasized state versus federal authority, not congressional versus executive. Danger to America from state excesses in foreign affairs had helped bring the Constitutional Convention to Philadelphia in 1787. Since colonial days the states had been reluctant to bear their fair shares of military burdens unless actually attacked, but willing themselves to provoke Indians, European powers, and their sister states. Separate diplomatic activity by them and their violations of national treaties were frequent. This disunity and provocative behavior invited foreign aggression. Jefferson wrote Washington early in the Philadelphia Convention about the need "to make our states as one to all foreign concerns," and Madison concluded that "if we are to be one nation in any respect, it clearly ought to be in respect to other nations."

The skimpy attention given congressional and executive war powers in 1787-1788 resulted from the short shrift given foreign affairs as a whole. The only aspects that received real attention were war and treaties. Emphasis went to treaties because peace was expected to be the customary state for the new nation. America would avoid aggressive war abroad and enjoy in turn "an insulated situation" from the great powers of Europe. In Alexander Hamilton's words: "Europe is at a great distance from us. Her colonies in our vicinity will be likely to continue too much disproportioned in strength to be able to give us any dangerous annoyance. Extensive military establishments cannot in this position be necessary to our security." This placid view of foreign relations precluded any focused look at the use of American force abroad, except for defensive naval action to protect the Atlantic coast and American commerce.

In fact, what the framers and ratifiers feared most was that the executive would use the military for tyrannical

Scene at the Signing of the Constitution

purposes at home, possibly to make himself a hereditary prince, not that he would use it for dangerous foreign adventures. Debate centered on whether it was safe to allow the president to command troops personally in the field, whether he might use standing armies to overthrow the republic, and whether he should be allowed to pardon traitors since their crimes might be efforts to help him seize power. Indeed, for some of the framers and ratifiers, the demons lurking in military matters were not even executive, but rather congressional: the legislators were said to hold both the purse and the sword, and thus were feared as incipient military despots. For these constitutional delegates the remedy was an America wholly dependent on state militia, state officers, and state military appropriations.

In short, the problems and assumptions of 1787-1788 did not anticipate all of ours. They were those of a small, divided people eager for national unity but fearful of federal tyranny. Domestic rebellion and foreign invasion were their "war" concerns. More important for them were safeguards against a military coup at home than military preparedness during peace. Greatly more than we, they valued state authority over national, legislative power over executive. They preferred peace and political isolation to a world made safe for America. The institutional arrangements developed in 1787-1788 reflected these values and needs. A small, elite branch of Congress (the Senate) was planned as a full participant with the president in whatever American diplomacy might arise. State militia were to be the backbone of national defense and Congress the arbiter of military policy, by governing the very existence of American armed forces and their commitment to conflict. The states and president would serve as interim defenders against sudden attack, pending opportunity for congressional decision; and the executive would act as first general and admiral when the legislators voted to fight.

The framers and ratifiers did intend a more effective national executive than had previously existed, influenced by their understanding of European practice and political theory, by prior legislative excesses in America, and by the dismal executive record of Revolutionary and Confederation legislatures. They wanted presidential aid in conducting negotiations, gathering intelligence, and in framing recommendations. They hoped to obtain an executive check on foolish or venal legislators, and they wanted the president to execute national policy. But with rare exception the framers and ratifiers did not mean to surrender congressional control over setting American policy and providing tools for its implementation. Their model was Parliament's seventeenth-century steps to curb the British king, and throughout their debates ran a persistent fear of executive despotism.

More specifically, the 1787-1788 debates show that the country was meant to be able to fight without a formal declaration of war, but not without prior congressional approval unless America was suddenly attacked. The framers and ratifiers also meant for the country to be able to use armed force on a limited basis, as well as for general hostilities. Defensive or retaliatory use of force, the sorts expected for America by the men of 1787-1788, tended in that era to be undeclared, limited engagements. In addition, the word "declare" was used loosely by the framers in ways equating it with "begin" or "authorize." Their grant of authority to Congress "to declare" war almost certainly was intended to give Congress control over all involvement of American forces in combat, except in response to sudden attack on this country.

In case of sudden attack, the text of the Constitution suggests that the framers expected state militia to bear the major brunt until Congress could act. Thus, the states are permitted to "engage in war" without prior congressional authorization if "actually invaded, or in such imminent danger as will not admit of delay" (Article I, section 10, clause 3). The only equivalent authority for the president comes not from the Constitution itself, but rather from a brief, confusing debate during the Philadelphia Convention that ended with the framers substituting the word "declare" for the word "make" in the Constitution's provision empowering Congress to declare war.

But if Congress could now "declare" rather than "make" war, it is not likely that the substitution implied much gain in the president's power. George Mason with his presidential phobias voted for the substitution, and the change later went through the ratification controversies unmentioned by the most rabid foes of the executive. The substitution may have been designed simply to prevent Congress from asserting control over the *conduct,* as well as the *initiation,* of a conflict. More likely, even if the change was intended to authorize emergency military action by the president, no mention was made of his defending against *imminent* attack, much less of his defending anything abroad. Most happily viewed for presidential war power, then, the framers' substitution of "declare" for "make" permits executive response to ongoing physical attack on American territory—conceivably, also, preemptive strikes by the president against impending attack—until Congress can decide what further steps should be taken.

The commander-in-chief clause, in turn, received little attention during the ratifying conventions. It was viewed as a modest grant of authority. Hamilton's limited "first general and admiral" interpretation reflected the consensus. During hostilities the president would set strategy and tactics, and his authority would inevitably grow during military crisis. But he would not commit America to hostilities except by signing authorizing legislation; and he would not make peace except as a participant with the Senate in the treaty process. Those who fought the commander-in-chief clause did so for fear that the president would use the army at home to make himself a tyrant. The Federalists replied with the need for single command during war, a lesson of the Revolution, and with the danger of placing it in an ambitious general rather than a civilian with a fixed term of office. They said that only the rare president would personally command troops and, anyway, there would be none for him to command unless Congress provided them.

Gouverneur Morris

Strong evidence exists that the framers and ratifiers expected the Senate, no less than the president, to govern those aspects of American foreign relations not committed to Congress as a whole. As the Constitution was being drafted, the Senate was given sole responsibility over treaties and ambassadors until the last two weeks of the Philadelphia Convention, when the president was suddenly joined with the Senate in dealing with both. The executive's capacity to receive foreign diplomats was ignored during the Philadelphia debates and dismissed as meaningless during the ratification process, and there was no suggestion that "the executive power" of Article II, section 1 conveyed authority over anything, other than the matters expressly assigned to the president by the Constitution.

But the 1780s were two hundred years ago, and we cannot know what the framers and ratifiers would have said in light of today's realities. What if they had realized that peace and isolation would not be America's customary condition; that the hazards, pace, and complexity of international affairs would burgeon, along with the country's capacity and need to influence events abroad; that treaties would not be the guts of our foreign relations; that the Senate would never be able to keep up with the president in diplomacy; that state militia could not replace federal forces; that the regular military would grow huge and stand during peace, little restrained by the need for

Congress to raise and fund it; and that the loyalty of naturalized citizens, the navigation of the Mississippi River, and other issues vital in the late 1700s would quickly fade?

We have only a sketchy idea, in any event, of what the constitutional delegates did say during the drafting and ratifying conventions of 1787-1788. The surviving records of their debates are often skimpy and confusing.

Further, fifty-five men participated in the four months of deliberation in Philadelphia, and many more took part in the state ratifying conventions. Interpretation of specific language varied among delegates. Because the Philadelphia Convention met in secret and its participants said little about it during the ratification process, delegates to the state conventions knew little about the views of the framers. It is not likely that most of those who voted in the federal and state conventions for the Constitution's war power provisions had a clearcut, common "intent" about their meaning.

Finally, the framers may have drafted with deliberate ambiguity, as a means of producing agreement among fractious delegates. Gouverneur Morris, very influential in drafting the final version of the document, explained that "it became necessary to select phrases which, pressing my own notions, would not alarm others." For men whose overriding objective was ratification of a constitution promising a more viable union, the precise meaning to be given ambiguous but generally acceptable language could await resolution in practice.

Objectives

In short, conclusions about the framers' and ratifiers' intent must be viewed with a cold and suspicious eye. Still, they do seem to have had certain basic objectives in mind. These objectives remain as compelling now as in 1787-1788. They are:

First, to ensure national defense. The Constitution empowers Congress to tax, to "provide for the common defense," and to call out the militia to "suppress insurrections and repel invasions." Habeas corpus may be suspended "when in cases of rebellion or invasion the public safety may require it." The states are guaranteed federal protection against invasion and permitted to fight without congressional authorization if in acute danger. Many congressional powers run to the care and tending of the national military, and the president is made commander in chief to ensure its effective use, including response to sudden attack. The Constitution flatly seeks the physical safety of the country. The defensive advantage of

American unity proved a prime selling point for the document during its struggle for ratification.

Second, to hinder use of the military for domestic tyranny. The framers and ratifiers were adamant that the war powers not encourage federal trampling on state and individual rights. The Constitution limits the purposes for which Congress may use state militia and provides that "a well regulated militia, being necessary to the security of a free state, the right of the people to keep and bear arms, shall not be infringed." It limits congressional army appropriations to two years, makes the commander in chief a civilian, and narrowly restricts suspension of habeas corpus.

Third, to hinder the use of the military for aggression abroad. Naively even for their own times, the framers and ratifiers anticipated peace for America. Exhausted by the Revolution, aware of the country's weakness, and inclined toward peace in principle, they hoped to avoid the perils of conflict unless they were unavoidably thrust upon the nation.

Fourth, to create and maintain national consensus behind American action for war or peace. The framers and ratifiers knew the burdens imposed on the country's prior military and diplomatic efforts by internal bickering. Based on experience during the Revolution and Confederation, they knew that if most citizens do not at least acquiesce in national policy, the country plunges into controversy, with grim impact on its effectiveness.

Fifth, to ensure democratic control over war and peace policy. Many of the framers and ratifiers felt public judgment was uninformed, irrational, and fickle. Similar fears were voiced about the House of Representatives as against the Senate and president. Because popular wisdom was thought to be especially lacking in foreign affairs, steps were taken to leave American diplomacy to the Senate and executive, neither of whom was directly elected by the voters under the 1787-1788 arrangements.

Nonetheless, consent of the governed was crucial to the framers and ratifiers. They feared the Senate and president precisely because of their separation from the people. Accordingly, the most fundamental war and peace decisions—whether to enter hostilities—were placed squarely under congressional control, and the House was awarded special power over federal money: one of the most basic tools of war.

Sixth, to encourage rational war and peace decisions. When to negotiate or fight, what to concede or demand, present the best-intentioned politicians with difficult choices as they try to protect America. The importance of rational decisions figured in the constitutional delegates' opposition to Confederation government and in their concern for an institutionally elite Senate and executive. They wanted informed, well-considered policy on war and peace.

Seventh, to permit continuity in American war and peace policy, when desirable, and its revision as necessary. Continuity leads to national credibility and predictability, both important to assure allies, deter enemies, and produce agreements with other countries. The framers and ratifiers worried about prior harm from the states' disruption of American foreign policy and from the inconsistency of Confederation Congresses. In matters of war and peace they recognized that discontinuity is safer by choice than by internal disarray and that a timely change in policy often has importance equal to its timely initiation. During the earliest years under the Constitution, the country backed away from military alliance with France, a step traumatic but calculated to avoid destruction of the fledgling republic in European struggles.

Eighth, to ensure American capacity to move toward war or peace rapidly or secretly when necessary, flexibly and proportionately always. There is often a need for speed and secrecy in negotiations and in the conduct of action, occasionally also in its initiation or termination. Flexibility (the capacity to act in a manner responsive to emerging circumstances) and proportionality (the avoidance of too little or too much reaction) are always vital to matters as intolerant of error as war and peace. The Constitution's text reflects concern for speed and secrecy in the provisions for anti-invasion action by states and for withholding sensitive congressional action from the public. The debate in 1787-1788 on the reflexes of the Senate and executive showed a keen appreciation of the objectives in question, as did the substitution of "declare" for "make" in the declaration-of-war clause so as to permit emergency action by the president to defend the country.

Ninth, to permit action for war or peace that has not yet been blessed by national consensus or democratic control. Sometimes public opinion of the moment is seriously wrong about how best to defend the country. To a limited extent, the constitutional delegates did expect the president and Senate in particular to act despite public opinion if essential in their view to the national interest.

Tenth, to permit the efficient setting and executing of war and peace policy. Consistent failure on either count undermines the wisest attempts at action. Bumbling national government invited constitution making in 1787-1788. Effective federal action in military and foreign affairs was a basic objective of the framers and ratifiers.

A strain of incompatibility does run among these ten war power objectives. Even if the national government were still a one-house assembly with both legislative and executive powers, it could not pay equal attention at once to speed and secrecy on the one hand and consensus and democratic control on the other. This incompatibility becomes more pronounced when the legislative and executive branches are separate, as they have been since 1789, each with a different ability to achieve the same objectives. For instance, a bow toward Congress as best to serve consensus and democratic control turns a back on the president and his comparative advantage for speed and secrecy. Which interests are to be preferred, since all cannot be sought with *equal* importance *at once?* The country has struggled mightily for an answer for almost two centuries.

With George Washington's inauguration, the United States quickly faced the vague language, grants of competing authority, and outright gaps in the war power provisions of the Constitution. Answers to many questions were needed if the new government was to operate. During a revolt at home might the president appear in the field, leave the seat of federal government to do so, and wield the pardon power to hasten peace? Might the executive wage war on threatening Indians without prior congressional approval? Which branch was to decide whether the United States would recognize the revolutionary French regime? Which was to interpret the Franco-American alliance and act on whether America would remain neutral in the ongoing European conflict? How were our military and diplomatic establishments to be created, organized, and administered? And what was to be the relationship among the president, Senate, and House in treaty making, in controlling official channels of communication with other nations, and in otherwise setting American diplomatic and military policy?

President Washington

On these and other scores, Washington's eight years as president provided the country with one of its richest troves of war power precedent. The president soon began to dominate American communications with other governments and the setting of our foreign policy, including the determination of when and how to negotiate treaties and whether to become involved in foreign conflicts. The Senate never grasped the diplomatic role expected for it during the constitutional conventions. The president also took the lead in setting American military policy, though with greater deference to Congress than on the diplomatic front. At times, however, Washington chose to fight without clearly having prior congressional authorization. And during the Whiskey Rebellion of 1794, the president did appear in the field, at the head of the national forces, using both his presence on horseback and his pardon power to quell the revolt.

The legislators, in turn, set up diplomatic and military establishments through which the president could work his will (a federal army of 840 men when Washington took office had grown to 7,108 when he left). Congress often provided the president with sweeping delegations of authority over diplomatic and military matters. It acquiesced in his withholding

from Congress of certain sensitive information, and it agreed
that the president alone might remove (and thus control) senior
executive officials, though their appointment required the
consent of the Senate. While Congress did wield far more
influence over American war and peace in the late 1700s than
it does now, its influence even then paled in comparison to the
congressional dominance anticipated by the framers and
ratifiers. Indeed, the first eight years of experience under the
Constitution split the war powers between the president and
Congress in ways more similar to their division in 1985 than to
the division sketched by the constitutional conventions in 1787-
1788.

W. Taylor Reveley III is a partner in the law firm of Hunton & Williams, Richmond,
Virginia. He studied the war powers while at the Woodrow Wilson International Center
for Scholars and the Council on Foreign Relations. This article was based upon his
book, *War Powers of the President and Congress: Who Holds the Arrows and Olive
Branch?* (University Press of Virginia, 1981).

War Powers in Nineteenth-Century America: Abraham Lincoln and His Heirs

Harold M. Hyman

As the Constitution's Bicentennial approaches, we learn painfully that sensitive public issues such as war powers cannot easily be resolved by neat references to specific clauses of the Constitution. A century and a quarter ago, Lincoln's generation tested the purposes to which president, Congress, and Supreme Court might apply or restrain the war powers. Perhaps this review of their experiences will help us to move closer to a point the poet T. S. Eliot described in his last *Quartet:* "The end of our exploring will be to arrive where we started and see the place for the first time."

"King Linkum I," according to antiwar Democrats, was a racemixing dictator who aimed to centralize, militarize, and mongrelize the Union of states. This description of Lincoln as dictator began to be heard very soon after the Civil War began. In order to prevent Washington from becoming entirely encircled by pro-secession state governments in Maryland and Delaware, and to ensure the transit of loyal troops to the isolated capital, Lincoln, beginning in April 1861, ordered federal soldiers to arrest activist secessionists, saboteurs, and guerrillas in those areas. In peacetime, such activities would have been clearly unconstitutional. He later extended similar temporary orders to other northern areas of uncertain allegiance. And, as Union soldiers occupied parcels of Dixie, Lincoln transformed such early improvisations into coherent policies on military governments, military emancipations, and military reconstructions of state governments. He based them all on the Constitution's scattered clauses on the war powers, those of the commander in chief, and other emergency provisions.

A Military Dictator

249

The Democrats' charges about military dictatorship received endorsement from the chief justice of the Supreme Court only weeks after the Civil War started. Among the civilians that Union troops arrested by Lincoln's authority was John Merryman, the young son of an influential Maryland family. Merryman was an avowed secessionist who, when arrested, was reportedly engaged in preparing an armed troop for Confederate service, an action not then a state or even a federal crime except under the Constitution's unworkable treason clause. Federal soldiers jailed him in historic Fort McHenry. This allegedly guiltless "prisoner of state," though locked up in an "American Bastille," nevertheless enjoyed access to his family's lawyer (a globally unique privilege, then or since, for captives in civil wars). The lawyer rushed to Washington and returned to Baltimore with the chief justice of the United States, Roger B. Taney, himself a Marylander and a devout Democrat. Taney held a special session of his circuit court in order to hear a petition, captioned *Ex parte Merryman,* for the prisoner's release on a habeas corpus writ. On Lincoln's orders, the fort's commander refused to honor Taney's writ. The chief justice thereupon lambasted the president in an opinion that he had printed in the newspapers, creating a deep well of constitutional rhetoric from which anti-administration spokesmen drew support.

Taney insisted in *Merryman* that no war existed because the Constitution allowed only Congress to declare war. Therefore the military arrests were twice illegal, first, because, legally, there was no war, and second, because only Congress had the power to suspend the habeas corpus writ. Aside from the swollen role for the judiciary this opinion asserted, Tancy's interpretation treated the Constitution as inelastic and not adaptable save through the fixed procedures of amendments: Its separations of power and functions between the branches of government were high and unbridgeable, and its provisions for emergencies, though written in 1787, were the only ones that authorities of 1861 might use. Though Lincoln refused to obey the chief justice, Taney's *Merryman* opinion received such warm reception in Union states, especially among Democratic lawyers, that Lincoln sometimes despaired about the failure of constitutional history to offer remedies for present ills.

Had Lincoln obeyed Taney in May 1861, the Confederacy conceivably could have won its bid for independence. Lincoln's surprising readiness to act in the existing crisis awoke leaders of the legal community and the general public from the despair into which many had descended during the secession winter. Excited by Lincoln's vigor and forthrightness, constitutional specialists responded quickly and accurately that civil wars were never declared, that gray areas existed between declared and undeclared wars, and that Lincoln's policies sustained

Abraham Lincoln

Roger B. Taney

Chief Justice Taney

rather than threatened Congress and the courts. Republican legalists insisted that though jurists might create constitutional abstractions, more accountable officials had to deal with the real world. Republicans said the Taney formula offered the nation no relevant means of self-defense against secession activists, and that the Constitution had to allow alternatives between acquiescence in national dismemberment and dictatorship.

Clearly individuals suffered from the arrests and other war power policies. But it appears that their imprisonments were brief, uncruel, and open rather than secret. Political criticism flourished everywhere in Union states during the War and Reconstruction years, and competitive two-party politics travelled to occupied southern states in the Union army's knapsacks. The dynamic war aims of Lincoln's party came to center on enlarging, not diminishing the electorates of both the Union states and the crumpling Confederate states. Unrigged, calendared elections and unfettered courts, including Taney's, operated almost as if no war existed. Neither Congress nor the majority of Union voters, in overwhelmingly fair elections, repudiated Lincoln, his policies, or his party, even after he used the war power to free slaves, recruit blacks into Union ranks, and reconstruct whole states and their local subdivisions. Himself as keen a defender of constitutional rights and legal processes as nineteenth-century America was capable of producing, Lincoln never apologized for the abrasive and politically risky arbitrary arrests.

Indeed, so far from apologizing for the arrests, Lincoln defended their necessity and constitutionality and argued that he had kept them to a risky minimum. The Constitution's war-emergency clauses existed to give the nation a reasonable capacity for self-defense, and implicitly sanctioned the arrests. Lincoln and those who agreed with him argued that necessity justified the president and commander in chief in invoking the Constitution against disloyalists because the secessionists of 1861 had left behind them in Union states, often in official positions, spies, informers, suppliers, and aiders and abettors of rebellion. These miscreants cloaked themselves in the Bill of Rights and habeas corpus, Lincoln claimed, and he had to lift that cloak.

And so the *Merryman* confrontation, although shocking even to supporters, contrasted happily with the nation's weakness in preceding weeks, when it failed to sustain the tiny garrison of Fort Sumter in one of its own harbors. It spurred many persons to climb aboard the war power bandwagon, including abolitionists, who now discerned in this president's use of emergency powers a possible link between arbitrary arrests and emancipation, and between reunion and a reconstructed or reformed nation.

Nevertheless, Lincoln's policies did greatly enlarge executive war and commander-in-chief powers, and this enlargement allowed Democrats to depict Lincoln as a wielder of unconstitutional power, especially since his policies differed so sharply with those of his predecessor, James Buchanan. During his lameduck months as president (November 1860-March 1861), while the Deep South's states seceded, Buchanan could find no resources in the Constitution to deal even with outgoing states much less a shooting war. So constrained, Buchanan allowed a significant segment of the nation's civil and military professionals to resign positions and go with their states, without impediment from the United States government.

Lincoln's Constitutional Understanding

Whence came Lincoln's understandings of the Constitution's war-emergency powers, which he so swiftly and unerringly applied to sustain national authority? Attorney Lincoln, a prominent commercial lawyer, shared his profession's concerns about individuals' legal rights to the profits of their labor and capital, and the social instabilities between liberty, authority, and anarchy developing since the French Revolution. These concerns made some lawyers try to achieve justice as well as stability, through lawsuits and politics. But even to abolitionist lawyers, private property was sacred, and American high court case law, especially the slavery-related decisions climaxing in *Dred Scott* (1857), sustained slaveowners' rights to property far more than other individuals' civil rights or liberties. Prewar lawyers were encouraged, however, by the growth of "equity" law—a judicial system based upon prevailing notions of fairness and justice.

Equity flowered as certain statutes and judicial decisions proved to be irrelevant or unjust to litigants and harmful to society, especially in light of swiftly changing social conditions. Flexibility and adaptation to change were what made equity law attractive to leading lawyers. Precisely such concerns had inspired the framers to gather in 1787. Apparently it was not difficult for Lincoln and numerous lawyers in Union states, upon news of Sumter, to extend analogous professional views to the escalating crisis, and to justify presidential decisions by a conception of the general welfare.

Further, before 1861, Lincoln had educated himself about a president's power to initiate and carry on a war, though a foreign one. A one-term Whig congressman in 1846, he opposed President James K. Polk's policies leading to war with Mexico. It appears at first glance that Lincoln reversed his position on presidential war powers between the time of his criticism of Polk and 1861. But Lincoln was not denying the nation's power when castigating Polk. Instead, he decried Polk's misuses of that power in diplomacy and assignments of troops to combat before the war declaration. Thereafter, as an early Republican, Lincoln accepted the central public policy inspiring the organization of his party, namely, the constitutional authority to exclude slave property from its territories, an authority that

Taney denied in the *Dred Scott* decision. In short, both equity and territorial questions stressed the possibility that the Constitution was more than a network of negatives but was also an instrument to release power.

The most telling intellectual support that Lincoln and many other lawyers brought to the Civil War derived from the idea that the nation possessed positive powers and duties under the Constitution to preserve itself and to seek justice. Self-defense as a right and duty of government had roots in the turbulent histories of England and its American colonies, and in the ideas of Locke, Montesquieu, Blackstone, and other writers. Such writings had embedded into democratic thought the premise that in real emergencies, normal procedures could give way to arbitrary ones, but also that incumbent authorities had to remain accountable for their policies during crises. These mixtures of views underlay Lincoln's forthright war

The outbreak of the rebellion in the United States in 1861

policies, in which coercion and democracy coexisted, though with risk to the latter.

Lincoln as president drew comfort from the spirit of Alexander Hamilton's *Federalist* No. 23, written to justify the proposed Constitution's war-emergency provisions. These powers, Hamilton had insisted, "ought to exist without limitation, because it is impossible to foresee or define the extent and variety of national emergencies, or the correspondent variety of the means which may be necessary to satisfy them." Lincoln knew also of George Washington's martial suppression of the Whiskey Rebellion and the fact that the revered Jefferson had dispatched anti-pirate naval expeditions to the shore of Tripoli and, like John Adams before him, sustained American naval commanders who, in undeclared mini-wars, fought French and British warships. In 1812, Congress and President James Madison stressed the self-defense theme heavily in the formal declaration of war against Britain, and in subsequent debates

John Tyler

on statutory controls over enemy aliens. All these precedents received Republicans' attention, as did the fact that by 1815, when that declared war ended in what Americans could at least claim was a victory, the foundation existed for a legal theory of emergency powers.

Foreign affairs, continuing to affect American policies, brought forward President James Monroe's Declaration of 1823 against future European colonization in Central and South America. From Monroe to Lincoln, presidents had dispatched many navy-marine units to distant shores, to combat private offenders such as pirates, to protect merchants and missionaries, to open trade, to advance science, and to stake claims to empire. Congress, providing funds and rules for the military services as the Constitution required, rarely objected to these distant, obscure, and brief exercises of national, executive, commander-in-chief powers. At home, the military functioned all but invisibly on the western frontiers against Indians, and in the Atlantic and Gulf coastal forts designed to fend off a future British oceanic assault that never came.

Lincoln's generation grew up applauding, if not always agreeing with, these nationalist implications of both general and constitutional history, even though Lincoln, like most Whigs, was suspicious of over-vigorous presidents, and critical of the ill-famed Sedition Acts of the Federalist party in 1799-1800. (No similar statute became public policy in the Civil War and Reconstruction).

A dozen years before the Civil War began, Chief Justice Taney himself had drawn many of these strands of American history together. In 1841-1842, Thomas Dorr and his supporters established a state government in Rhode Island in opposition to the existing one, as a response to a dispute over suffrage limitations. President Tyler offered federal support to the old government. A court case emerged from the conflict, *Luther v. Borden* (1849). In *Luther,* Taney created a "doctrine" of legitimate self-defense by a government threatened by civil war, which the justice tried to ignore in his own *Merryman* opinion. Taney, in *Luther,* held that judges could not decide essentially political questions such as which government was legitimate in a state. A state (and, by implication, the nation) had legitimate duties to defend itself when attacked by armed force from within or outside. The uprising in Rhode Island in 1842, Taney continued, was a war, though not a declared one between nations. The incumbent government rightfully resorted to the contemporary usages of war, including military arrests of activist civilian dissidents, to defend itself.

Lincoln and other Republican legalists would not let Taney forget *Luther,* especially when antiwar, anti-emancipation Democrats paraded *Merryman* before the public. For himself, as the Civil War ground on, Taney secretly wrote decisions without cases, declaring unconstitutional military emancipation, reconstruction, and conscription. But his brethren, in the 1863 *Prize Cases* decision, rejected, if only by a 5-4 margin, a chance to advance the chief justice's negative views, by sustaining the prior duties of the Congress and president to determine the existence of armed threats to the nation and to choose the appropriate means to meet those threats. On balance, subsequent Supreme Court verdicts sustained Lincoln's position and helped to make the Lincoln White House years the central ones in the history of war powers.

Lincoln's Heirs   They remained central in part because, almost at one after Appomattox, Andrew Johnson, Lincoln's successor, proved to be unwilling to use national power to sustain blacks' rights in states, and adopted *Merryman*-like positions. However, from the 1870s through the early 1980s, presidents exploited Lincolnian precedents. In domestic crises presidents used troops to break strikes, control essential industries, initiate internal security programs, and obstruct anti-Vietnam War activists. In foreign affairs, presidents after Lincoln cited his elastic doctrines of executive power to sustain their assignments of troops to numerous obscure, often hazardous "gunboat diplomacy" duties abroad. Some of these interventions profoundly and permanently affected our foreign relations. Without war declarations, American troops fought many "presidential wars," including those against Chinese Boxers, Philippine nationalists, Mexican border raiders, Bolshevik revolutionaries, Vietnamese anticolonialists, and Central American insurrectionists. Korea, Vietnam, Lebanon, and Grenada attest that we still know no fixed formulas for using the commander in chief's powers abroad. (The 1973 War Powers Act remains an uncertain reed for Congress to use as a staff.)

Yet, despite these imprecisions, over the past century, assertions have issued from the White House that presidents, in order to respond swiftly, must remain untethered in using war-crisis powers both domestically and abroad. Opponents repeat the equally precise response that the Constitution is never silent and that its constraints govern at all times; moreover, they

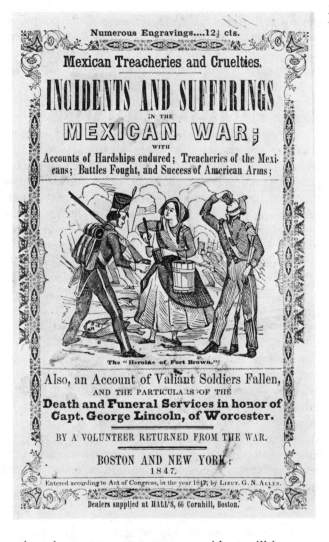

Numerous Engravings....12½ cts.

Mexican Treacheries and Cruelties.

INCIDENTS AND SUFFERINGS

IN THE

MEXICAN WAR;

WITH

Accounts of Hardships endured; Treacheries of the Mexicans; Battles Fought, and Success of American Arms;

The "Heroine of Fort Brown."

Also, an Account of Valiant Soldiers Fallen,

AND THE PARTICULARS OF THE

Death and Funeral Services in honor of Capt. George Lincoln, of Worcester.

BY A VOLUNTEER RETURNED FROM THE WAR.

BOSTON AND NEW YORK:
1847.

Entered according to Act of Congress, in the year 1847, by LIEUT. G. N. ALLEN.

Dealers supplied at HALL'S, 66 Cornhill, Boston.

argue, unless they do govern, a runaway president will become a military dictator, as Lincoln allegedly did.

Was Lincoln a dictator? Distinguished scholars, describing him as America's first "constitutional dictator," implicitly dignified the ultra-Democrats' partisan accusations of the 1860s. But if dictatorship is measured by unaccountability, deliberate and wholesale cruelties, and contempt for constitutionalism, Lincoln was no dictator. This conclusion appears to be the more valid when considering the coercive and punitive policies that nineteenth-century dictators (not to mention those of the twentieth century) imposed on dissenters and losers during and after civil wars. These policies commonly included gang executions and even attempts at genocide, mass torturings, imprisonments, property confiscations, exilings, suppressions and censorships of the press, disfranchisements, and, in the rare places where elections existed, cancellations or manipulations of ballotings. On such a scale, Lincoln rates no place at all.

Should historians absolve Lincoln of responsibility for creating precedents that later presidents used to excess, because he lacked intent to harm, and, though exercising war powers in unprecedented ways, nevertheless kept himself and his subordinates accountable to all traditional constraints of the democratic process? Or is he less subject to criticism because his laudable, and rare, educability allowed him to escalate his uses of war powers from "mere" internal security functions to higher ones, especially emancipation?

It is sensible to absolve Lincoln from the "dictator" accusation, and to perceive that he himself was so wretched at the need to use the war power that he expected his successors to avoid recourse to it, especially in an arbitrary manner or if anything less than fundamental, immediate dangers threatened government and society. Our national history since Appomattox suggests that he was too optimistic on this last assumption. Still, in December 1863, Lincoln reminded Congress and the nation that "we must not lose sight of the fact that the war power is still our main reliance." Much remains to be learned from the Civil War and Reconstruction experience with war-emergency powers, so central in the development of this "main reliance," before presidents, congressmen, jurists, or historians interpret them with excessive confidence.

SUGGESTED ADDITIONAL READING H. M. Hyman and W. M. Wiecek, *Equal Justice Under Law: Constitutional Development, 1835-1875* (1982) offers details and extended sources for further reading on the nineteenth century. The enormous literature on the war powers that spun off from Vietnam is best evaluated in *The Tethered Presidency: Congressional Restraints on Executive Power*, ed. T. M. Franck (1981).

Harold M. Hyman holds the William P. Hobby chair of history at Rice University. His most recent book, with William Wiecek, is *Equal Justice Under Law*.

Vietnam and the Constitution: The War Power Under Johnson and Nixon

Michal R. Belknap

During the national agony known as the Vietnam War, Presidents Lyndon Johnson and Richard Nixon came under fire almost as intense as that directed at American military units in Southeast Asia. Among the charges leveled against them were allegations of unconstitutional conduct. In fact, Johnson and Nixon were guilty neither of massively misemploying their authority as commander in chief nor of abusing presidential war powers. Although often condemned for failing to obtain a congressional declaration of war, they had the support of twentieth-century practice and opinion in contending that it was for the president to decide when and against whom the United States should commit its armed forces to battle. Furthermore, neither Johnson nor Nixon claimed, as had some of their predecessors, that the war powers of their office gave them the authority to subject large aspects of American domestic life to executive control. These much-vilified presidents may deserve censure for fighting the wrong war in the wrong place at the wrong time, but they were not guilty of fighting that war unconstitutionally.

Precedent

It had never been quite clear what the framers of the Constitution meant when they provided in Article I, section 8, "The Congress shall have Power . . . to declare war. . . ." The declaration of war was a medieval custom associated with chivalry, which required one belligerent to notify another formally before commencing hostilities against it. By the time of the Constitutional Convention in 1787, this practice had fallen into disuse, and of the approximately 140 wars fought in the world between 1700 and 1907 (when the Hague Conference adopted a convention providing that hostilities might not be commenced without a formal warning), only a handful were declared. The draft of the Constitution prepared by the Committee on Detail gave Congress the power to "make" war, but the full Convention changed that word to "declare." It seems unlikely that the Convention intended thereby to restrict Congress only to giving formal notification of America's intention to fight or to initiating the minority of wars in which a declaration was employed. Probably, it made the change to allow the president to respond immediately if the nation were attacked. Unfortunately, debate on this issue was brief and opaque. By employing a word whose meaning was at best ambiguous, the Convention made it possible for presidents to argue later that it was constitutional for them to commence, on their own initiative, all wars which were not "declared."

In any event, by making the president the "Commander in Chief of the Army and Navy . . . ," the Convention conceded to the executive the real power to decide when and against whom the United States would fight whether or not the war is "declared." Congress declared war on Mexico in 1846, but only after being informed by President James K. Polk that Mexico already had initiated hostilities by attacking American troops. In fact, Polk, who was seeking a pretext for war, had provoked the Mexican attack by ordering the Army into disputed territory to which Mexico's claim was considerably stronger than that of the United States.

Other presidents have used their authority as commander in chief to deploy American military forces in ways which, although not causing a declared war, have resulted in fighting and even loss of life. In 1801, for example, Thomas Jefferson started a naval conflict with the Barbary pirates by spurning their demands for increased "protection money" and ordering the Navy and Marines to North Africa.

Presidential War-Making

Six decades later, the Supreme Court gave backhanded legal recognition to such presidentially initiated "wars." In 1861, Abraham Lincoln launched the fighting between the North and South by dispatching a relief expedition to Fort Sumter. He made the resulting conflict a war under international law by ordering the Navy to blockade southern ports. In upholding the legality of that action, the Supreme Court employed language useful to later champions of presidential war-making. Whether a congressional declaration was necessary to make a non-civil war legal as a matter of domestic constitutional law was not really an issue in the *Prize Cases*

(1863), which involved a dispute over international law. In its opinion, though, the Court proclaimed that a president was bound "to resist force by force," and to do so "without waiting for any special legislative authority." He could wage war without waiting "for Congress to baptize it with a name."

During the twentieth century, presidents advanced toward the sort of executive takeover of the war-initiating function that this language seemed to sanction. McKinley moved only a little way in that direction, and he did so with the explicit permission of Congress. On April 20, 1898, the House and Senate adopted a resolution recognizing the independence of the Spanish colony of Cuba and demanding that Spain relinquish its authority over that island and withdraw its military and naval forces. At the same time, Congress directed the president to use the Army and Navy to carry its resolution into effect. In other words, Congress issued an ultimatum, then left it to the president to decide what action the United States should take if its demands were not met. Spain responded to the resolution by

The battle of Quasimas near Santiago, June 1898

President Franklin Roosevelt signing war declaration, 1941

breaking diplomatic relations. On April 22, McKinley proclaimed a naval blockade of Cuba, and that same day an American warship fired across the bow of a Spanish steamer. On April 24, Spain declared war on the United States, and the following day Congress adopted a second resolution, which announced that a state of war had existed between the two countries since the twenty-first.

Like the Spanish-American War, World War I had explicit congressional sanction. In April 1917, Woodrow Wilson, an admirer of the British parliamentary system who believed a president should govern by leading Congress, asked for and obtained a declaration of war against Germany. Had the House and Senate refused his request, Americans might still have found themselves fighting Germans. Earlier, a Senate filibuster had prevented Wilson from obtaining congressional authorization to put guns, and Navy men to fire them, on merchant vessels. In March he took that step on his own. It was a move likely to result in American ships shooting it out with German submarines, whether or not Congress declared war.

During the period 1939-1941 Franklin Roosevelt went much further than Wilson had, reducing congressional declaration to little more than a formality. Congress voted for war against Japan only after the Japanese bombed Pearl Harbor on December 7, 1941, and for hostilities against Germany and

Italy only after those countries announced they would join their Axis ally in its fight against the United States. Long before December 1941, however, this country had ceased to be neutral in the military conflicts already raging in Asia and Europe. Roosevelt had assisted China in its fight with Japan by subjecting the Japanese to escalating economic pressure and had made America into a virtual arsenal for Britain in her war against Nazi Germany. On his own authority, he transferred fifty destroyers to the British in exchange for some Western Hemisphere bases and with congressional authorization lent and leased American war materiel to Britain. Besides taking actions likely to provoke the Axis powers into attacking the United States, Roosevelt initiated combat against Germany. He ordered the Navy to convoy supplies bound for the British Isles and to fire on German submarines that tried to interfere. Several months before Pearl Harbor, the United States was already engaged in a shooting war with Germany in the North Atlantic. Of the two-year period which preceded December 7, 1941, political scientist Edward S. Corwin said in *Total War and the Constitution* (1947), "The initiative throughout was unremittingly with the President."

In June 1950 a president dispensed entirely with the declaration of war, leading the United States into major military conflict without even consulting Congress. When North Korea attacked South Korea, Harry Truman simply ordered American air, naval, and ground forces into combat against the Communist aggressors. Explaining to legislative leaders why he had proceeded this way, Truman declared, "I just had to act as Commander in Chief, and I did." When the tide of battle began to run strongly against the United States, Representative Frederic R. Coudert, Jr., introduced a resolution against sending additional military forces abroad without the prior approval of Congress. Conservative Republican senator Robert Taft endorsed his position, but a host of other prominent senators from both parties, among them Paul Douglas, Arthur Vandenberg, Wayne Morse, and J. William Fulbright, defended Truman's right to send American forces anywhere he felt the security of the United States required.

By 1950 it was obvious to perceptive legislators that, whatever the members of the Constitutional Convention may have intended, the real power to determine whether or not this country went to war lay with the president. Lawyers and scholars had grasped this reality too. In 1941 University of California law professor Harry Willmer Jones observed:

"Champions of the authority of Congress have long been aware that bold presidential exercise of the power of command over the armed forces may make somewhat unreal the constitutional power of Congress to declare war."

By the early 1960s this state of affairs was widely regarded as a good thing. Victory in World War II had vindicated Roosevelt's pre-Pearl Harbor initiatives and discredited the isolationists who had criticized him for bypassing Congress. In the wake of that conflict, prominent international and constitutional lawyers took the position that the congressional power to declare war was really little more than the authority to announce to the rest of the world that the United States was engaged in hostilities. The development of atomic weapons, and of planes and rockets capable of delivering them from one continent to another, seemed to make essential vesting war-making power in a single individual, who could act quickly and decisively to meet an enemy challenge. Historians, such as Arthur Schlesinger, Jr., and political scientists, such as Richard Neustadt, praised the emergence of the "strong" presidency. Meanwhile, international law authority Pittman B. Potter, unaware of how naive and even ridiculous his views would appear by the 1980s, observed in 1954 that while the president did have a large measure of discretion, it was after all "subject to the obligation to use a large measure of prudence . . . and not to involve us in another World War without more than ample justification."

It was in this climate of opinion that Lyndon Johnson went to Congress after the Tonkin Gulf incident in August 1964 seeking a resolution expressing congressional approval and support for "the determination of the President, as commander in chief to take all necessary measures to repel any armed attack against the forces of the United States and to prevent further aggression." Johnson did not believe the Constitution required him to obtain authorization from Congress before taking military action in Vietnam, but he thought such a resolution would be politically useful. It would show the Communists that America was united behind its commander in chief and enable him to avoid the sort of partisan criticism Truman had received for his unilateral action in Korea. Although Dwight Eisenhower had sought similar expressions of congressional support during the Formosa and Middle East crises of the 1950s, several prominent senators maintained that the president already had sufficient authority to use force in Vietnam. The commander in chief needed no legislative endorsement, they insisted. Among the proponents of this thesis was Senator Fulbright, by now chairman of the Foreign Relations Committee and later one of the sharpest critics of Johnson's Southeast Asian policies.

Such critics often faulted LBJ for failing to obtain a declaration of war from Congress before sending hundreds of thousands of troops to South Vietnam and launching a massive bombing campaign against North Vietnam, but this objection

Public Law 93-148
93rd Congress, H. J. Res. 542
November 7, 1973

Joint Resolution

Concerning the war powers of Congress and the President.

Resolved by the Senate and House of Representatives of the United States of America in Congress assembled,

War Powers Resolution.

SHORT TITLE

SECTION 1. This joint resolution may be cited as the "War Powers Resolution".

PURPOSE AND POLICY

SEC. 2. (a) It is the purpose of this joint resolution to fulfill the intent of the framers of the Constitution of the United States and insure that the collective judgment of both the Congress and the President will apply to the introduction of United States Armed Forces into hostilities, or into situations where imminent involvement in hostilities is clearly indicated by the circumstances, and to the continued use of such forces in hostilities or in such situations.

(b) Under article I, section 8, of the Constitution, it is specifically provided that the Congress shall have the power to make all laws necessary and proper for carrying into execution, not only its own powers but also all other powers vested by the Constitution in the Government of the United States, or in any department or officer thereof.

USC prec. title 1.

(c) The constitutional powers of the President as Commander-in-Chief to introduce United States Armed Forces into hostilities, or into situations where imminent involvement in hostilities is clearly indicated by the circumstances, are exercised only pursuant to (1) a declaration of war, (2) specific statutory authorization, or (3) a national emergency created by attack upon the United States, its territories or possessions, or its armed forces.

CONSULTATION

SEC. 3. The President in every possible instance shall consult with Congress before introducing United States Armed Forces into hostilities or into situations where imminent involvement in hostilities is clearly indicated by the circumstances, and after every such introduction shall consult regularly with the Congress until United States Armed Forces are no longer engaged in hostilities or have been removed from such situations.

REPORTING

SEC. 4. (a) In the absence of a declaration of war, in any case in which United States Armed Forces are introduced—

(1) into hostilities or into situations where imminent involvement in hostilities is clearly indicated by the circumstances;

87 STAT. 555

(2) into the territory, airspace or waters of a foreign nation, while equipped for combat, except for deployments which relate solely to supply, replacement, repair, or training of such forces; or

87 STAT. 556

(3) in numbers which substantially enlarge United States

The War Powers Resolution

A search and destroy mission in Vietnam, June 1967

was seldom heard until after the futility of the war revealed itself late in the Johnson administration. As Professor Graham T. Allison has pointed out, had the War Powers Resolution, passed by Congress in 1973 to prevent "any more Vietnams," been in force a decade earlier, it would not have kept America from becoming militarily involved in Southeast Asia; Johnson's actions were initially popular, and he could easily have obtained the congressional authorization required for the troops he sent to Vietnam in 1965 to remain there. Furthermore, the president's conduct was in line with pre-1964 thinking and presidential practice.

So for the most part were the actions of Richard Nixon, which included expanding the war by invading neutral Cambodia in 1970.* In justifying the Cambodian incursion as an exercise of the powers of the commander in chief, then assistant attorney general William Rehnquist took a position actually more restrained than Truman's. As Rehnquist argued, Nixon's invasion was, at least in part, a tactical move designed to protect American forces already fighting in Vietnam from attacks launched by the enemy out of sanctuaries across the border in Cambodia. Truman, on the other hand, had started a brand new war when he sent U.S. troops off to engage the North Koreans in 1950. Nixon did break new and dubious ground, but only when he continued to fight in Southeast Asia despite clear expressions of congressional opposition to the war, such as the 1971 repeal of the Tonkin Gulf Resolution.

Arthur Schlesinger, Jr., is hardly warranted in asserting in the *The Imperial Presidency* (1973): "Both Johnson and Nixon ... indulged in presidential warmaking beyond the wildest dreams of their predecessors." What bothers Schlesinger is the character of the conflict which one of these presidents escalated** and the other prolonged and expanded. He finds their conduct distinguishable from that of Lincoln, Roosevelt, and Truman primarily because, unlike Nixon and Johnson, those men involved the nation in just wars. That distinction may be a valid one, but it is not a constitutional one.

----

* Like thousands of college students of my generation, I participated in protests against the Cambodian incursion. I do not mean here to endorse it (or the Vietnam War as a whole) as either morally justified or politically wise.

** President Truman sent the first American military personnel to Vietnam. The number of U.S. advisors in that country, which stood at less than 700 at the end of the Eisenhower administration, was raised to more than 16,000 by John F. Kennedy. Besides increasing the number of American men in Vietnam from that level to about 550,000, Johnson also changed the U.S. role there in two significant ways: he introduced American ground combat units into the fighting in the South and he initiated the bombing of the North.

War Powers "At Home"

Although Johnson was a domineering individual and Nixon's efforts to enhance the prerogatives of the presidency sometimes suggested dictatorial ambitions, neither Vietnam president was as "imperial" in his use of presidential war power on the domestic front as predecessors who have fared far better at the hands of historians such as Schlesinger. Lincoln, for example, used the war power to justify spending money never appropriated by Congress, locking up disloyal civilians, and even freeing the slaves. Indeed, the domestic presidential "war power" was largely his creation. Lincoln manufactured it by linking the commander-in-chief clause, apparently intended by those who wrote the Constitution only to make the president the head of the Army and Navy, to the provision in Article II, section 3 directing the chief executive to "take care that the laws be faithfully executed." Together, Lincoln insisted, these clauses gave him sufficient authority not only to fight the civil war but also to deal effectively with all of the domestic problems it created. In his hands, the commander-in-chief clause became a constitutional grant to the president of almost unlimited emergency powers.

Lincoln was, of course, fighting a unique internal war in which the very survival of the nation was at stake. The extraordinary circumstances which he confronted justified the extraordinary measures which he took. By the end of the nineteenth century, though, commentators were pointing to his actions as examples of what any wartime president could do. They generalized Lincoln's conduct into a broad domestic presidential war power, available during foreign as well as civil wars.

This concept went largely untested during the Spanish-American War. That conflict, which ended victoriously only a few months after it began, was too brief and required too little in the way of economic and manpower mobilization to provide much occasion for assertions of presidential prerogative on the home front.

World War I was different. It was a cataclysmic world conflict in which several nations (although certainly not the United States) were battling for survival. Hence, it seemed to require extraordinary measures to ensure victory. Furthermore, national war efforts in an industrial age had become so heavily dependent on the economic base supporting them that a dozen workers had to labor at home to keep a single soldier fighting at the front. Under such circumstances, the use of unprecedented methods could not be restricted to the battlefield.

Wilson responded to the challenge of World War I with a more sweeping domestic exercise of presidential power than anything seen since Lincoln's day. In a speech accepting the 1920 Republican nomination, Warren G. Harding complained that due to anxieties inspired by the war emergency, "every safeguard was swept away. In the name of democracy we established autocracy."

Woodrow Wilson

Harding's partisan recollections were not entirely fair to his Democratic predecessor. Rather than relying largely on the inherent powers of the commander in chief, as Lincoln had done, Wilson went to the legislative branch and got it to delegate sweeping authority to the chief executive. Congress gave him the power not only to draft men into the Army and Navy, but also to regulate food production, set fuel prices, license businesses, seize railroads, telegraph, and telephone lines, take over factories, censor the mails, and even imprison critics of the government and opponents of the war.

Although the scope of the authority which Congress delegated to Wilson was breathtaking, he sometimes found it inadequate, or at least too slow in coming. Consequently, the president took a number of actions for which statutory authorization was lacking, justifying them as exercises of his own war powers. The most important of these was the establishment of the powerful War Industries Board, which extended a large measure of supervision over much of American business.

During World War II, Roosevelt relied even more than had Wilson on the war powers of the presidency itself. Congress was again generous in delegating authority to the executive, but FDR did many things, even during the period September 1939 to December 1941, for which he lacked statutory authority. These ranged from creating a host of new federal agencies to lengthening the work week to 48 hours. The president insisted he had the inherent power to seize defense plants in danger of being idled by strikes and took over several before Congress got around to enacting legislation clearly giving him the authority to do this. The Justice Department argued moreover that Roosevelt's war powers provided a legal basis for Army seizure of Montgomery Ward, despite the tenuous connection between a consumer mail order house and the national military effort.

The war powers Roosevelt claimed were even greater than those he actually exercised. On September 7, 1942, he declared that if Congress did not repeal a statutory provision which was undermining the government's efforts to combat inflation, the "responsibilities of the president in war time to protect the nation" would justify him in refusing to carry out the offensive law. Corwin sharply criticized this message, lambasting Roosevelt for claiming he had the right to suspend the Constitution. Other commentators reacted differently, insisting that the nation's involvement in a "total war" justified, even required, such extreme examples of executive leadership. Neither Congress nor the judiciary, they believed, should sit in judgment of the commander in chief. The Supreme Court probably agreed, for it tended to treat many domestic actions of the President—like excluding Japanese-Americans from the West Coast and closing the civilian courts to captured enemy saboteurs—as part of his military conduct of the war, and consequently as matters in which judges should not interfere.

Like Roosevelt before him, Truman relied on extra-statutory authority to establish new agencies and give additional powers to old ones during the Korean conflict. In April 1952, when a nationwide strike threatened to shut down the steel industry and restrict the flow of war materiel to Korea, he ordered the Secretary of Commerce to seize the steel mills. In doing this, Truman relied upon what he insisted were the inherent powers of the president in a "defense emergency" (a rationale, however, with which the Supreme Court did not agree).

Johnson and Nixon managed the home front quite differently. In July 1967, when a railroad strike interfered with the movement of ammunition and military equipment to ports of embarkation to Vietnam, LBJ asked Congress for legislation to end the work stoppage and resolve the underlying labor-management dispute. When Nixon called out military reservists to deliver the mail during a 1970 postal strike, he cited as his authority for taking this action not the commander-in-chief clause but a statute. In imposing a ninety-day wage-price freeze the following year, he relied not on presidential war power but on stand-by authority which Congress had bestowed upon the president in 1970. It is true that when trying to justify some of the more dubious conduct of his administration, Nixon liked to refer frequently to the demands of "national security," but in managing the home front, neither he nor Johnson relied on the war power. As a matter of fact, the Vietnam presidents seldom even mentioned it in a domestic context.

There are probably three reasons for their failure to make greater use of the war power. One is the Supreme Court's decision in *Youngstown Sheet and Tube Co. v. Sawyer* (1952).

Harry S Truman

In that case, the Court held that Truman lacked the authority to seize the steel mills. Since every member of the six-man majority wrote a separate opinion, it is difficult to say precisely why, but clearly only the three dissenters accepted Truman's contention that the inherent powers of the presidency provided sufficient support for his action. Two other justices might have agreed with them, had Congress not already provided a remedy for such strikes in the Taft-Hartley Act. They and two additional colleagues insisted, however, that a president had no right to ignore a statute. After 1952 the prudent course for a cautious chief executive was to cite statutory authority for any action likely to be challenged.

Richard M. Nixon

The growing unpopularity of the war in Vietnam also gave Johnson and Nixon plenty of reason for caution. In February 1968, LBJ chose to deal with the inflation which the war had ignited by setting up a cabinet committee to study the problem. His staff already had made a detailed analysis of the wage and price controls imposed by Truman during the Korean conflict, and many months earlier the White House Office of Emergency Preparedness had drafted the executive orders and legislation necessary to impose a variety of constraints on an overheating economy. Like the head of that agency, Johnson seems to have feared how the public might react to the idea of economic controls. Consequently, he opted for another study of inflation rather than for meaningful action to halt it. Even Nixon had to be prodded toward wage and price controls by a Congress dominated by the Democratic opposition.

Although both the *Youngstown* decision and fear of negative public reaction help to explain why Nixon and Johnson seldom resorted to presidential war power, there is another more important reason for their failure to make it their main reliance: absence of any real need to do so. By the 1960s, the statute books contained hundreds of laws which delegated often quite broad powers to the executive during a national emergency. To lawyers and judges of the era prior to 1939, only a military emergency would have justified the redistribution of power for which these statutes provided. Roosevelt erased almost completely the "bright line" between war and peace fundamental to their constitutional thought. By the time Pearl Harbor was attacked, he already had proclaimed both a limited state of national emergency (in September 1939) and an unlimited one (in May 1941). The precise legal significance of either proclamation was never entirely clear. The states of emergency which they created did not end with the fighting in

September 1945. It was years before the victorious Allies managed to sign a peace treaty with Japan, and they were never able to conclude one with a divided Germany. Rather than terminating decisively, World War II dissolved imperceptibly into the developing Cold War between the United States and the Soviet Union. Neither psychologically nor legally did the country ever completely return to a state of peace. Roosevelt's proclamations remained in effect until 1952. By then Truman had declared a new state of emergency. That one did not end with the Korean conflict which had inspired it, but

Lyndon B. Johnson

remained in effect at least until 1978.*** By the time Johnson escalated the Vietnam War in 1965, emergency government had become for the United States, as senators Frank Church and Charles McC. Mathias would note a few years later, the norm. Neither Johnson nor Nixon had any real need to resort to special constitutional powers, arguably available only during a declared war. They could instead rely upon the vast and ill-defined statutory emergency power which Congress had bestowed upon the executive in bits and pieces, which by 1974 (as the staff of a Senate committee headed by Church and Mathias discovered), numbered at least 470 separate laws.

Unlike Lincoln, the Vietnam presidents had no need to make the war power their main reliance on the home front. They did point to their constitutional authority as commander in chief to justify plunging the country into military engagement not previously authorized by Congress, but in doing so Johnson and Nixon were merely following in the footsteps of Lincoln, Roosevelt, and Truman. They were implementing concepts accepted, and even applauded, by most lawyers, scholars, and politicians before the Vietnam debacle itself called them into question. Thus, condemning Johnson and Nixon for unconstitutional conduct is scapegoating—it personalizes responsibility for a national mistake. Had Nixon and Johnson defeated Hitler or freed four million black slaves, few would charge them with abusing the war powers of the presidency. They behaved no more unconstitutionally than their predecessors. They were just less successful.

*** In the National Emergencies Act of 1976, Congress provided for the termination, two years after the enactment of that law, of all powers possessed by the president as a result of the existence of any declaration of emergency. This law does not purport, however, to withdraw or repeal such declarations themselves. Consequently, one can argue that the national emergency which Truman declared in 1950 is technically still in existence.

Michal R. Belknap, a member of the history department at the University of Georgia, served during the 1984-1985 academic year as Richard J. Hughes Distinguished Visiting Professor of Law at Seton Hall University. The author of *Cold War Political Justice* (1977), he is presently working on a book which will examine the effects of twentieth-century warfare on the Constitution.

What Constitutional Changes Do Americans Want?

Austin Ranney

Although some forums looked seriously at the heritage of American independence, many of the activities inspired by the 1976 Bicentenary of the American Revolution fitted Webster's definition of "celebrations": they "held up for public acclaim" and "demonstrated satisfaction by festivities." There were no conferences, articles, or books asking whether American independence has been a good thing, or whether it fits the conditions of the twentieth century, or whether we should rejoin the British crown.

In sharp contrast, many of the activities now being generated by the approaching Bicentenary of the Constitution are cerebrations. Scholarly undertakings, such as Project '87 and the American Enterprise Institute's Study of the Constitution, are holding conferences and producing books and articles (such as this) asking how and why the constitutional system of today differs from the system designed in 1787. In addition, a number of more activist groups, such as the Committee on the Constitutional System co-chaired by Lloyd Cutler and Douglas Dillon, are considering what changes need to be made in the Constitution to make it better able to cope with today's problems. And at least eleven proposals for amending the Constitution, ranging from equal rights for women to a mandatory balanced federal budget, are now at various levels on the nation's agenda. Indeed, the balanced budget amendment needs the support of only two more state legislatures to require Congress to call the first national constitutional convention since 1787. Accordingly, while we may commit some sins in observing the Constitution's Bicentenary, they are not likely to include smugness or mindlessness.

Most of the current cerebrations focus on what constitutional changes *should* be made, and pay little or no heed to how much popular support particular proposals are likely to attract. Such a focus seems entirely appropriate for scholars who wish only to describe, analyze, and explain the existing constitutional system. But scholars and other citizens who wish to *change* their system cannot escape considerations of how much popular support their proposals have now and how much more can be mobilized. This article is intended to be a modest contribution to discussions of constitutional change by reviewing some relevant data from public opinion polls; for, with all the perils of biased questions, skewed answers, and misleading interpretations that bedevil the polls, they still provide the best evidence we have on how our mass publics feel about proposals for changes in the Constitution.

A first glance at the poll data quickly shows that survey respondents are receptive to some proposals for constitutional change, divided on others, and resistant to still others. Hence it seems useful to proceed by identifying the main types of current proposals and seeing what the polls reveal about the level of popular support for each.

Proposals to Institute Substantive Policies

Some of the most prominent current proposals for constitutional amendments do not seek fundamental changes in the structure of government or the processes by which public policy is made. Rather, they attempt to change certain policies made by the president, the Congress, and/or the courts; or they seek to institute policies that those policy makers are unwilling to adopt. Until recently the Equal Rights Amendment received far more attention than any other in this category, and the polls have shown consistently that about two-thirds of the public approve the amendment. However, after its passage by Congress in 1972, its proponents were unable to persuade the legislatures of three-fourths of the states to ratify it, falling short by three states. Since the most recent ratification deadline expired in 1982, one effort to get Congress to re-propose it has failed, and it has recently received less attention from the national news media.

It has been replaced on center stage by the balanced budget amendment. By July of 1984 the legislatures of thirty-two states—just two fewer than the two-thirds required by the Constitution—have submitted petitions to Congress requesting that a constitutional convention be held to propose an amendment requiring the federal government to adopt balanced budgets except in times of national emergencies. It is too early to say whether two more states will join the petitioners, or whether the courts will regard the petitions already submitted as binding on Congress (many of them differ from the others in one respect or another), or whether Congress will respond by calling a convention or by submitting its own amendment to the states, or whether thirty-eight states would ratify such an amendment however proposed. Be that as it may, it is clear that the general idea has strong public support: for example, a 1983 Gallup poll showed 71 percent in favor and only 21 percent opposed, and other polls have produced similar results.

Another amendment in this category that has aroused strong passions is the proposal, which has a number of variants, to reverse a Supreme Court ruling by allowing states to hold organized prayers, on public school property during school

New York City, ca. 1913

hours, for children attending public schools. (Perhaps we should note in passing that Herbert Stein, the well-known economist, has proposed that the two amendments be consolidated into one providing that all school children be required to pray for a balanced budget.) This general idea also has strong public support: an NBC/AP poll in 1982 showed 72 percent in favor of "allowing organized prayers in public schools" and 28 percent opposed. However, in 1984 a proposed amendment to that end received the support of only fifty-six senators, eleven short of the necessary two-thirds majority, and for the moment the proposal is dormant (as is a related proposal to allow "silent prayers" during school hours).

Another well-publicized amendment intended to reverse a Supreme Court decision is one that would prohibit, or allow the states to prohibit, abortions except when necessary to save the mother's life. This is the only one of the amendments strongly supported by conservative and Moral Majority leaders that is opposed by the general public: a Louis Harris poll in 1982 showed 33 percent in favor and 61 percent opposed. Moreover, perhaps in keeping with this sentiment, an amendment recommended by the Senate Judiciary Committee in 1984 failed to win the necessary two-thirds majority from the whole chamber.

Proposals to Increase Direct Popular Control of Government

In their capacity as scholars if not as citizens, most historians, political scientists, and legal scholars are likely to be more interested in the pending proposals to change one aspect or another of the Constitution's decision-making processes. One group includes proposals that seek to increase direct popular control of the national government in various ways. One of the most familiar items in this category is the perennial proposal to abolish the electoral college and institute direct popular election of the president. A 1981 Louis Harris poll showed 77 percent in favor of such an amendment and 21 percent opposed. Yet when such a proposal, strongly backed by President Jimmy Carter, was voted on by the Senate in 1979, it was supported by only fifty-one senators—well short of the number needed to submit it to the states.

A number of amendments are also being proposed to "democratize" the presidential nominating process, although none has yet gotten past the committee stage in Congress. Several proposed amendments would replace the present gaggle of state presidential primaries, caucuses, and conventions with a series of regional primaries. A recent Gallup poll reported 66 percent in favor of such a change and 24 percent opposed. Another proposal would go even further by mandating that both parties choose their presidential nominees in one-day national primaries. This proposal has received less attention recently, but a 1980 Gallup poll showed 66 percent in favor and 24 percent opposed.

Perhaps the most radical of the "democratizing" amendments is one proposed by former senator James Abourezk and representatives Guy Vander Jagt and James Jones in 1977 to establish legislation by popular initiative on the national level comparable to the systems now operating in many of the states. Their amendment failed to get out of committee in either chamber, but a Gallup poll at the time showed 57 percent in favor and 21 percent opposed.

One other proposal that might be placed in this category is the amendment to give the District of Columbia two senators and at least one representative, all with full voting rights, in Congress. This proposal received the necessary two-thirds approval by both houses of Congress in 1978, but the amendment died in August 1985, when its statutory ratification expired. Only sixteen states had ratified, well short of the thirty-eight needed. I have been unable to find a national public poll on the proposal, but the leaders of the "D.C. voting rights" movement have apparently given up on it and have shifted their efforts to getting the District admitted to the union as a full-fledged state.

Proposals to Make Government Less Political and/or More Efficient

While not uninterested in many of the proposals for constitutional change in the first two categories, scholars have generally conferred, lectured, and written considerably more about proposals in a third category—those that seek, in one way or another, to overcome the fragmentation of power, internal antagonisms, and weakness of leadership they see in our constitutional structure so as to make it capable of developing, adopting, and implementing truly coherent and consistent policies. These proposals, in turn, can be divided into four main subgroups:

1. *By Limiting Tenure in Office.* A number of people believe that one of the worst aspects of our present constitutional system is the fact that the terms of some or all of our national elected officials are so short that they are forced to spend most of their time and energies in office on running for reelection and thus have too little time to develop and work for long-range programs. Accordingly, one much-discussed pro-

British Parliament buildings

posal, advocated by former president Jimmy Carter among others, would change the president's term of office from four years to six and make him ineligible for reelection. The public, however, is apparently torn between the desire to have a president "above politics" and the desire to have a president they can turn out of office in less than six years if they do not like him: a 1982 Gallup poll showed 49 percent in favor of the single six-year term and 47 percent opposed.

They are less divided about proposals for limiting the terms of members of Congress: a 1982 Gallup poll showed 61 percent in favor and 32 percent opposed to an amendment to limit both representatives and senators to a total of twelve years in office.

2. *By Giving the President an Item Veto over Appropriations.* Despite the reformed congressional budgetary process adopted in the mid-1970s, the polls show that most people blame Congress more than the president for the soaring expenditures and deficits of recent years. It is therefore not surprising that a proposed amendment to give the president the power to veto individual items in appropriations bills—a power now enjoyed by the governors of forty-four states—was shown by a 1983 Gallup poll to be approved by 67 percent and opposed by 25 percent.

3. *By Bridging the Separation of Powers.* A number of eminent reformers believe that the greatest deficiency in our constitutional system is the separation of powers between the president and Congress and the consequent endemic discord in their dealings with each other. Few reformers propose to remedy this congenital incapacity by the root-and-branch substitution of a British-style parliamentary system, but many advocate the construction of a series of bridges between the two branches comparable to those in Westminster. For example, some urge that cabinet members be given seats and voices in Congress. Others propose that the president be required to choose cabinet members from among members of Congress. Still others advocate giving the president the power to dissolve Congress and call a new election whenever necessary to break a deadlock.

It would be illuminating to know how ordinary Americans feel about the specific proposals and about the general idea of substituting British-style concentration of powers for our traditional separation of powers. Unfortunately, I am unable to find recent polls that bear directly on these questions, but perhaps public attitudes on the fourth subgroup of proposals can cast at least some indirect light on whether Americans want a more coherent and disciplined constitutional system.

4. *By Establishing Responsible Party Government.* Ever since the 1870s a succession of distinguished American writers—Woodrow Wilson, Frank Goodnow, E. E. Schattschneider, David Broder, and James MacGregor Burns, among others—have argued that America badly needs a more effective and responsible governing system, one that is capable of developing and carrying out coherent programs of public policy and accepting the responsibility for the programs' consequences. Most of them have agreed that formally replacing our presidential system with some version of the Westminster model is not only politically impossible but institutionally

unnecessary. They say that we can get the same results much more easily by developing outside the written Constitution a system of "responsible party government." That system has three basic requirements: First, after each election one party must be in control of both the presidency and the Congress. Second, all the majority party's members in both branches must act together cohesively on all policy matters. And third, at each election the governing party must be held fully responsible, *as a party* and not as a collection of independent officeholders, for how well or badly the party has exercised its stewardship. With such responsible parties, these writers say, we can achieve truly coherent and democratic government without changing a word of the written Constitution.

How do the American people feel about responsible party government? I have been able to find only one piece of direct evidence from the public opinion polls, and the circumstances in which the questions were asked are worth recalling. As the 1976 election approached, the United States had had divided party control of the national government (a president of one party and a Congress controlled by the other) for sixteen of the thirty years since World War II. The Louis Harris organization wanted to know whether the public thought that, aside from the individual merits of Gerald Ford and Jimmy Carter, it would be good to have both the presidency and the Congress controlled by the same party. So they asked their respondents a question bearing directly upon the first condition of responsible party government—one-party control:

> In general, do you think it is better for the country to have Congress under the control of one party and the White House under the control of another party so that there is a way for each to keep the other under control, or do you think it is better to have the Congress and the White House under the control of the same political party so that the business of the federal government can be done more effectively?

They asked the question in August and again in November after the election. On both occasions the respondents divided almost evenly:

	August	November
Favor divided control	40%	39%
Favor same-party control	38	45
Not sure	22	16

Harris reported that those who preferred same-party control gave as reasons, "Real problems of the country will be neglected in the stalemate that takes place between the White House and Congress"; and "Real reforms to make the federal government more efficient won't be enacted." Respondents favoring divided control commented, "It's a good way to be sure that one party can't get away with corruption and misuse of power in office"; and "the growth of big government and big federal spending can be prevented better."

The voters' choices in national elections since World War II provide additional evidence. From 1946 to 1982 there were a total of nineteen congressional elections and therefore nineteen opportunities to choose Congresses controlled by the president's party. Only nine produced same-party control of both houses of Congress and the White House. So it seems that divided party control, not same-party control, has been the more normal situation in American government.

This state of affairs is possible, of course, only if a good many voters regularly split their tickets, and that is just what they have done. Survey evidence shows that in the 1960 election only 35 percent of the voters voted split tickets, but in 1964 the proportion rose to 57 percent, in 1968 it was 66 percent, and in 1972 it was 67 percent. I estimate that the level remained at about two-thirds in the 1976 and 1980 presidential elections. Evidently, then, achieving same-party control of the national government's three elective agencies is not highly valued by well over half of the American electórate.

Neither the polling nor the voting data provide conclusive **Conclusion** evidence about what kinds of constitutional change Americans want, but the survey answers are suggestive. For example, it is clear that survey respondents are considerably more receptive than members of Congress to constitutional change. We have reviewed eleven proposed constitutional amendments that have recently been introduced in Congress. Substantial majorities of the general public have favored nine of the eleven (ERA, balanced budgets, school prayers, direct election of presidents, regional presidential primaries, a national presidential primary, national initiative, limiting terms of senators and representatives, and presidential item veto). Popular majorities have rejected only one proposal (outlawing abortions), and respondents were evenly divided on another (a single six-year presidential term). By contrast, Congress has sent only one of these proposals (ERA) to the states for ratification; it has given two others less than the necessary two-thirds majorities; and it has taken no action on the others. On this showing, then, there is considerably more resistance to constitutional change in the Congress than in the general public.

Be that as it may, is there any common theme underlying the changes survey respondents favor and reject? I believe there is. They approve proposals to require a balanced federal budget and to give the president the power to veto individual items in appropriations bills, both of which are intended to restrain federal spending. They approve leaving it up to each state and locality to decide for itself whether it wishes to have school prayers. They *dis*approve a federally imposed ban on abortion, evidently preferring to leave the matter to private decision.

They also approve a number of proposals to give the people more direct power over national public officials, by direct nomination and election of the president, by limiting congressmen's tenure in office, and by giving the people the power to bypass Congress and legislate by popular initiative.

These proposals are all intended to limit the reach and power of the national government in one way or another. It should not surprise us that survey respondents favor them, for they are entirely in keeping with what the polls have been telling us is the prevailing popular mood since the late 1960s. It remains to be seen whether that mood will persist and, if so, whether it will become strong enough to overcome the continuing reluctance of Congress to make very many or very drastic constitutional changes of any kind. And that, in turn, will determine whether the United States will celebrate the Bicentenary of the Philadelphia Convention mainly by celebrating and cerebrating about the Constitution or by changing it.

Austin Ranney, a former president of the American Political Science Association and member of the Joint Committee of Project '87, is an adjunct professor of political science at the University of California, Berkeley, and an adjunct scholar of the American Enterprise Institute for Public Policy Research. His recent works include *Channels of Power: The Impact of Television on American Politics.*

Chronology of Bicentennial Dates
from the End of the American Revolution
to the Ratification of the Bill of Rights

After the Continental Congress voted in favor of independence from Great Britain on July 2, 1776, and adopted the Declaration of Independence on July 4, it took up the proposal of Richard Henry Lee for a "plan of confederation." On July 12, 1776, a congressional committee presented "Articles of Confederation and Perpetual Union," which the Congress debated for more than a year. The body adopted the Articles of Confederation on November 15, 1777, and submitted them to the thirteen states for ratification, which had to be unanimous. By March 1, 1781, all the states had given their assent. The Articles of Confederation gave limited powers to the federal government; important decisions required a super-majority of nine states. Congress could declare war and compact peace, but could not levy taxes, or regulate trade between the states or between any state and a foreign country. All amendments had to be adopted without dissenting votes. In 1786, James Madison described the Articles as "nothing more than a treaty of amity and of alliance between independent and sovereign states." As attempts to amend the Articles proved fruitless, and interstate disputes over commercial matters multiplied, the weaknesses of the Articles of Confederation as a fundamental charter became apparent. The march toward a new form of government began.

September 3, 1783: Articles of Peace ending hostilities between Great Britain and the United States are signed by Britain in Paris.

November 25, 1783: British troops evacuate New York City.

December 23, 1783: George Washington resigns his commission as commander in chief of American forces and takes leave "of all the employments of public life."

March 25-28, 1785: Mount Vernon Conference. George Washington hosts a meeting at Mount Vernon of four commissioners from Maryland and four from Virginia to discuss problems relating to the navigation of the Chesapeake Bay and the Potomac River. After negotiating agreements, the commissioners recommend to their respective legislatures that annual conferences be held on commercial matters and

287

that Pennsylvania be invited to join Maryland and Virginia to discuss linking the Chesapeake and the Ohio River.

January 16, 1786: Virginia's legislature adopts a statute for religious freedom, originally drafted by Thomas Jefferson and introduced by James Madison. The measure protects Virginia's citizens against compulsion to attend or support any church and against discrimination based upon religious belief. The law serves as a model for the First Amendment to the United States Constitution.

January 21, 1786: Virginia's legislature invites all the states to a September meeting in Annapolis to discuss commercial problems.

August 7, 1786: The Congress of the Confederation considers a motion offered by Charles Pinckney of South Carolina to amend the Articles of Confederation in order to give Congress more control over foreign affairs and interstate commerce. Because amendments to the Articles require the unanimous consent of the states, an unlikely eventuality, Congress declines to recommend the changes.

September 11-14, 1786: Annapolis Convention. New York, New Jersey, Delaware, Pennsylvania, and Virginia send a total of twelve delegates to the conference which had been proposed by Virginia in January to discuss commercial matters. (New Hampshire, Massachusetts, Rhode Island, and North Carolina send delegates but they fail to arrive in time.) The small attendance makes discussion of commercial matters fruitless. On September 14, the convention adopts a resolution drafted by Alexander Hamilton asking all the states to send representatives to a new convention to be held in Philadelphia in May of 1787. This meeting will not be limited to commercial matters but will address all issues necessary "to render the constitution of the Federal Government adequate to the exigencies of the Union."

February 4, 1787: The End of Shays' Rebellion. General Benjamin Lincoln, leading a contingent of 4,400 soldiers enlisted by the Massachusetts governor, routs the forces of Daniel Shays. A destitute farmer, Shays had organized a rebellion against the Massachusetts government, which had failed to take action to assist the state's depressed farm population. The uprisings, which had begun in the summer of 1786, are completely crushed by the end of February. The Massachusetts legislature, however, enacts some statutes to assist debt-ridden farmers. The disorder fuels concern about the need for an effective central government.

February 21, 1787: The Congress of the Confederation cautiously endorses the plan adopted at the Annapolis Convention for a new meeting of delegates from the states "for the sole and express purpose of revising the Articles of Confederation and reporting to Congress and the several legislatures such alterations and provisions therein."

May 25, 1787: Opening of the Constitutional Convention. On May 25, a quorum of delegates from seven states arrives in Philadelphia in response to the call from the Annapolis Convention, and the meeting convenes. Ultimately, representatives from all the states but Rhode Island attend. Of the fifty-five participants, over half are lawyers, and twenty-nine have attended college. The distinguished public figures include George Washington, James Madison, Benjamin Franklin, George Mason, Gouverneur Morris, James Wilson, Roger Sherman, and Elbridge Gerry.

May 29, 1787: Virginia Plan Proposed. On the fifth day of the meeting, Edmund Randolph, a delegate from Virginia, offers fifteen resolutions making up the "Virginia plan" of Union. Rather than amending the Articles of Confederation, the proposal describes a completely new organization of government, including a bicameral legislature which represents the states proportionately, with the lower house elected by the people and the upper house chosen by the lower body from nominees proposed by the state legislatures; an executive chosen by the legislature; a judiciary branch; and a council composed of the executive and members of the judiciary branch with a veto over legislative enactments.

June 15, 1787: New Jersey Plan Proposed. Displeased by Randolph's plan which placed the smaller states in a disadvantaged position, William Paterson proposes instead only to modify the Articles of Confederation. The New Jersey plan gives Congress power to tax and to regulate foreign and interstate commerce and establishes a plural executive (without veto power) and a supreme court.

June 19, 1787: After debating all the proposals, the Convention decides not merely to amend the Articles of Confederation but to devise a new national government. The question of equal versus proportional representation by states in the legislature now becomes the focus of the debate.

June 21, 1787: The Convention adopts a two-year term for representatives.

June 26, 1787: The Convention adopts a six-year term for senators.

July 12, 1787: The Connecticut Compromise (I). Based upon a proposal made by Roger Sherman of Connecticut, the Constitutional Convention agrees that representation in the lower house should be proportional to a state's population (the total of free residents ["excluding Indians not taxed"] and three-fifths of "all other persons," i.e., slaves).

July 13, 1787: Northwest Ordinance. While the Constitutional Convention meets in Philadelphia, the Congress of the Confederation crafts another governing instrument for the territory north of the Ohio River. The Northwest Ordinance, written largely by Nathan Dane of

Massachusetts, provides for interim governance of the territory by congressional appointees (a governor, secretary, and three judges), the creation of a bicameral legislature when there are 5,000 free males in the territory, and ultimately, the establishment of three to five states on an equal footing with the states already in existence. Freedom of worship, right to trial by jury, and public education are guaranteed, and slavery prohibited.

July 16, 1787: The Connecticut Compromise (II). The Convention agrees that each state should be represented equally in the upper chamber.

August 6, 1787: The five-man committee appointed to draft a constitution based upon twenty-three "fundamental resolutions" drawn up by the convention between July 19 and July 26 submits its document which contains twenty-three articles.

August 6-September 10, 1787: The Great Debate. The Convention debates the draft constitution.

August 16, 1787: The Convention grants to Congress the right to regulate foreign trade and interstate commerce.

August 25, 1787: The Convention agrees to prohibit Congress from banning the foreign slave trade for twenty years.

August 29, 1787: The Convention agrees to the fugitive slave clause.

September 6, 1787: The Convention adopts a four-year term for the president.

September 8, 1787: A five-man committee, comprising William Samuel Johnson (chair), Alexander Hamilton, James Madison, Rufus King, and Gouverneur Morris, is appointed to prepare the final draft.

September 12, 1787: The committee submits the draft, written primarily by Gouverneur Morris, to the Convention.

September 13-15, 1787: The Convention examines the draft clause by clause and makes a few changes.

September 17, 1787: All twelve state delegations vote approval of the document. Thirty-nine of the forty-two delegates present sign the engrossed copy, and a letter of transmittal to Congress is drafted. The Convention formally adjourns.

September 20, 1787: Congress receives the proposed Constitution.

September 26-27, 1787: Some representatives seek to have Congress censure the Convention for failing to abide by Congress' instruction only to revise the Articles of Confederation.

September 28, 1787: Congress resolves to submit the Constitution to special state ratifying conventions. Article VII of the document stipulates that it will become effective when ratified by nine states.

October 27, 1787: The first *Federalist* paper appears in New York City newspapers, one of eighty-five to argue in favor of the adoption of the new frame of government. Written by Alexander Hamilton, James Madison, and John Jay, the essays attempt to counter the arguments of Anti-Federalists, who fear a strong centralized national government.

December 7, 1787: Delaware ratifies the Constitution, the first state to do so, by unanimous vote.

December 12, 1787. Pennsylvania ratifies the Constitution in the face of considerable opposition. The vote in convention is 46 to 23.

December 18, 1787: New Jersey ratifies unanimously.

January 2, 1788: Georgia ratifies unanimously.

January 9, 1788: Connecticut ratifies by a vote of 128 to 40.

February 6, 1788: The Massachusetts convention ratifies by a close vote of 187 to 168, after vigorous debate. Many Anti-Federalists, including Sam Adams, change sides after Federalists propose nine amendments, including one which would reserve to the states all powers not "expressly delegated" to the national government by the Constitution.

March 24, 1788: Rhode Island, which had refused to send delegates to the Constitutional Convention, declines to call a state convention and holds a popular referendum instead. Federalists do not participate, and the voters reject the Constitution, 2,708 to 237.

April 28, 1788: Maryland ratifies by a vote of 63 to 11.

May 23, 1788: South Carolina ratifies by a vote of 149 to 73.

June 21, 1788: New Hampshire becomes the ninth state to ratify, by a vote of 57 to 47. The convention proposes twelve amendments.

June 25, 1788: Despite strong opposition led by Patrick Henry, Virginia ratifies the Constitution by 89 to 79. James Madison leads the fight in favor. The convention recommends a bill of rights, composed of twenty articles, in addition to twenty further changes.

July 2, 1788: The President of Congress, Cyrus Griffin of Virginia, announces that the Constitution has been ratified by the requisite nine states. A committee is appointed to prepare for the change in government.

July 26, 1788: New York ratifies by vote of 30 to 27 after Alexander Hamilton delays action, hoping that news of ratification from New Hampshire and Virginia would influence Anti-Federalist sentiment.

August 2, 1788: North Carolina declines to ratify until the addition to the Constitution of a bill of rights.

September 13, 1788: Congress selects New York as the site of the new government and chooses dates for the appointment of and balloting by presidential electors, and for the meeting of the first Congress under the Constitution.

September 30, 1788:   Pennsylvania chooses its two senators, Robert Morris and William Maclay, the first state to do so. Elections of senators and representatives continue through August 31, 1790, when Rhode Island concludes its elections.

October 10, 1788:   The Congress of the Confederation transacts its last official business.

January 7, 1789:   Presidential electors are chosen by ten of the states that have ratified the Constitution (all but New York).

February 4, 1789:   Presidential electors vote; George Washington is chosen as president, and John Adams as vice-president.

March 4, 1789:   The first Congress convenes in New York, with eight senators and thirteen representatives in attendance, and the remainder en route.

April 1, 1789:   The House of Representatives, with thirty of its fifty-nine members present, elects Frederick A. Muhlenberg of Pennsylvania to be its speaker.

April 6, 1789:   The Senate, with nine of twenty-two senators in attendance, chooses John Langdon of New Hampshire as temporary presiding officer.

April 30, 1789:   George Washington is inaugurated as the nation's first president under the Constitution. The oath of office is administered by Robert R. Livingston, chancellor of the State of New York, on the balcony of Federal Hall, at Wall and Broad Streets in New York City.

July 27, 1789:   Congress establishes the Department of Foreign Affairs (later changed to Department of State).

August 7, 1789:   Congress establishes the War Department.

September 2, 1789:   Congress establishes the Treasury Department.

September 22, 1789:   Congress creates the office of Postmaster General.

September 24, 1789:   Congress passes the Federal Judiciary Act, which provides for a chief justice and five associate justices of the Supreme Court and which establishes three circuit courts and thirteen district courts. It also creates the office of the Attorney General.

September 25, 1789:   Congress submits to the states twelve amendments to the Constitution, in response to the five state ratifying conventions that had emphasized the need for immediate changes.

November 20, 1789:   New Jersey ratifies ten of the twelve amendments, the Bill of Rights, the first state to do so.

November 21, 1789: As a result of congressional action to amend the Constitution, North Carolina ratifies the original document, by a vote of 194 to 77.

December 19, 1789: Maryland ratifies the Bill of Rights.

December 22, 1789: North Carolina ratifies the Bill of Rights.

January 25, 1790: New Hampshire ratifies the Bill of Rights.

January 28, 1790: Delaware ratifies the Bill of Rights.

February 24, 1790: New York ratifies the Bill of Rights.

March 10, 1790: Pennsylvania ratifies the Bill of Rights.

May 29, 1790: Rhode Island ratifies the Constitution, by a vote of 34 to 32.

June 7, 1790: Rhode Island ratifies the Bill of Rights.

July 16, 1790: George Washington signs legislation selecting the District of Columbia as the permanent national capital, to be occupied in 1800. Philadelphia will house the government in the intervening decade.

December 6, 1790: All three branches of government assemble in Philadelphia.

January 10, 1791: Vermont ratifies the Constitution.

March 4, 1791: Vermont is admitted to the Union as the fourteenth state.

November 3, 1791: Vermont ratifies the Bill of Rights.

December 15, 1791: Virginia ratifies the Bill of Rights, making it part of the United States Constitution.

Three of the original thirteen states did not ratify the Bill of Rights until the 150th anniversary of its submission to the states. Massachusetts ratified on March 2, 1939; Georgia on March 18, 1939; and Connecticut on April 19, 1939.

Principal Sources: Richard B. Morris, ed. *Encyclopedia of American History* (New York: Harper & Row, 1976); Samuel Eliot Morison, *The Oxford History of the American People* (New York: Oxford University Press, 1965).

The Constitution of the United States

The Preamble

We the People of the United States, in Order to form a more perfect Union, establish Justice, insure domestic Tranquility, provide for the common defence, promote the general Welfare, and secure the Blessings of Liberty to ourselves and our Posterity, do ordain and establish this Constitution for the United States of America.

Article I

Section 1

All legislative Powers herein granted shall be vested in a Congress of the United States, which shall consist of a Senate and House of Representatives.

Section 2

1. The House of Representatives shall be composed of Members chosen every second Year by the People of the several States, and the Electors in each State shall have the Qualifications requisite for Electors of the most numerous Branch of the State Legislature.

2. No Person shall be a Representative who shall not have attained to the age of twenty five Years, and been seven Years a Citizen of the United States, and who shall not, when elected, be an Inhabitant of that State in which he shall be chosen.

3. [Representatives and direct Taxes shall be apportioned among the several States which may be included within this Union, according to their respective Numbers, which shall be determined by adding to the whole Number of free Persons, including those bound to Service for a Term of Years, and excluding Indians not taxed, three fifths of all other Persons.][1] The actual Enumeration shall be made within three Years after the first Meeting of the Congress of the United States, and within every subsequent Term of ten Years, in such Manner as they shall by Law direct. The Number of Representatives shall not exceed one for every thirty Thousand, but each State shall have at Least one Representative; and until such enumeration shall be made, the State of New Hampshire shall be entitled to chuse three, Massachusetts eight, Rhode-Island and Providence Plantations one, Connecticut five, New-York six, New Jersey

four, Pennsylvania eight, Delaware one, Maryland six, Virginia ten, North Carolina five, South Carolina five, and Georgia three.

4. When vacancies happen in the Representation from any State, the Executive Authority thereof shall issue Writs of Election to fill such Vacancies.

5. The House of Representatives shall chuse their Speaker and other Officers; and shall have the sole Power of Impeachment.

Section 3

1. The Senate of the United States shall be composed of two Senators from each State, [chosen by the Legislature thereof,][2] for six Years; and each Senator shall have one Vote.

2. Immediately after they shall be assembled in Consequence of the first Election, they shall be divided as equally as may be into three Classes. The Seats of the Senators of the first Class shall be vacated at the Expiration of the second Year, of the second Class at the Expiration of the fourth Year, and of the third Class at the Expiration of the sixth Year, so that one third may be chosen every second Year; [and if Vacancies happen by Resignation, or otherwise, during the Recess of the Legislature of any State, the Executive thereof may make temporary Appointments until the next Meeting of the Legislature, which shall then fill such Vacancies].[3]

3. No Person shall be a Senator who shall not have attained to the Age of thirty Years, and been nine Years a Citizen of the United States, and who shall not, when elected, be an Inhabitant of that State for which he shall be chosen.

4. The Vice President of the United States shall be President of the Senate, but shall have no Vote, unless they be equally divided.

5. The Senate shall chuse their other Officers, and also a President pro tempore, in the Absence of the Vice President, or when he shall exercise the Office of President of the United States.

6. The Senate shall have the sole Power to try all Impeachments. When sitting for that Purpose, they shall be on Oath or Affirmation. When the President of the United States is tried the Chief Justice shall preside: And no Person shall be convicted without the Concurrence of two thirds of the Members present.

7. Judgment in Cases of Impeachment shall not extend further than to removal from Office, and disqualification to hold and enjoy any Office of honor, Trust or Profit under the United States: but the Party convicted shall nevertheless be liable and subject to Indictment, Trial, Judgment and Punishment, according to Law.

Section 4

1. The Times, Places and Manner of holding Elections for Senators

and Representatives, shall be prescribed in each State by the Legislature thereof; but the Congress may at any time by Law make or alter such Regulations, except as to the Places of chusing Senators.

2. The Congress shall assemble at least once in every Year, and such Meeting shall [be on the first Monday in December],[4] unless they shall by Law appoint a different Day.

Section 5

1. Each House shall be the Judge of the Elections, Returns and Qualifications of its own Members, and a Majority of each shall constitute a Quorum to do Business; but a smaller Number may adjourn from day to day, and may be authorized to compel the Attendance of absent Members, in such Manner, and under such Penalties as each House may provide.

2. Each House may determine the Rules of its Proceedings, punish its Members for disorderly Behaviour, and, with the Concurrence of two thirds, expel a Member.

3. Each House shall keep a Journal of its Proceedings, and from time to time publish the same, excepting such Parts as may in their Judgment require Secrecy; and the Yeas and Nays of the Members of either House on any question shall, at the Desire of one fifth of those Present, be entered on the Journal.

4. Neither House, during the Session of Congress, shall, without the Consent of the other, adjourn for more than three days, nor to any other Place than that in which the two Houses shall be sitting.

Section 6

1. The Senators and Representatives shall receive a Compensation for their Services, to be ascertained by Law, and paid out of the Treasury of the United States. They shall in all Cases, except Treason, Felony and Breach of the Peace, be privileged from Arrest during their Attendance at the Session of their respective Houses, and in going to and returning from the same; and for any Speech or Debate in either House, they shall not be questioned in any other Place.

2. No Senator or Representative shall, during the Time for which he was elected, be appointed to any civil Office under the Authority of the United States, which shall have been created, or the Emoluments whereof shall have been encreased during such time; and no Person holding any Office under the United States, shall be a Member of either House during his Continuance in Office.

Section 7

1. All Bills for raising Revenue shall originate in the House of

Representatives; but the Senate may propose or concur with amendments as on other Bills.

2. Every Bill which shall have passed the House of Representatives and the Senate, shall, before it become a Law, be presented to the President of the United States; If he approve he shall sign it, but if not he shall return it, with his Objections to that House in which it shall have originated, who shall enter the Objections at large on their Journal, and proceed to reconsider it. If after such Reconsideration two thirds of that House shall agree to pass the Bill, it shall be sent, together with the Objections, to the other House, by which it shall likewise be reconsidered, and if approved by two thirds of that House, it shall become a Law. But in all such Cases the Votes of both Houses shall be determined by yeas and Nays, and the Names of the Persons voting for and against the Bill shall be entered on the Journal of each House respectively. If any Bill shall not be returned by the President within ten Days (Sunday excepted) after it shall have been presented to him, the Same shall be a Law, in like Manner as if he had signed it, unless the Congress by their Adjournment prevent its Return, in which Case it shall not be a Law.

3. Every Order, Resolution, or Vote to which the Concurrence of the Senate and House of Representatives may be necessary (except on a question of Adjournment) shall be presented to the President of the United States; and before the Same shall take Effect, shall be approved by him, or being disapproved by him, shall be repassed by two thirds of the Senate and House of Representatives, according to the Rules and Limitations prescribed in the Case of a Bill.

Section 8

1. The Congress shall have Power To lay and collect Taxes, Duties, Imposts and Excises, to pay the Debts and provide for the common Defence and general Welfare of the United States; but all Duties, Imposts and Excises shall be uniform throughout the United States;

2. To borrow Money on the credit of the United States;

3. To regulate Commerce with foreign Nations, and among the several States, and with the Indian Tribes;

4. To establish an uniform Rule of Naturalization, and uniform Laws on the subject of Bankruptcies throughout the United States;

5. To coin Money, regulate the Value thereof, and of foreign Coin, and fix the Standard of Weights and Measures;

6. To provide for the Punishment of counterfeiting the Securities and current Coin of the United States;

7. To establish Post Offices and post Roads;

8. To promote the Progress of Science and useful Arts, by securing for limited Times to Authors and Inventors the exclusive Right to their respective Writings and Discoveries;

9. To constitute Tribunals inferior to the supreme Court;

10. To define and punish Piracies and Felonies commited on the high Seas, and Offences against the Law of Nations;

11. To declare War, grant Letters of Marque and Reprisal, and make Rules concerning Captures on Land and Water;

12. To raise and support Armies, but no Appropriation of Money to that Use shall be for a longer Term than two Years;

13. To provide and maintain a Navy;

14. To make Rules for the Government and Regulation of the land and naval Forces;

15. To provide for calling forth the Militia to execute the Laws of the Union, suppress Insurrections and repel Invasions;

16. To provide for organizing, arming, and disciplining, the Militia, and for governing such Part of them as may be employed in the Service of the United States, reserving to the States respectively, the Appointment of the Officers, and the Authority of training the Militia according to the discipline prescribed by Congress;

17. To exercise exclusive Legislation in all Cases whatsoever, over such District (not exceeding ten Miles square) as may, by Cession of Particular States, and the Acceptance of Congress, become the Seat of the Government of the United States, and to exercise like Authority over all Places purchased by the Consent of the Legislature of the State in which the Same shall be, for the Erection of Forts, Magazines, Arsenals, dock-Yards, and other needful Buildings; — And

18. To make all Laws which shall be necessary and proper for carrying into Execution the foregoing Powers, and all other Powers vested by this Constitution in the Government of the United States, or in any Department or Officer thereof.

Section 9

1. The Migration or Importation of such Persons as any of the States now existing shall think proper to admit, shall not be prohibited by the Congress prior to the Year one thousand eight hundred and eight, but a Tax or duty may be imposed on such Importation, not exceeding ten dollars for each Person.

2. The Privilege of the Writ of Habeas Corpus shall not be suspended, unless when in Cases of Rebellion or Invasion the public Safety may require it.

3. No Bill of Attainder or ex post facto Law shall be passed.

4. No capitation, or other direct, Tax shall be laid, unless in Proportion to the Census of Enumeration herein before directed to be taken.[5]

5. No Tax or Duty shall be laid on Articles exported from any State.

6. No Preference shall be given by any Regulation of Commerce or

Revenue to the Ports of one State over those of another; nor shall Vessels bound to, or from, one State, be obliged to enter, clear or pay Duties in another.

7. No Money shall be drawn from the Treasury, but in Consequence of Appropriations made by Law; and a regular Statement and Account of the Receipts and Expenditures of all public Money shall be published from time to time.

8. No Title of Nobility shall be granted by the United States: And no Person holding any Office of Profit or Trust under them, shall, without the Consent of the Congress, accept of any present, Emolument, Office, or Title, of any kind whatever, from any King, Prince or foreign State.

Section 10

1. No State shall enter into any Treaty, Alliance, or Confederation; grant Letters of Marque and Reprisal; coin Money; emit Bills of Credit; make any Thing but gold and silver Coin a Tender in Payment of Debts; pass any Bill of Attainder, ex post facto Law, or Law impairing the Obligation of Contracts, or grant any Title of Nobility.

2. No State shall, without the Consent of the Congress, lay any Imposts or Duties on Imports or Exports, except what may be absolutely necessary for executing it's inspection Laws: and the net Produce of all Duties and Imposts, laid by any State on Imports or Exports, shall be for the Use of the Treasury of the United States; and all such Laws shall be subject to the Revision and Controul of the Congress.

3. No State shall, without the Consent of Congress, lay any Duty of Tonnage, keep Troops, or Ships of War in time of Peace, enter into any Agreement or Compact with another State, or with a foreign Power, or engage in War, unless actually invaded, or in such imminent Danger as will not admit of delay.

Article II

Section 1

1. The executive Power shall be vested in a President of the United States of America. He shall hold his Office during the Term of four Years, and, together with the Vice President, chosen for the same Term, be elected, as follows.

2. Each State shall appoint, in such Manner as the Legislature thereof may direct, a Number of Electors, equal to the whole Number of Senators and Representatives to which the State may be entitled in the Congress: but no Senator or Representative, or Person holding an Office of Trust or Profit under the United States, shall be appointed an Elector.

3. [The Electors shall meet in their respective States, and vote by Ballot for two Persons, of whom one at least shall not be an Inhabitant of the same State with themselves. And they shall make a List of all the Per-

sons voted for, and of the Number of Votes for each; which List they shall sign and certify, and transmit sealed to the Seat of the Government of the United States, directed to the President of the Senate. The President of the Senate shall, in the Presence of the Senate and House of Representatives, open all the Certificates, and the Votes shall then be counted. The Person having the greatest Number of Votes shall be the President, if such Number be a Majority of the whole Number of Electors appointed; and if there be more than one who have such Majority, and have an equal Number of Votes, then the House of Representatives shall immediately chuse by Ballot one of them for President; and if no Person have a Majority, then from the five highest on the list the said House shall in like Manner chuse the President. But in chusing the President, the Votes shall be taken by States, the Representation from each State having one Vote; a quorum for this Purpose shall consist of a Member or Members from two thirds of the States, and a Majority of all the States shall be necessary to a Choice. In every Case, after the Choice of the President, the Person having the greatest Number of Votes of the Electors shall be the Vice President. But if there should remain two or more who have equal Votes, the Senate shall chuse from them by Ballot the Vice President.] [6]

4. The Congress may determine the Time of chusing the Electors, and the Day on which they shall give their Votes; which Day shall be the same throughout the United States.

5. No Person except a natural born Citizen, or a Citizen of the United States, at the time of the Adoption of this Constitution, shall be eligible to the Office of President; neither shall any Person be eligible to that Office who shall not have attained to the Age of thirty five Years, and been fourteen Years a Resident within the United States.

6. In Case of the Removal of the President from Office, or of his Death, Resignation, or Inability to discharge the Powers and Duties of the said Office,[7] the Same shall devolve on the Vice President, and the Congress may by Law provide for the Case of Removal, Death, Resignation or Inability, both of the President and Vice President, declaring what Officer shall then act as President, and such Officer shall act accordingly, until the Disability be removed, or a President shall be elected.

7. The President shall, at stated Times, receive for his Services, a Compensation, which shall neither be encreased nor diminished during the Period for which he shall have been elected, and he shall not receive within that Period any other Emolument from the United States, or any of them.

8. Before he enter on the Execution of his Office, he shall take the following Oath or Affirmation: — "I do solemnly swear (or affirm) that I will faithfully execute the Office of President of the United States, and

will to the best of my Ability, preserve, protect and defend the Constitution of the United States."

Section 2

1. The President shall be Commander in Chief of the Army and Navy of the United States, and of the Militia of the several States, when called into the actual Service of the United States; he may require the Opinion, in writing, of the principal Officer in each of the executive Departments, upon any Subject relating to the Duties of their respective Offices, and he shall have Power to grant Reprieves and Pardons for Offenses against the United States, except in Cases of Impeachment.

2. He shall have Power, by and with the Advice and Consent of the Senate, to make Treaties, provided two thirds of the Senators present concur; and he shall nominate, and by and with the Advice and Consent of the Senate, shall appoint Ambassadors, other public Ministers and Consuls, Judges of the supreme Court, and all other Officers of the United States, whose Appointments are not herein otherwise provided for, and which shall be established by Law: but the Congress may by Law vest the Appointment of such inferior Officers, as they think proper, in the President alone, in the Courts of Law, or in the Heads of Departments.

3. The President shall have Power to fill up all Vacancies that may happen during the Recess of the Senate, by granting Commissions which shall expire at the End of their next Session.

Section 3

He shall from time to time give to the Congress Information of the State of the Union, and recommend to their Consideration such Measures as he shall judge necessary and expedient; he may, on extraordinary Occasions, convene both Houses, or either of them, and in Case of Disagreement between them, with Respect to the Time of Adjournment, he may adjourn them to such Time as he shall think proper; he shall receive Ambassadors and other public Ministers; he shall take Care that the Laws be faithfully executed, and shall Commission all the Officers of the United States.

Section 4

The President, Vice President and all Civil Officers of the United States, shall be removed from office on Impeachment for, and Conviction of, Treason, Bribery, or other high Crimes and Misdemeanors.

Article III

Section 1

The judicial Power of the United States, shall be vested in one supreme Court, and in such inferior Courts as the Congress may from time to time ordain and establish. The Judges, both of the supreme and inferior Courts, shall hold their Offices during good Behaviour, and shall, at stated Times, receive for their Services, a Compensation, which shall not be diminished during their Continuance in Office.

Section 2

1. The judicial Power shall extend to all Cases, in Law and Equity, arising under this Constitution, the Laws of the United States, and Treaties made, or which shall be made, under their Authority; — to all Cases affecting Ambassadors, other public Ministers and Consuls; — to all Cases of admiralty and maritime Jurisdiction; — to Controversies to which the United States shall be a Party; — to Controversies between two or more States; — between a State and Citizens of another State;[8] — between Citizens of different States; — between Citizens of the same State claiming Lands under Grants of different States, and between a State, or the Citizens thereof, and foreign States, Citizens or Subjects.[8]

2. In all Cases affecting Ambassadors, other public Ministers and Consuls, and those in which a State shall be Party, the supreme Court shall have original Jurisdiction. In all the other Cases before mentioned, the supreme Court shall have appellate Jurisdiction, both as to Law and Fact, with such Exceptions, and under such Regulations as the Congress shall make.

3. The Trial of all Crimes, except in cases of Impeachment, shall be by Jury; and such Trial shall be held in the State where the said Crimes shall have been committed; but when not committed within any State, the Trial shall be at such Place or Places as the Congress may by Law have directed.

Section 3

1. Treason against the United States, shall consist only in levying War against them, or in adhering to their Enemies, giving them Aid and Comfort. No Person shall be convicted of Treason unless on the Testimony of two Witnesses to the same overt Act, or on Confession in open Court.

2. The Congress shall have Power to declare the Punishment of Treason, but no Attainder of Treason shall work Corruption of Blood, or Forfeiture except during the Life of the Person attainted.

Article IV

Section 1

Full Faith and Credit shall be given in each State to the public Acts, Records, and judicial Proceedings of every other State. And the Congress may by general Laws prescribe the Manner in which such Acts, Records and Proceedings shall be proved, and the Effect thereof.

304

Section 2

1. The Citizens of each State shall be entitled to all Privileges and Immunities of Citizens in the several States.

2. A Person charged in any State with Treason, Felony, or other Crime, who shall flee from Justice, and be found in another State, shall on Demand of the executive Authority of the State from which he fled, be delivered up, to be removed to the State having Jurisdiction of the Crime.

3. [No Person held to Service or Labour in one State, under the Laws thereof, escaping into another, shall, in Consequence of any Law or Regulation therein, be discharged from such Service or Labour, but shall be delivered up on Claim of the Party to whom such Service or Labour may be due.][9]

Section 3

1. New States may be admitted by the Congress into this Union; but no new State shall be formed or erected within the Jurisdiction of any other State; nor any State be formed by the Junction of two or more States, or Parts of States, without the Consent of the Legislatures of the States concerned as well as of the Congress.

2. The Congress shall have Power to dispose of and make all needful Rules and Regulations respecting the Territory or other Property belonging to the United States; and nothing in this Constitution shall be so construed as to Prejudice any Claims of the United States, or of any particular State.

Section 4

The United States shall guarantee to every State in this Union a Republican Form of Government, and shall protect each of them against Invasion; and on Application of the Legislature, or of the Executive (when the Legislature cannot be convened) against domestic Violence.

Article V

The Congress, whenever two thirds of both Houses shall deem it necessary, shall propose Amendments to this Constitution, or, on the Application of the Legislatures of two thirds of the several States, shall call a Convention for proposing Amendments, which, in either Case, shall be valid to all Intents and Purposes, as Part of this Constitution, when ratified by the Legislatures of three fourths of the several States, or by Conventions in three fourths thereof, as the one or the other Mode of Ratification may be proposed by the Congress; Provided [that no Amendment which may be made prior to the Year One thousand eight hundred and eight shall in any Manner affect the first and fourth Clauses in the Ninth Section of the first Article; and][10] that no State, without its Consent, shall be deprived of its equal Suffrage in the Senate.

Article VI

1. All Debts contracted and Engagements entered into, before the Adoption of this Constitution, shall be as valid against the United States under this Constitution, as under the Confederation.

2. This Constitution, and the Laws of the United States which shall be made in Pursuance thereof; and all Treaties made, or which shall be made, under the Authority of the United States, shall be the supreme Law of the Land; and the Judges in every State shall be bound thereby, any Thing in the Constitution or Laws of any State to the Contrary notwithstanding.

3. The Senators and Representatives before mentioned, and the Members of the several State Legislatures, and all executive and judicial Officers, both of the United States and of the several States, shall be bound by Oath or Affirmation, to support this Constitution; but no religious Test shall ever be required as a Qualification to any Office or public Trust under the United States.

Article VII

The Ratification of the Conventions of nine States, shall be sufficient for the Establishment of this Constitution between the States so ratifying the Same. Done in Convention by the Unanimous Consent of the States present the Seventeenth Day of September in the Year of our Lord one thousand seven hundred and Eighty seven and of the Independence of the United States of America the Twelfth In witness whereof We have hereunto subscribed our Names, George Washington, President and deputy from Virginia.

New Hampshire:	John Langdon, Nicholas Gilman.
Massachusetts:	Nathaniel Gorham, Rufus King.
Connecticut:	William Samuel Johnson, Roger Sherman.
New York:	Alexander Hamilton
New Jersey:	William Livingston, David Brearley, William Paterson, Jonathan Dayton.
Pennsylvania:	Benjamin Franklin, Thomas Mifflin, Robert Morris, George Clymer,

Thomas FitzSimons,
Jared Ingersoll,
James Wilson,
Gouverneur Morris.

Delaware:

George Read,
Gunning Bedford Jr.,
John Dickinson,
Richard Bassett,
Jacob Broom.

Maryland:

James McHenry,
Daniel of St. Thomas Jenifer,
Daniel Carroll.

Virginia:

John Blair,
James Madison Jr.

North Carolina:

William Blount,
Richard Dobbs Spaight,
Hugh Williamson.

South Carolina:

John Rutledge,
Charles Cotesworth Pinckney,
Charles Pinckney,
Pierce Butler.

Georgia:

William Few,
Abraham Baldwin.

[The language of the original Constitution, not including the Amendments, was adopted by a convention of the states on September 17, 1787, and was subsequently ratified by the states on the following dates: Delaware, December 7, 1787; Pennsylvania, December 12, 1787; New Jersey, December 18, 1787; Georgia, January 2, 1788; Connecticut, January 9, 1788; Massachusetts, February 6, 1788; Maryland, April 28, 1788; South Carolina, May 23, 1788; New Hampshire, June 21, 1788.

Ratification was completed on June 21, 1788.

The Constitution subsequently was ratified by Virginia, June 25, 1788; New York, July 26, 1788; North Carolina, November 21, 1789; Rhode Island, May 29, 1790; and Vermont, January 10, 1791.]

The Amendments

Amendment I

*(First ten amendments
ratified December 15, 1791.)*

Congress shall make no law respecting an establishment of religion, or prohibiting the free exercise thereof; or abridging the freedom of speech, or of the press; or the right of the people peaceably to assemble, and to petition the Government for a redress of grievances.

Amendment II

A well regulated Militia, being necessary to the security of a free State, the right of the people to keep and bear Arms, shall not be infringed.

Amendment III

No Soldier shall, in time of peace be quartered in any house, without the consent of the Owner, nor in time of war, but in a manner to be prescribed by law.

Amendment IV

The right of the people to be secure in their persons, houses, papers, and effects, against unreasonable searches and seizures, shall not be violated, and no Warrants shall issue, but upon probable cause, supported by Oath or affirmation, and particularly describing the place to be searched, and the persons or things to be seized.

Amendment V

No person shall be held to answer for a capital, or otherwise infamous crime, unless on a presentment or indictment of a Grand Jury, except in cases arising in the land or naval forces, or in the Militia, when in actual service in time of War or public danger; nor shall any person be subject for the same offence to be twice put in jeopardy of life or limb; nor shall be compelled in any criminal case to be a witness against himself, nor be deprived of life, liberty, or property, without due process of law; nor shall private property be taken for public use, without just compensation.

Amendment VI

In all criminal prosecutions, the accused shall enjoy the right to a speedy and public trial, by an impartial jury of the State and district wherein the crime shall have been committed, which district shall have been previously ascertained by law, and to be informed of the nature and cause of the accusation; to be confronted with the witnesses against him; to have compulsory process for obtaining witnesses in his favor, and to have the Assistance of Counsel for his defence.

Amendment VII

In Suits at common law, where the value in controversy shall exceed twenty dollars, the right of trial by jury shall be preserved, and no fact tried by a jury, shall be otherwise re-examined in any Court of the United States, than according to the rules of the common law.

Amendment VIII

Excessive bail shall not be required, nor excessive fines imposed, nor cruel and unusual punishments inflicted.

Amendment IX

The enumeration in the Constitution, of certain rights, shall not be construed to deny or disparage others retained by the people.

Amendment X

The powers not delegated to the United States by the Constitution, nor prohibited by it to the States, are reserved to the States respectively, or to the people.

Amendment XI

(Ratified February 7, 1795)

The Judicial power of the United States shall not be construed to extend to any suit in law or equity, commenced or prosecuted against one of the United States by Citizens of another State, or by Citizens or Subjects of any Foreign State.

Amendment XII

(Ratified June 15, 1804)

The Electors shall meet in their respective states and vote by ballot for President and Vice-President, one of whom, at least, shall not be an inhabitant of the same state with themselves; they shall name in their ballots the person voted for as President, and in distinct ballots the person voted for as Vice-President, and they shall make distinct lists of all persons voted for as President, and of all persons voted for as Vice-President, and of the number of votes for each, which lists they shall sign and certify, and transmit sealed to the seat of the government of the United States, directed to the President of the Senate; — The President of the Senate shall, in the presence of the Senate and House of Representatives, open all the certificates and the votes shall then be counted; — The person having the greatest number of votes for President, shall be the President, if such number be a majority of the whole number of Electors appointed; and if no person have such majority, then from the persons having the highest numbers not exceeding three on the list of those voted for as President, the House of Representatives shall choose immediately, by ballot, the President. But in choosing the President, the votes shall be taken by states, the representation from each state having one vote; a quorum for this purpose shall consist of a member or members from two-thirds of the states, and a majority of all the states shall be necessary to a choice. [And if the House of Representatives shall not choose a President whenever the right of choice shall devolve upon them, before the fourth day of March next following, then the Vice-President shall act as President, as in the case of the death or other constitutional disability of the President —][11] The person having the greatest number of votes as Vice-President, shall be the Vice-President, if such number be a majority of the whole number of Electors appointed, and if no person have a majority, then from the two highest numbers on the list, the Senate shall choose the Vice-President; a quorum for the purpose shall consist of two-thirds of the whole number of Senators, and a majority of the whole number shall be necessary to a choice. But no person constitutionally ineligible to the office of President shall be eligible to that of Vice-President of the United States.

Amendment XIII
(Ratified December 6, 1865)
Section 1
Neither slavery nor involuntary servitude, except as a punishment for crime whereof the party shall have been duly convicted, shall exist within the United States, or any place subject to their jurisdiction.

Section 2
Congress shall have power to enforce this article by appropriate legislation.

Amendment XIV
(Ratified July 9, 1868)
Section 1
All persons born or naturalized in the United States and subject to the jurisdiction thereof, are citizens of the United States and of the State wherein they reside. No State shall make or enforce any law which shall abridge the privileges or immunities of citizens of the United States; nor shall any State deprive any person of life, liberty, or property, without due

process of law; nor deny to any person within its jurisdiction the equal protection of the laws.

Section 2
Representatives shall be apportioned among the several States according to their respective numbers, counting the whole number of persons in each State, excluding Indians not taxed. But when the right to vote at any election for the choice of electors for President and Vice President of the United States, Representatives in Congress, the Executive and Judicial officers of a State, or the members of the Legislature thereof, is denied to any of the male inhabitants of such State, being twenty-one years of age,[12] and citizens of the United States, or in any way abridged, except for participation in rebellion, or other crime, the basis of representation therein shall be reduced in the proportion which the number of such male citizens shall bear to the whole number of male citizens twenty-one years of age in such State.

Section 3
No person shall be a Senator or Representative in Congress, or elector of President and Vice President, or hold any office, civil or military, under the United States, or under any State, who, having previously taken an oath, as a member of Congress, or as an officer of the United States, or as a member of any State legislature, or as an executive or judicial officer of any State, to support the Constitution of the United States, shall have engaged in insurrection or rebellion against the same, or given aid or comfort to the enemies thereof. But Congress may by a vote of two-thirds of each House, remove such disability.

Section 4
The validity of the public debt of the United States, authorized by law, including debts incurred for payment of pensions and bounties for services in suppressing insurrection or rebellion, shall not be questioned. But neither the United States nor any State shall assume or pay any debt or obligation incurred in aid of insurrection or rebellion against the United States, or any claim for the loss or emancipation of any slave; but all such debts, obligations and claims shall be held illegal and void.

Section 5
The Congress shall have power to enforce, by appropriate legislation, the provisions of this article.

Amendment XV
(Ratified February 3, 1870)
Section 1
The right of citizens of the United States to vote shall not be denied

or abridged by the United States or by any State on account of race, color, or previous condition of servitude.

Section 2

The Congress shall have power to enforce this article by appropriate legislation.

Amendment XVI
(Ratified February 3, 1913)

The Congress shall have power to lay and collect taxes on incomes, from whatever source derived, without apportionment among the several States, and without regard to any census or enumeration.

Amendment XVII
(Ratified April 8, 1913)

The Senate of the United States shall be composed of two Senators from each State, elected by the people thereof, for six years; and each Senator shall have one vote. The electors in each State shall have the qualifications requisite for electors of the most numerous branch of the State legislatures.

When vacancies happen in the representation of any State in the Senate, the executive authority of such State shall issue writs of election to fill such vacancies: *Provided,* That the legislature of any State may empower the executive thereof to make temporary appointments until the people fill the vacancies by election as the legislature may direct.

This amendment shall not be so construed as to affect the election or term of any Senator chosen before it becomes valid as part of the Constitution.

Amendment XVIII
(Ratified January 16, 1919)

Section 1

After one year from the ratification of this article the manufacture, sale, or transportation of intoxicating liquors within, the importation thereof into, or the exportation thereof from the United States and all territory subject to the jurisdiction thereof for beverage purposes is hereby prohibited.

Section 2

The Congress and the several States shall have concurrent power to enforce this article by appropriate legislation.

Section 3

This article shall be inoperative unless it shall have been ratified as

an amendment to the Constitution by the legislatures of the several
States, as provided in the Constitution, within seven years from the date
of the submission hereof to the States by the Congress.][13]

Amendment XIX
(Ratified August 18, 1920)

The right of citizens of the United States to vote shall not be denied
or abridged by the United States or by any State on account of sex.

Congress shall have power to enforce this article by appropriate
legislation.

Amendment XX
(Ratified January 23, 1933)

Section 1

The terms of the President and Vice President shall end at noon on
the 20th day of January, and the terms of Senators and Representatives
at noon on the 3d day of January, of the years in which such terms would
have ended if this article had not been ratified; and the terms of their successors shall then begin.

Section 2

The Congress shall assemble at least once in every year, and such
meeting shall begin at noon on the 3d day of January, unless they shall by
law appoint a different day.

Section 3[14]

If, at the time fixed for the beginning of the term of the President,
the President elect shall have died, the Vice President elect shall become
President. If a President shall not have been chosen before the time fixed
for the beginning of his term, or if the President elect shall have failed to
qualify, then the Vice President elect shall act as President until a
President shall have qualified; and the Congress may by law provide for
the case wherein neither a President elect nor a Vice President elect shall
have qualified, declaring who shall then act as President, or the manner in
which one who is to act shall be selected, and such person shall act
accordingly until a President or Vice President shall have qualified.

Section 4

The Congress may by law provide for the case of the death of any of
the persons from whom the House of Representatives may choose a
President whenever the right of choice shall have devolved upon them,
and for the case of the death of any of the persons from whom the Senate
may choose a Vice President whenever the right of choice shall have
devolved upon them.

Section 5

Sections 1 and 2 shall take effect on the 15th day of October following the ratification of this article.

Section 6

This article shall be inoperative unless it shall have been ratified as an amendment to the Constitution by the legislatures of three-fourths of the several States within seven years from the date of its submission.

Amendment XXI

(Ratified December 5, 1933)

Section 1

The eighteenth article of amendment to the Constitution of the United States is hereby repealed.

Section 2

The transportation or importation into any State, Territory or possession of the United States for delivery or use therein of intoxicating liquors, in violation of the laws thereof, is hereby prohibited.

Section 3

This article shall be inoperative unless it shall have been ratified as an amendment to the Constitution by conventions in the several States, as provided in the Constitution, within seven years from the date of the submission hereof to the States by the Congress.

Amendment XXII

(Ratified February 27, 1951)

Section 1

No person shall be elected to the office of the President more than twice, and no person who has held the office of President, or acted as President, for more than two years of a term to which some other person was elected President shall be elected to the office of the President more than once. But this Article shall not apply to any person holding the office of President when this Article was proposed by the Congress, and shall not prevent any person who may be holding the office of President, or acting as President, during the term within which this Article become operative from holding the office of President or acting as President during the remainder of such term.

Section 2

This Article shall be inoperative unless it shall have been ratified as an amendment to the Constitution by the legislatures of three-fourths of the several States within seven years from the date of its submission to the States by the Congress.

Amendment XXIII

(Ratified March 29, 1961)

Section 1

The District constituting the seat of Government of the United States shall appoint in such manner as the Congress may direct:

A number of electors of President and Vice President equal to the whole number of Senators and Representatives in Congress to which the District would be entitled if it were a State, but in no event more than the least populous State; they shall be in addition to those appointed by the States, but they shall be considered, for the purposes of the election of President and Vice President, to be electors appointed by a State; and they shall meet in the District and perform such duties as provided by the twelfth article of amendment.

Section 2

The Congress shall have power to enforce this article by appropriate legislation.

Amendment XXIV

(Ratified January 23, 1964)

Section 1

The right of citizens of the United States to vote in any primary or other election for President or Vice President, for electors for President or Vice President, or for Senator or Representative in Congress, shall not be denied or abridged by the United States or any State by reason of failure to pay any poll tax or other tax.

Section 2

The Congress shall have power to enforce this article by appropriate legislation.

Amendment XXV

(Ratified February 10, 1967)

Section 1

In case of the removal of the President from office or of his death or resignation, the Vice President shall become President.

Section 2

Whenever there is a vacancy in the office of the Vice President, the President shall nominate a Vice President who shall take office upon confirmation by a majority vote of both Houses of Congress.

Section 3

Whenever the President transmits to the President pro tempore of the Senate and the Speaker of the House of Representatives his written declaration that he is unable to discharge the powers and duties of his office, and until he transmits to them a written declaration to the contrary, such powers and duties shall be discharged by the Vice President as Acting President.

Section 4

Whenever the Vice President and a majority of either the principal officers of the executive departments or of such other body as Congress may by law provide, transmit to the President pro tempore of the Senate and the Speaker of the House of Representatives their written declaration that the President is unable to discharge the powers and duties of his office, the Vice President shall immediately assume the powers and duties of the office as Acting President.

Thereafter, when the President transmits to the President pro tempore of the Senate and the Speaker of the House of Representatives his written declaration that no inability exists, he shall resume the powers and duties of his office unless the Vice President and a majority of either the principal officers of the executive department or of such other body as Congress may by law provide, transmit within four days to the President pro tempore of the Senate and the Speaker of the House of Representatives their written declaration that the President is unable to discharge the powers and duties of his office. Thereupon Congress shall decide the issue, assembling within forty-eight hours for that purpose if not in session. If the Congress, within twenty-one days after receipt of the latter written declaration, or, if Congress is not in session, within twenty-one days after Congress is required to assemble, determines by two-thirds vote of both houses that the President is unable to discharge the powers and duties of his office, the Vice President shall continue to discharge the same as Acting President; otherwise, the President shall resume the powers and duties of his office.

Amendment XXVI
(Ratified July 1, 1971)
Section 1

The right of citizens of the United States, who are eighteen years of age or older, to vote shall not be denied or abridged by the United States or by any State on account of age.

Section 2

The Congress shall have power to enforce this article by appropriate legislation.

Notes

1. The part in brackets was changed by section 2 of the Fourteenth Amendment.
2. The part in brackets was changed by section 1 of the Seventeenth Amendment.
3. The part in brackets was changed by the second paragraph of the Seventeenth Amendment.
4. The part in brackets was changed by section 2 of the Twentieth Amendment.
5. The Sixteenth Amendment gave Congress the power to tax incomes.
6. The material in brackets has been superseded by the Twelfth Amendment.
7. This provision has been affected by the Twenty-fifth Amendment.
8. These clauses were affected by the Eleventh Amendment.
9. This paragraph has been superseded by the Thirteenth Amendment.
10. Obsolete.
11. The part in brackets has been superseded by section 3 of the Twentieth Amendment.
12. See the Twenty-sixth Amendment.
13. This Amendment was repealed by section 1 of the Twenty-first Amendment.
14. See the Twenty-fifth Amendment.

Source: U.S. Congress, House, Committee on the Judiciary, *The Constitution of the United States of America, As Amended Through July 1971,* H. Doc. 93-215, 93rd Cong., 2nd sess., 1974.

Illustration Acknowledgments

Museum; Dewitt Clinton, p. 158, painting by John Wesley Jarvis, c. 1816, National Portrait Gallery, Smithsonian Institution, Washington, D.C.; Sojourner Truth, p. 162, photograph by unidentified photographer, National Portrait Gallery, Smithsonian Institution, Washington, D.C.; Thomas Paine, p. 164, from the collection of Roger Butterfield, *The American Past*, Simon & Schuster, 1947; Paul Cuffe, p. 166, National Portrait Gallery, Smithsonian Institution, Washington, D.C.; Zachary Taylor, p. 168, Library of Congress; Daniel Webster, p. 169, Library of Congress; Anti-slavery Almanac, p. 172, Division of Political History, Smithsonian Institution, Washington, D.C.; Americanism poster, p. 179, Division of Political History, Smithsonian Institution, Washington, D.C.; Thomas Nast cartoon, *Harper's Weekly*, November 20, 1869, p. 180, Library of Congress; Know-Nothings songsheet, p. 183, Library of Congress; Chinese immigrants to the United States, p. 185, wood engraving in Frank Leslie's Sunday Magazine, March 1881, Library of Congress; Judge in chambers swearing in a new citizen, New York City, 1916, p. 187, Library of Congress; Japanese agricultural workers packing broccoli, March 1937, p. 188, Farm Security Administration, Library of Congress.

Part V

Charles Evans Hughes, p. 196, Supreme Court Historical Society; John Adams, p. 201, National Portrait Gallery, Smithsonian Institution, Washington, D.C.; Philadelphia newspaper account of the adjournment of the Constitutional Convention, p. 203, Library of Congress; Charles Sumner, p. 211, painting by Walter Ingalls, Library of Congress; Dred Scott, p. 213, National Park Service; Andrew Johnson, p. 214, Library of Congress; Thomas Nast cartoon, *Harper's Weekly*, September 1, 1866, p. 218, Library of Congress; *The Labor Herald*, July 1922, p. 223, Library of Congress; The Warren

Court, 1965, p. 225, Supreme Court Historical Society; Florence Kelley, p. 227, Library of Congress; Thomas Nast cartoon, *Harper's Weekly*, February 26, 1870, p. 230, Library of Congress.

Part VI

Scene at the Signing of the Constitution, p. 239, painting by Howard Chandler Christy, U.S. Capitol; Gouverneur Morris, p. 242, Library of Congress; George Washington, p. 246, engraving by Charles Saint-Mémin, 1800, National Portrait Gallery, Smithsonian Institution, Washington, D.C.; Abraham Lincoln, p. 251, photo by Mathew Brady, 1864, National Portrait Gallery, Smithsonian Institution, Washington, D.C.; Roger B. Taney, p. 252, photograph attributed to Mathew Brady, National Portrait Gallery, Smithsonian Institution, Washington, D.C.; The outbreak of the rebellion in the United States in 1861, p. 255, lithograph by Kimmel S. Forster, 1865, Library of Congress; John Tyler, p. 256, Library of Congress; Mexican War engravings, p. 259, Library of Congress; The battle of Quasimas near Santiago, June 1898, p. 263, lithograph by Kurz S. Allison, 1898, Library of Congress; President Franklin Roosevelt, 1941, p. 264, Library of Congress; A search and destroy mission in Vietnam, June 1967, p. 268, Department of the Army, Office of Public Affairs; Woodrow Wilson, p. 271, Library of Congress; Harry S Truman, p. 272, National Park Service, Record Group 79, National Archives; Richard M. Nixon, p. 273, The White House; Lyndon B. Johnson, p. 274, The White House.

Conclusion

New York City, ca. 1913, p. 279, photo by Harrrison Ewing, Library of Congress; British Parliament buildings, p. 282, Library of Congress.

Index